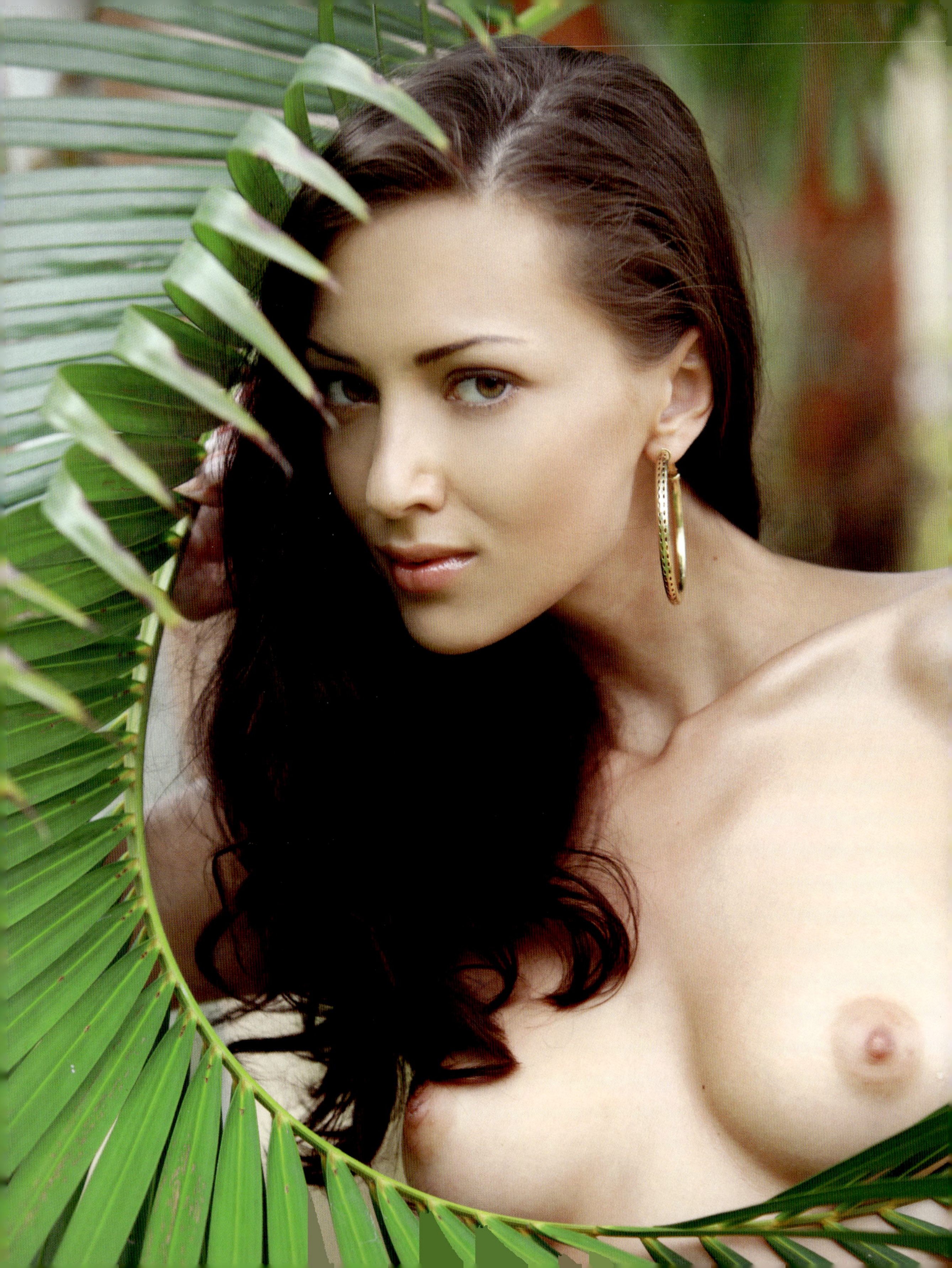

TOP MODELS OF

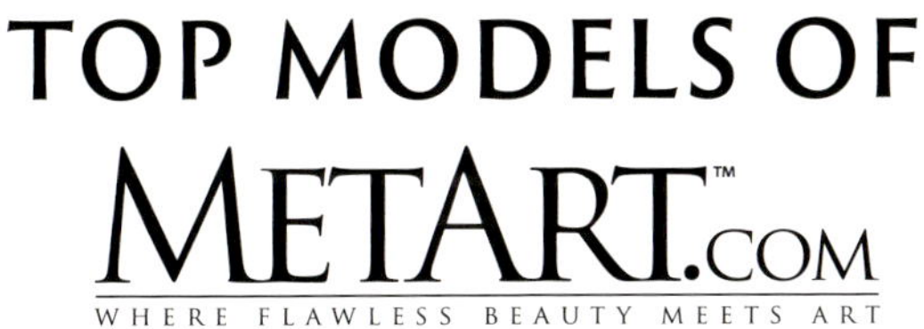

ANNA AJ

COLLECTED AND EDITED BY ISABELLA CATALINA

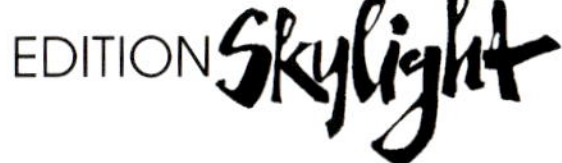

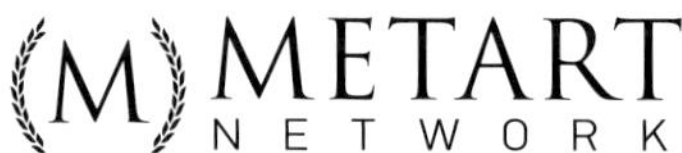

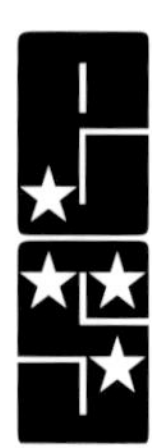

First edition 2024

EDITION SKYLIGHT
Rosengartenstrasse 13B
CH-8608 Bubikon / Zürich
Switzerland
info@edition-skylight.com
www.edition-skylight.com

ISBN 978-3-03766-695-1

Bibliographic information published by Die Deutsche Bibliothek
Die Deutsche Bibliothek lists this publication in the Deutsche Nationalbibliografie; detailed bibliographic data are available in the Internet at http://dnb.ddb.de.

Printed in Czech Republik

ANNA AJ IS NOT SHY TO SHOW HER STUNNING BEAUTY

"Hi, my name is Anna. I love chocolate, lying around in the sun, McDonald`s, animals and, of course my family. I really dislike overly nice people and oysters, they are both slimy! I was born in Ukraine in the wonderful city of Kiev. At school I was a very pugnacious girl; I always could protect myself, even if my offender was a boy. Since childhood I was interested in creative activities, I was fond of singing and dancing, I even solo for my relatives and neighbours.
However, together with age my hobbies changed a bit. At the present moment of my life I prefer extreme kinds of sport. I realize this hobby by fast driving a sporting car, or driving a sporting motorcycle. Exactly these minutes let me understand the fact that a human life can stop so quickly; however, the extreme and adrenaline that I get during driving let me think over about the sense of life. Therefore I try to live my life the way that not let me regret about anything."
With her delicate features, Anna could easily be mistaken for a porcelain doll. But make no mistake about it, she is far from fragile. Anna is comfortable in her skin, unafraid to bare all and show off the beauty she was born with. Her tiny body, accentuated by full breasts, is a testament to the beauty Ukrainian women are known for. Anna aspires to become a psychologist, deeply fascinated by the human mind. For Anna, life gains meaning when shared with someone else, and she looks forward to the meetings that destiny has in store for her.

"Hallo, mein Name ist Anna. Ich liebe Schokolade, in der Sonne zu liegen, McDonald's, Tiere und natürlich meine Familie. Ich mag übermäßig nette Leute und Austern wirklich nicht, sie sind beide schleimig! Ich wurde in der Ukraine in der wunderbaren Stadt Kiew geboren. In der Schule war ich ein sehr streitlustiges Mädchen; ich konnte mich immer schützen, auch wenn mein Angreifer ein Junge war. Seit meiner Kindheit interessierte ich mich für kreative Aktivitäten, ich liebte es zu singen und zu tanzen, ich trat sogar solo für meine Verwandten und Nachbarn auf. Allerdings haben sich meine Hobbys mit dem Alter etwas verändert. Im jetzigen Moment meines Lebens bevorzuge ich extreme Sportarten. Ich lebe dieses Hobby aus, indem ich schnell ein Sportauto oder ein Rennmotorrad fahre. Genau diese Minuten lassen mich verstehen, dass das menschliche Leben schnell enden kann; beim Fahren lassen mich der Nervenkitzel und das Adrenalin über den Sinn des Lebens nachdenken. Ich versuche, mein Leben so zu leben, dass ich nichts bereue."
Mit ihren feinen Gesichtszügen könnte man Anna leicht für eine Porzellanpuppe halten. Aber machen Sie keinen Fehler, sie ist alles andere als zerbrechlich. Anna hat überhaupt keine Hemmungen sich nackt zu präsentieren. Ihr kleiner Körper, betont durch perfekte, freche Brüste, zeigt genau die Schönheitsattribute, für die ukrainische Frauen bekannt sind. Anna strebt danach, Psychologin zu werden, da sie von der menschlichen Psyche fasziniert ist. Für Anna gewinnt das Leben an Bedeutung, wenn es mit jemand anderem geteilt wird, und sie freut sich auf die Begegnungen, die das Schicksal für sie bereithält.

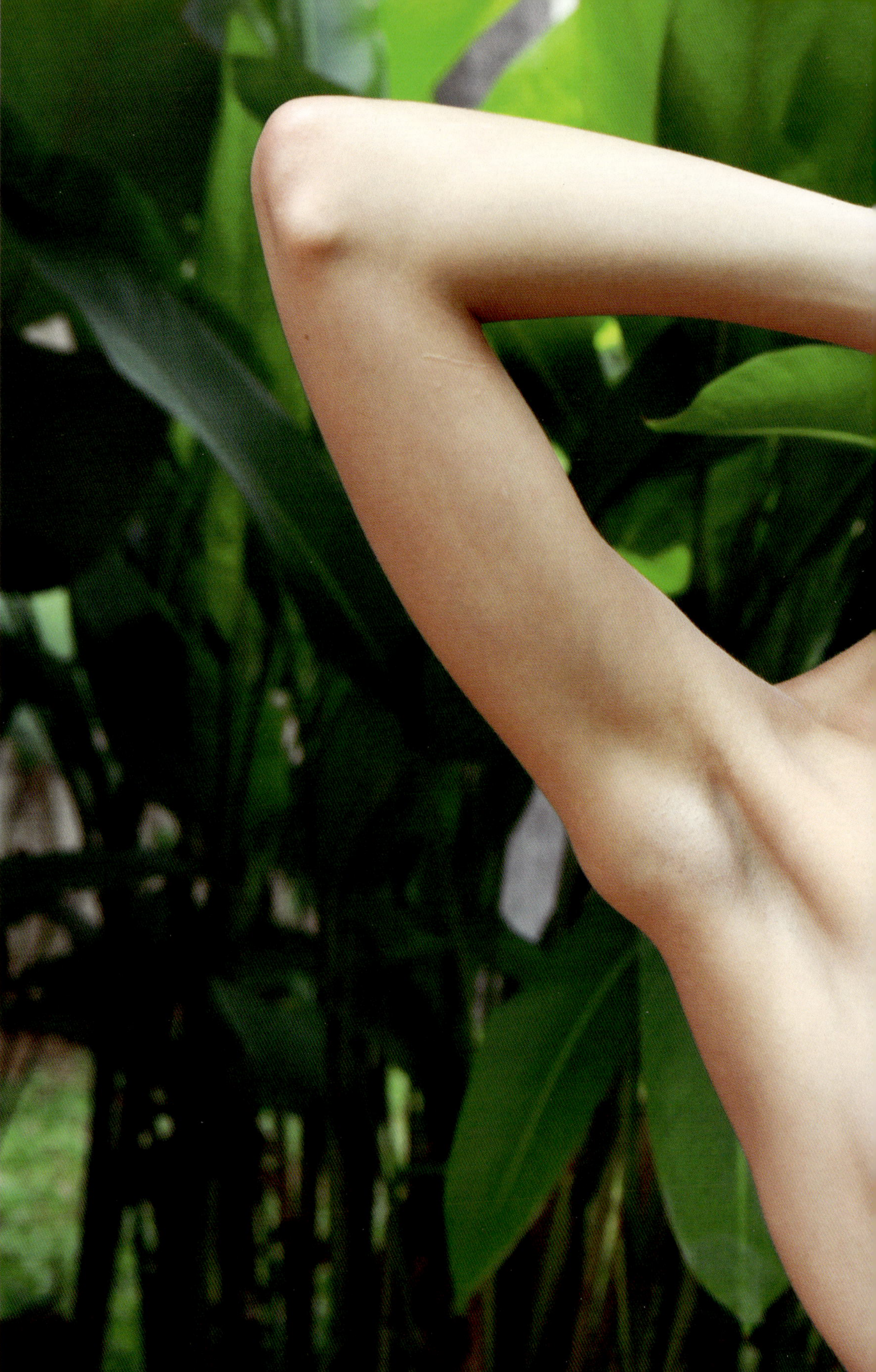

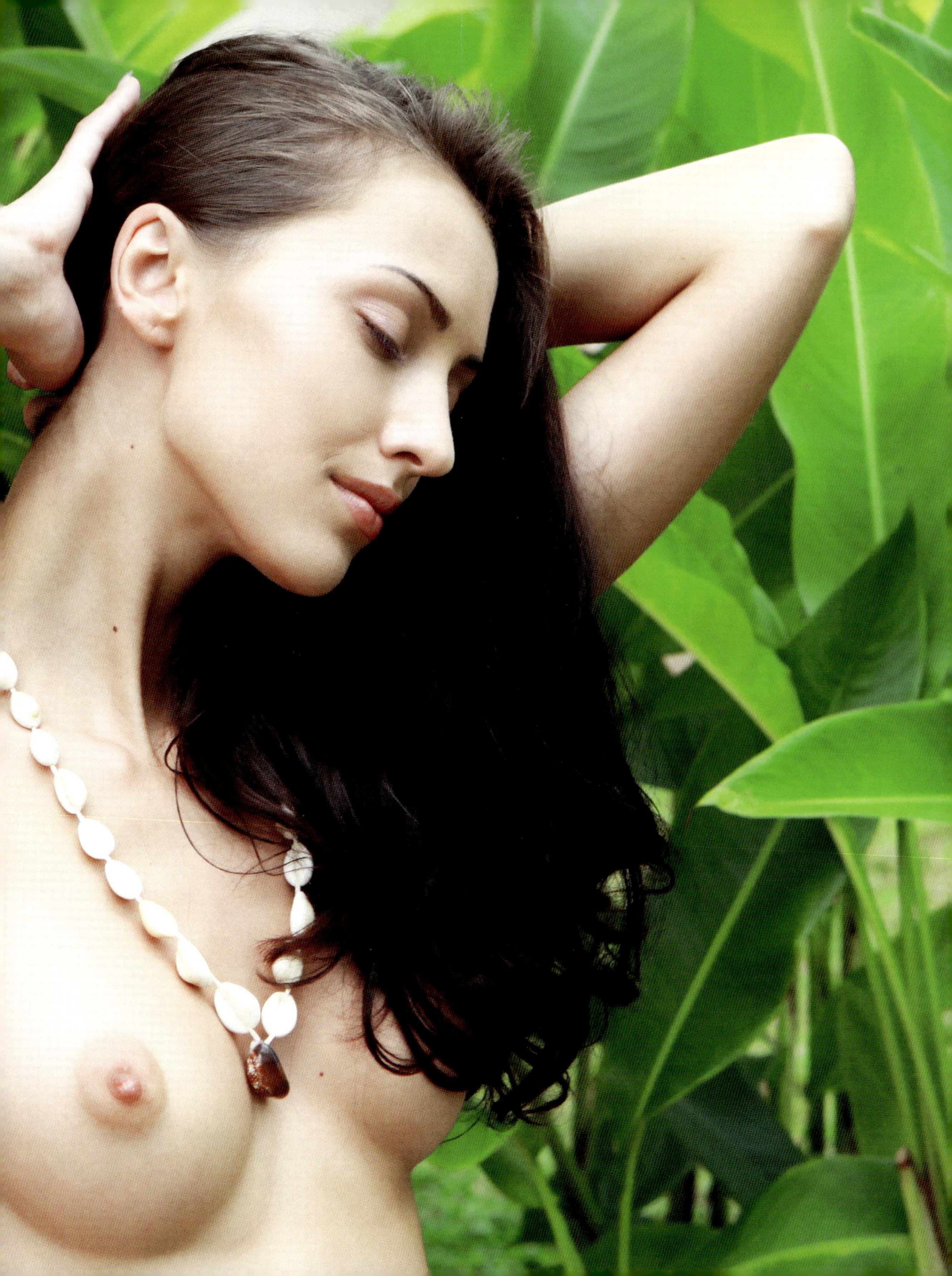

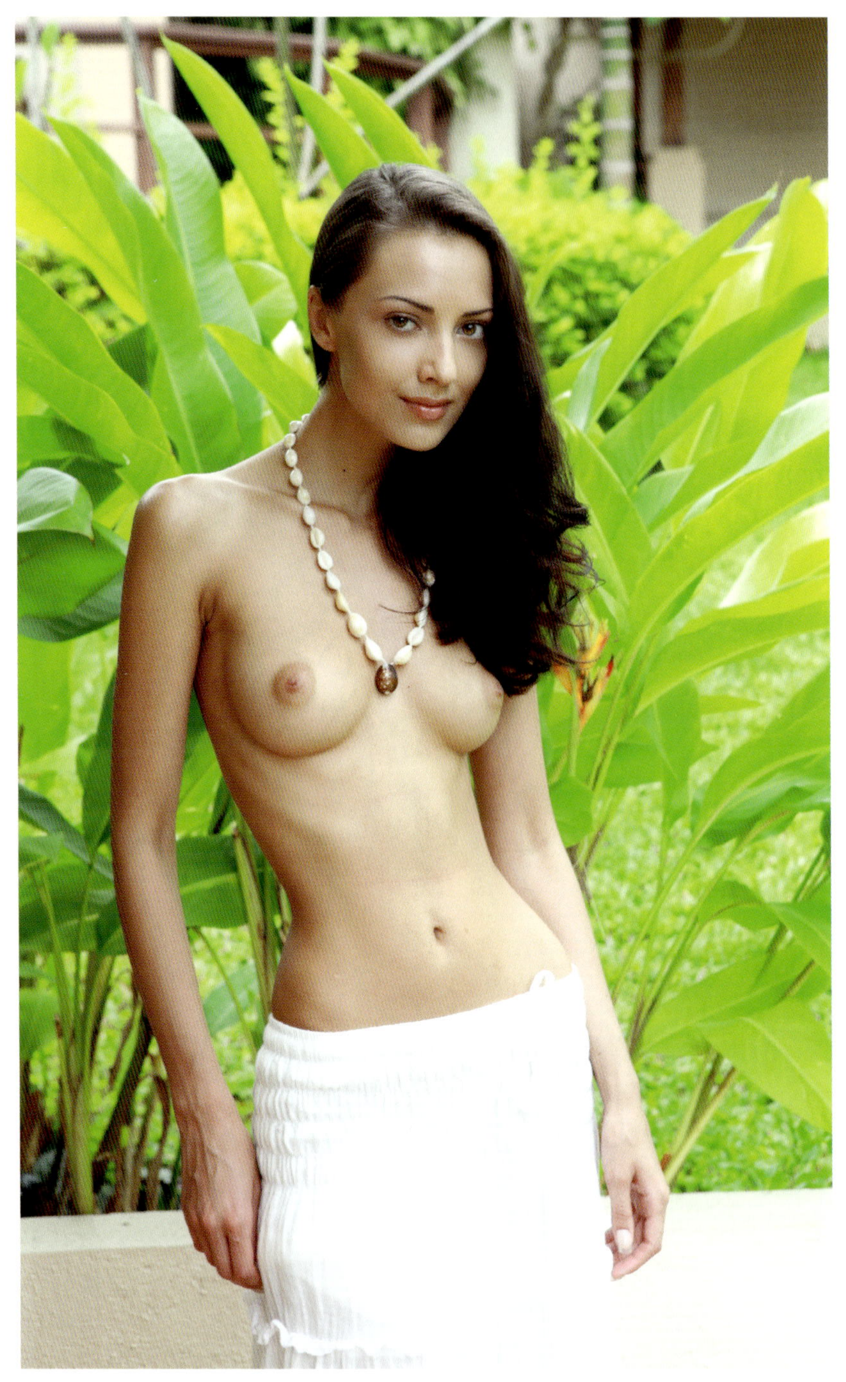

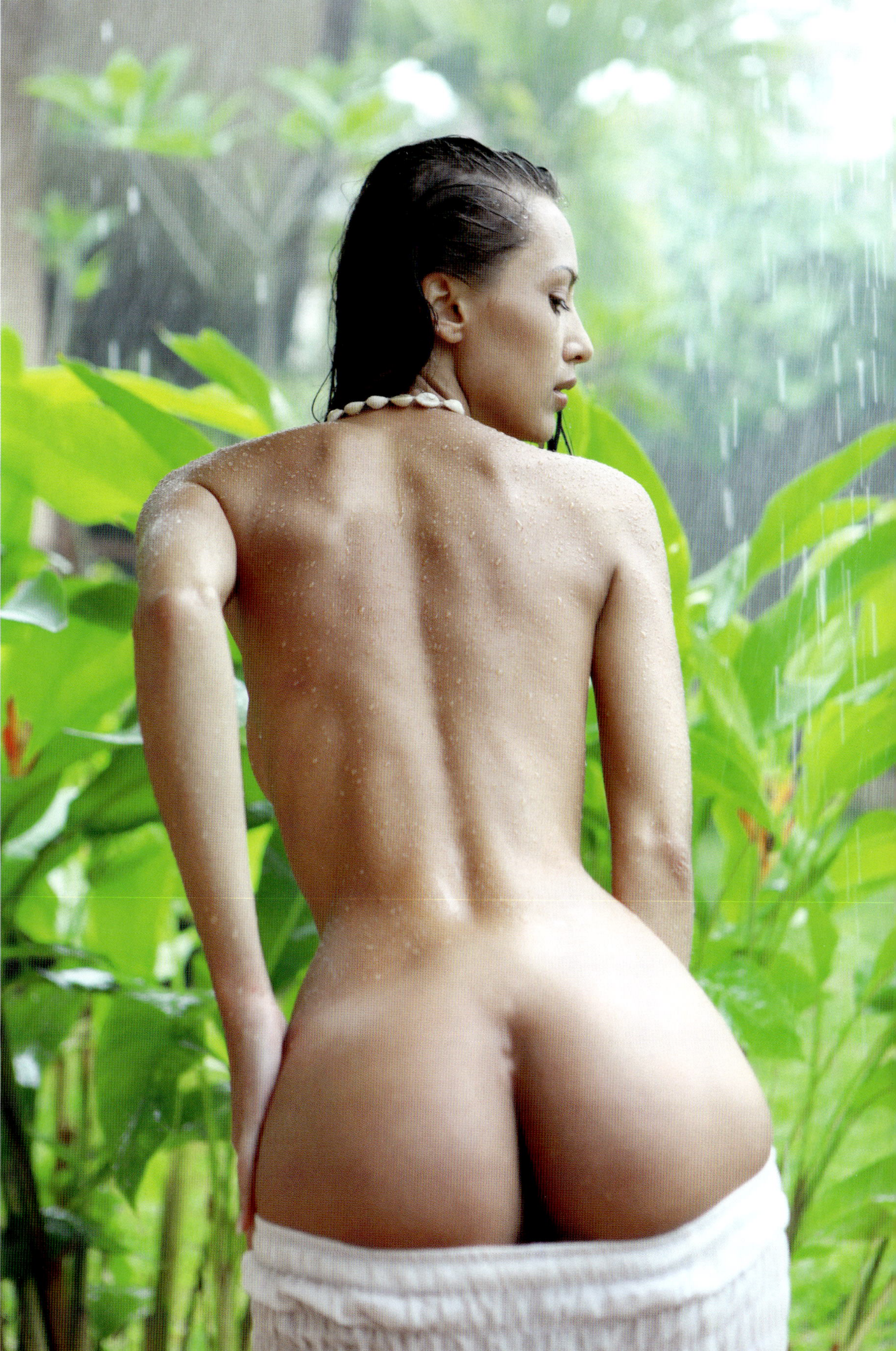

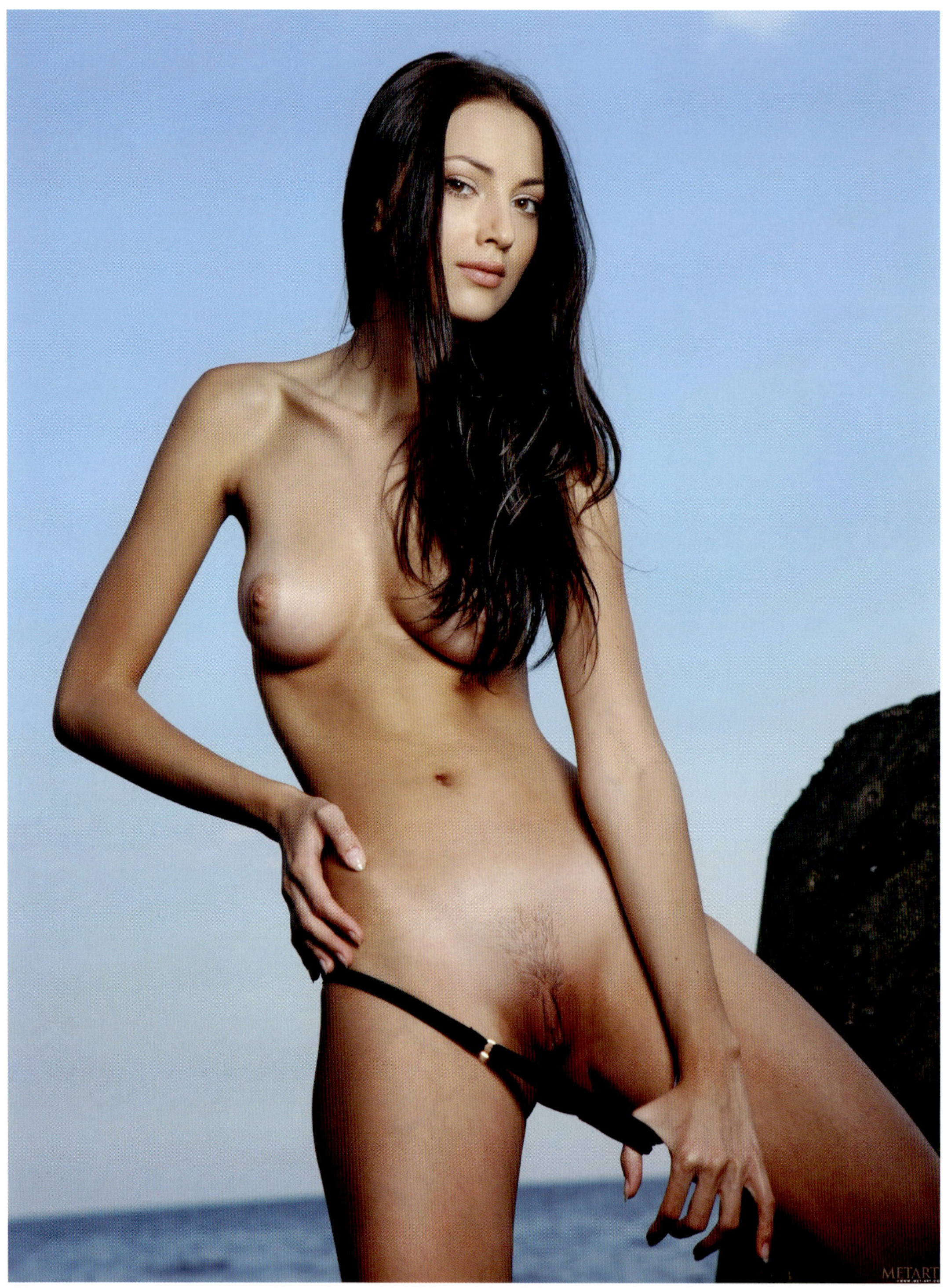
METART

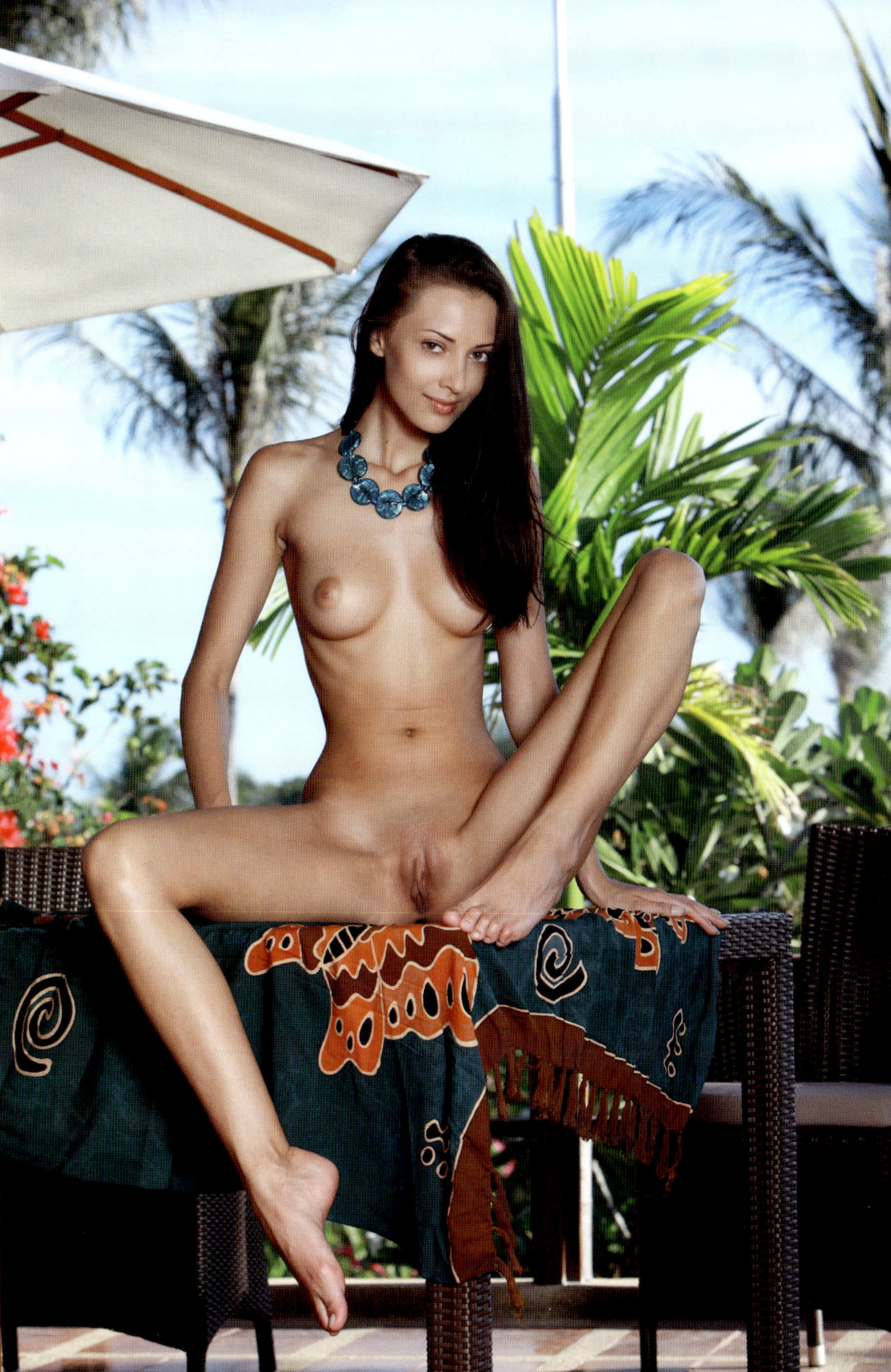

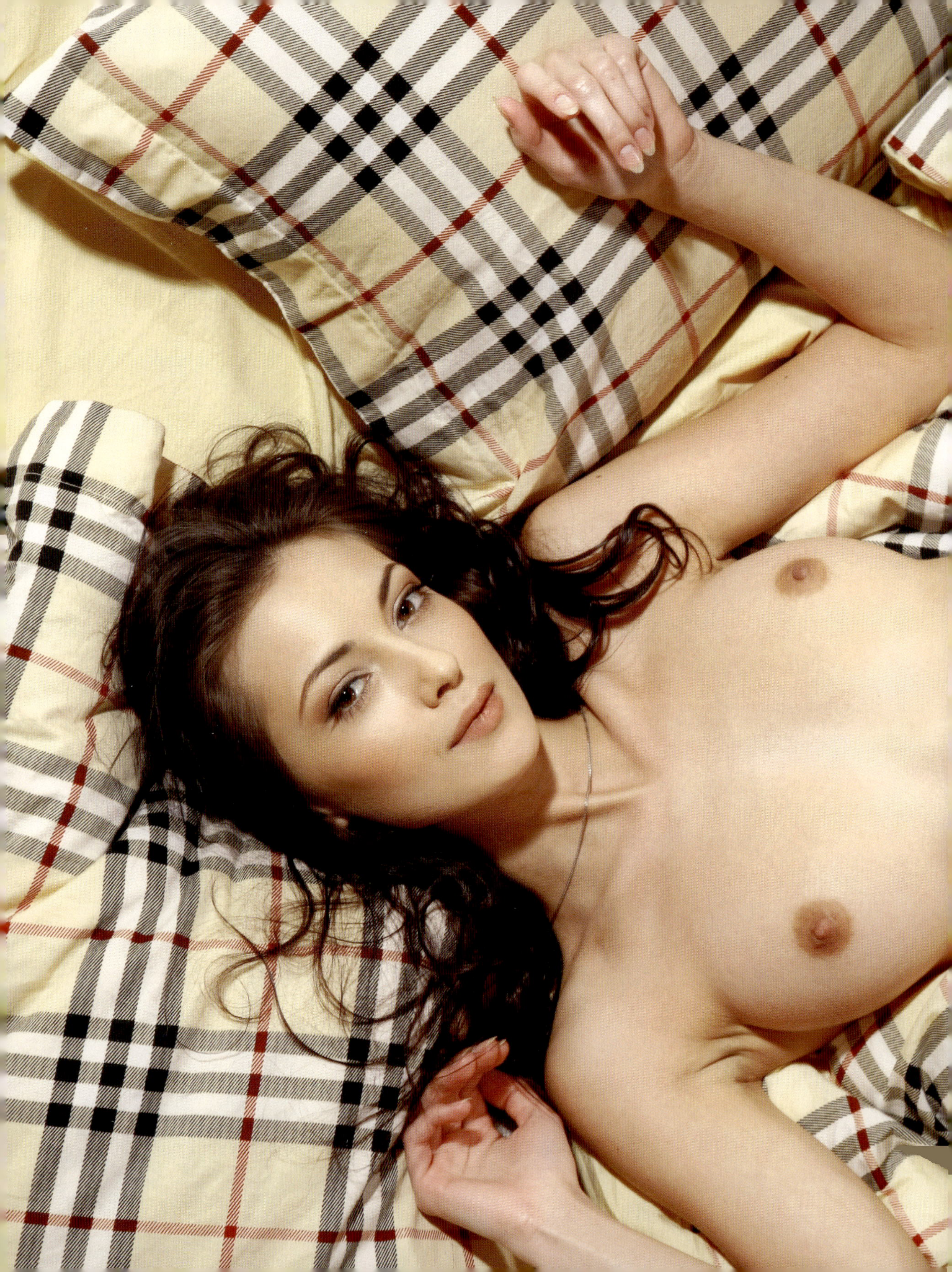

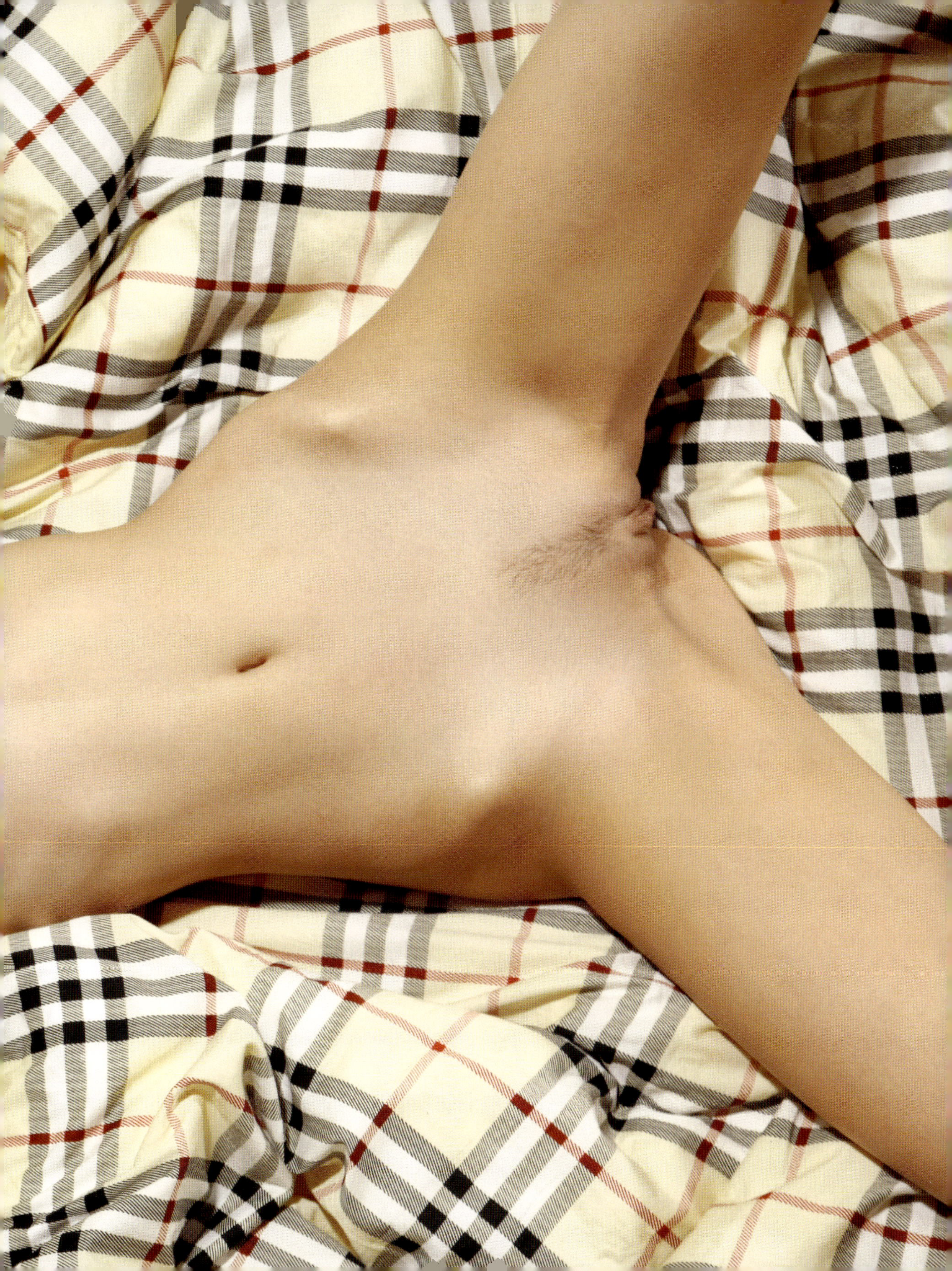

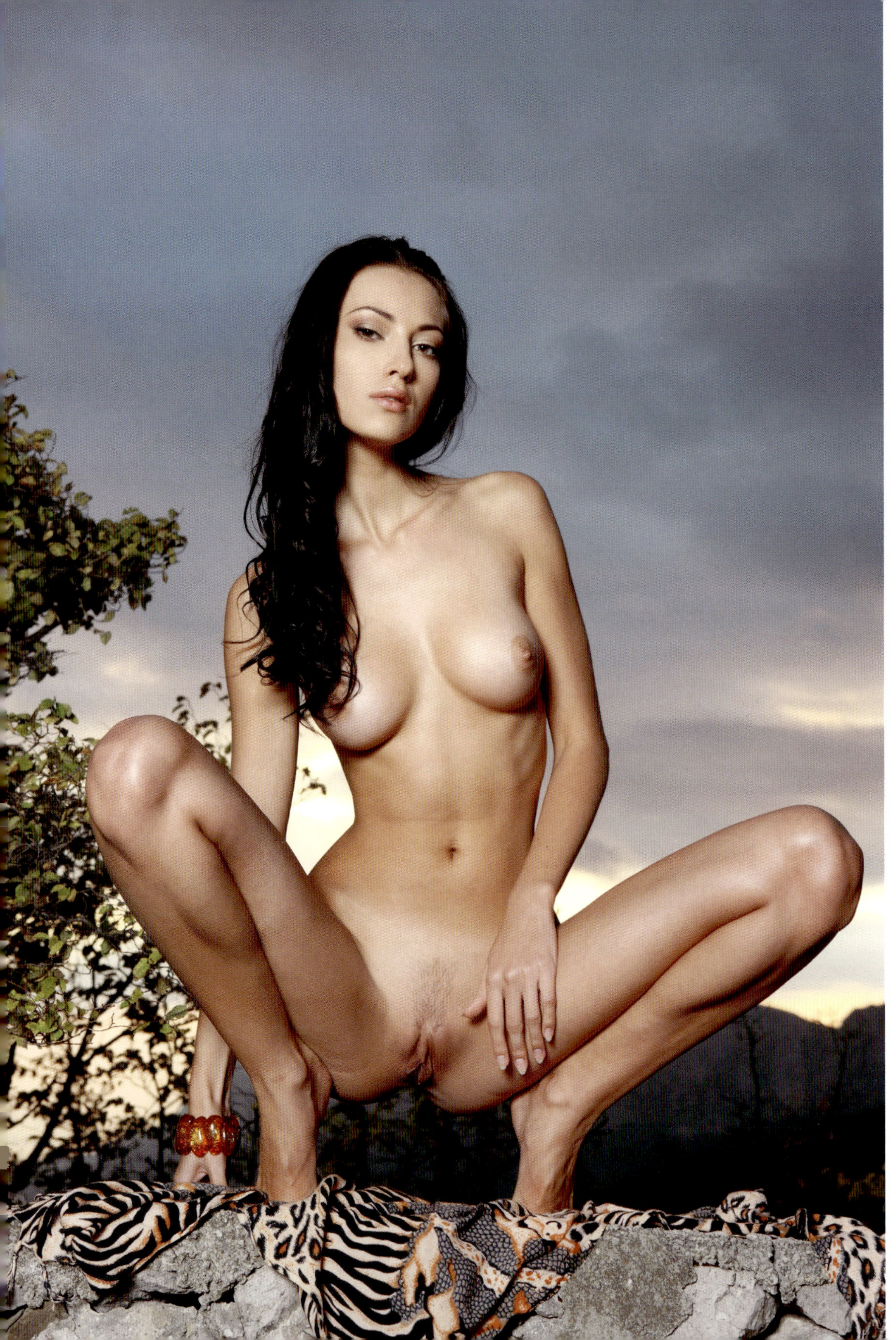

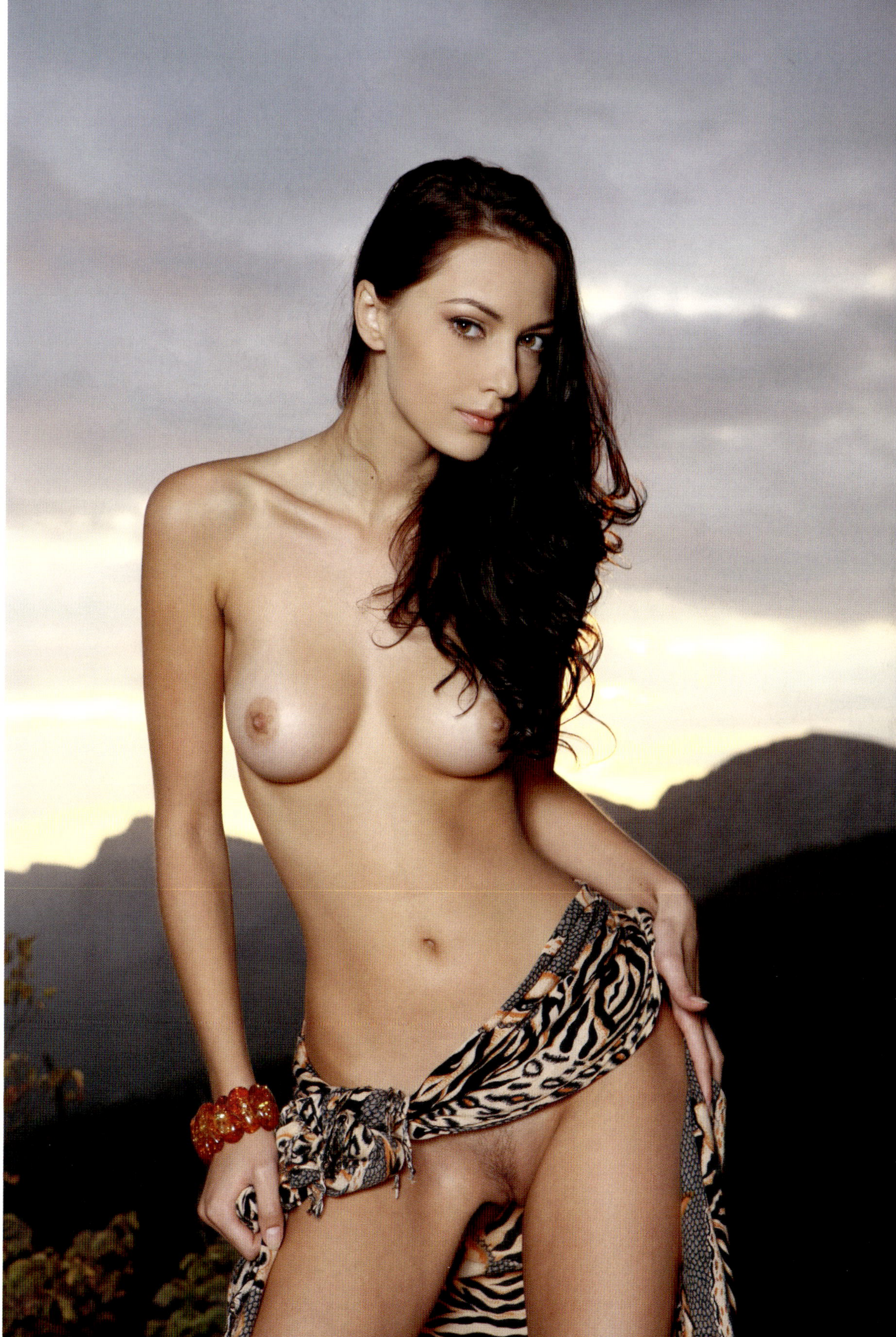

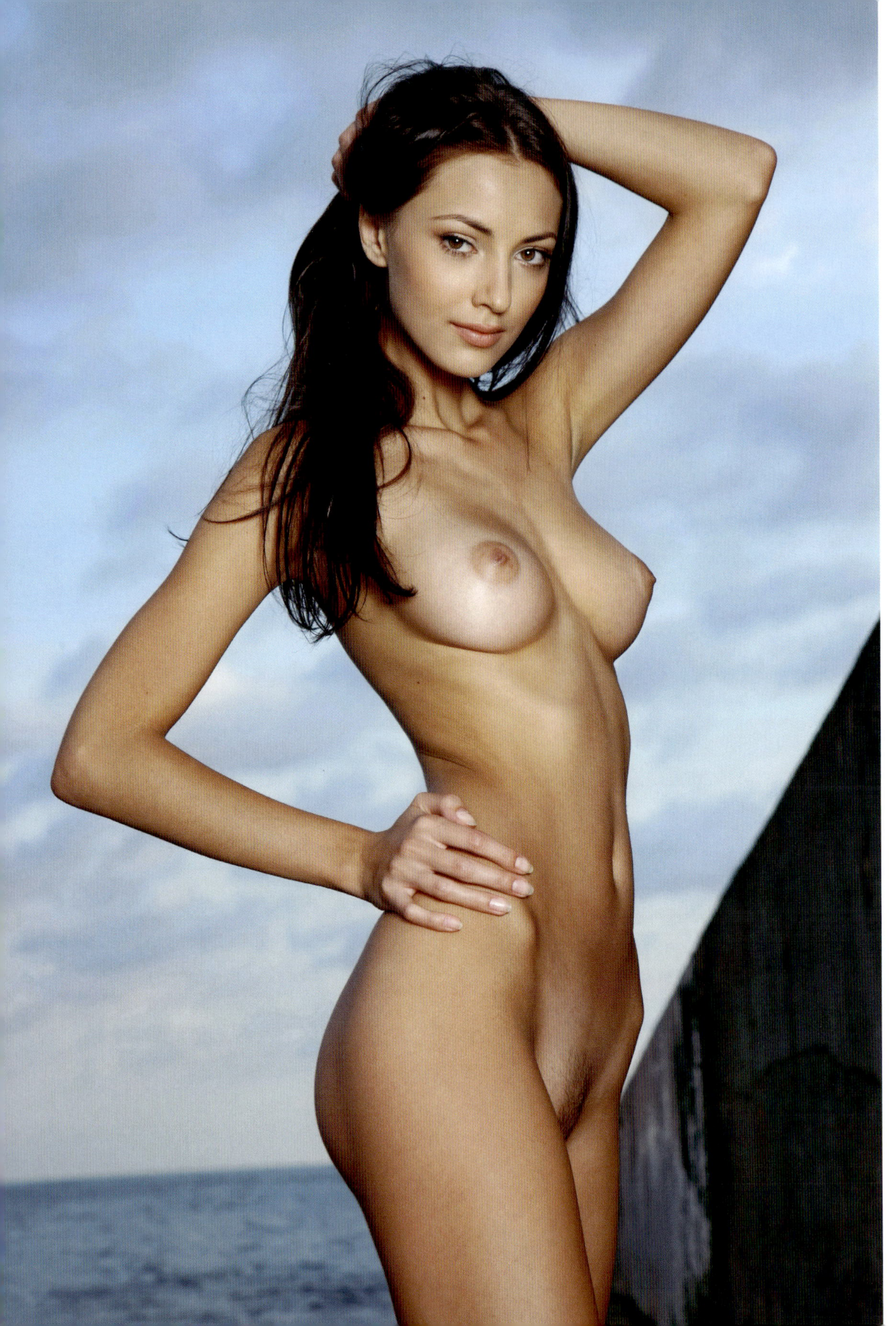

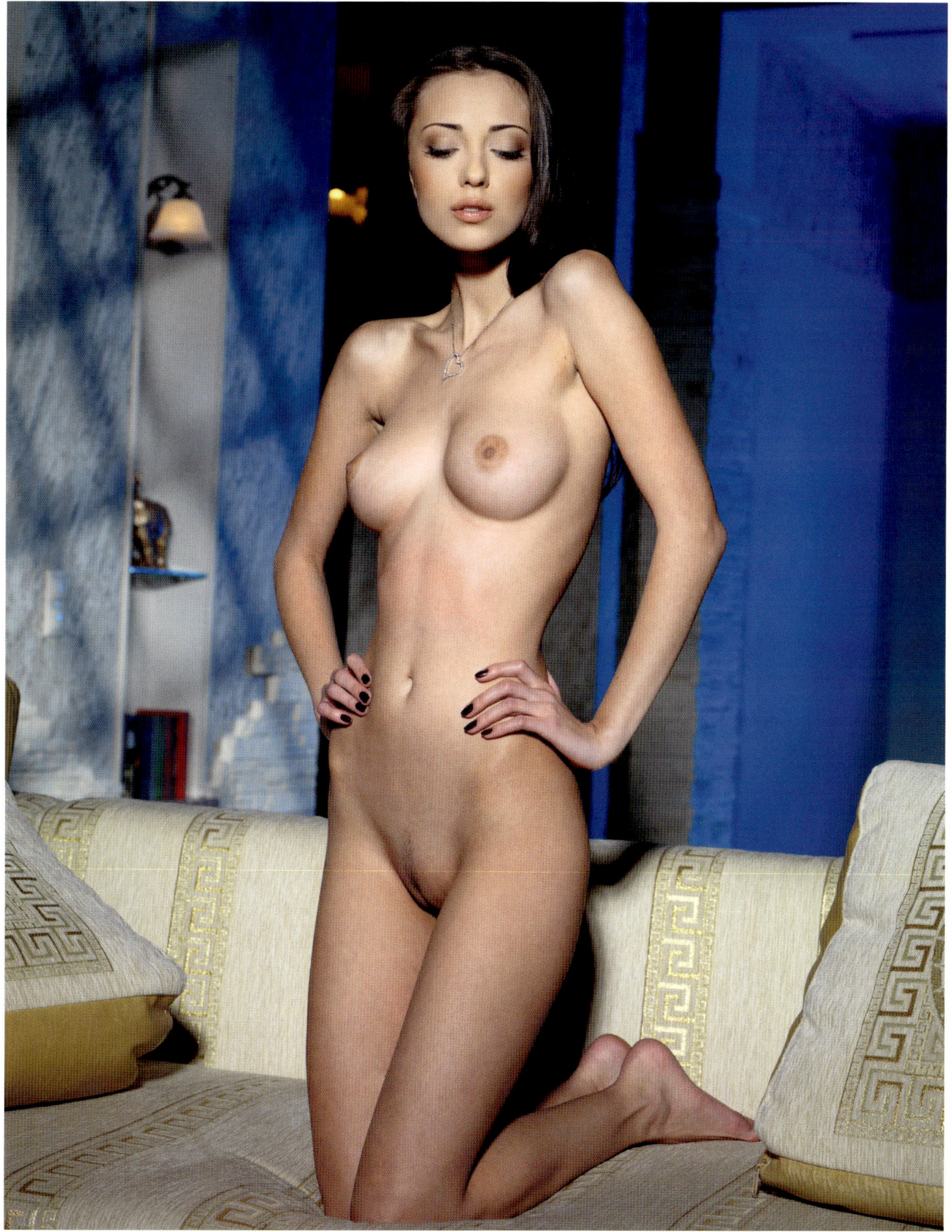

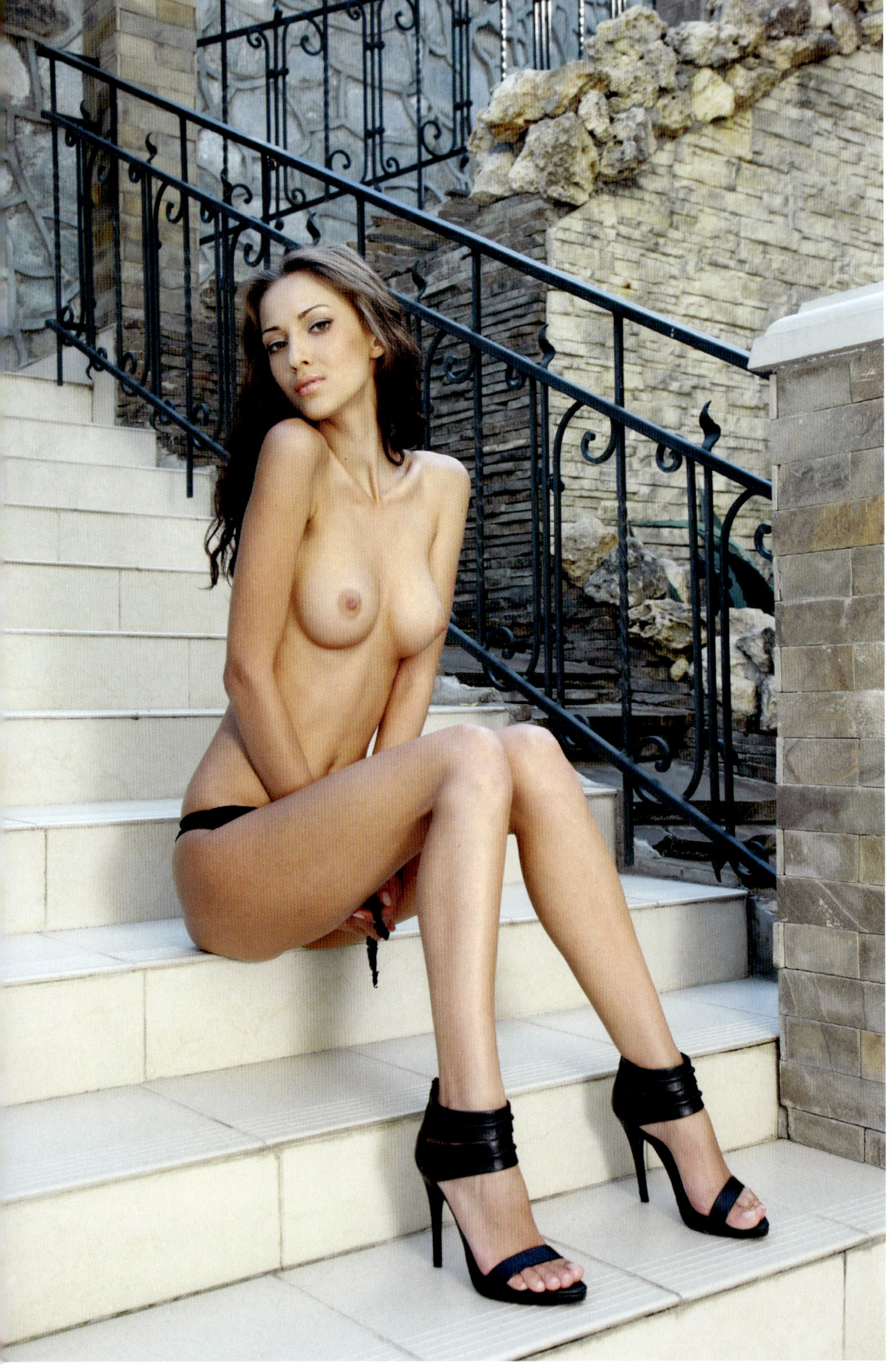

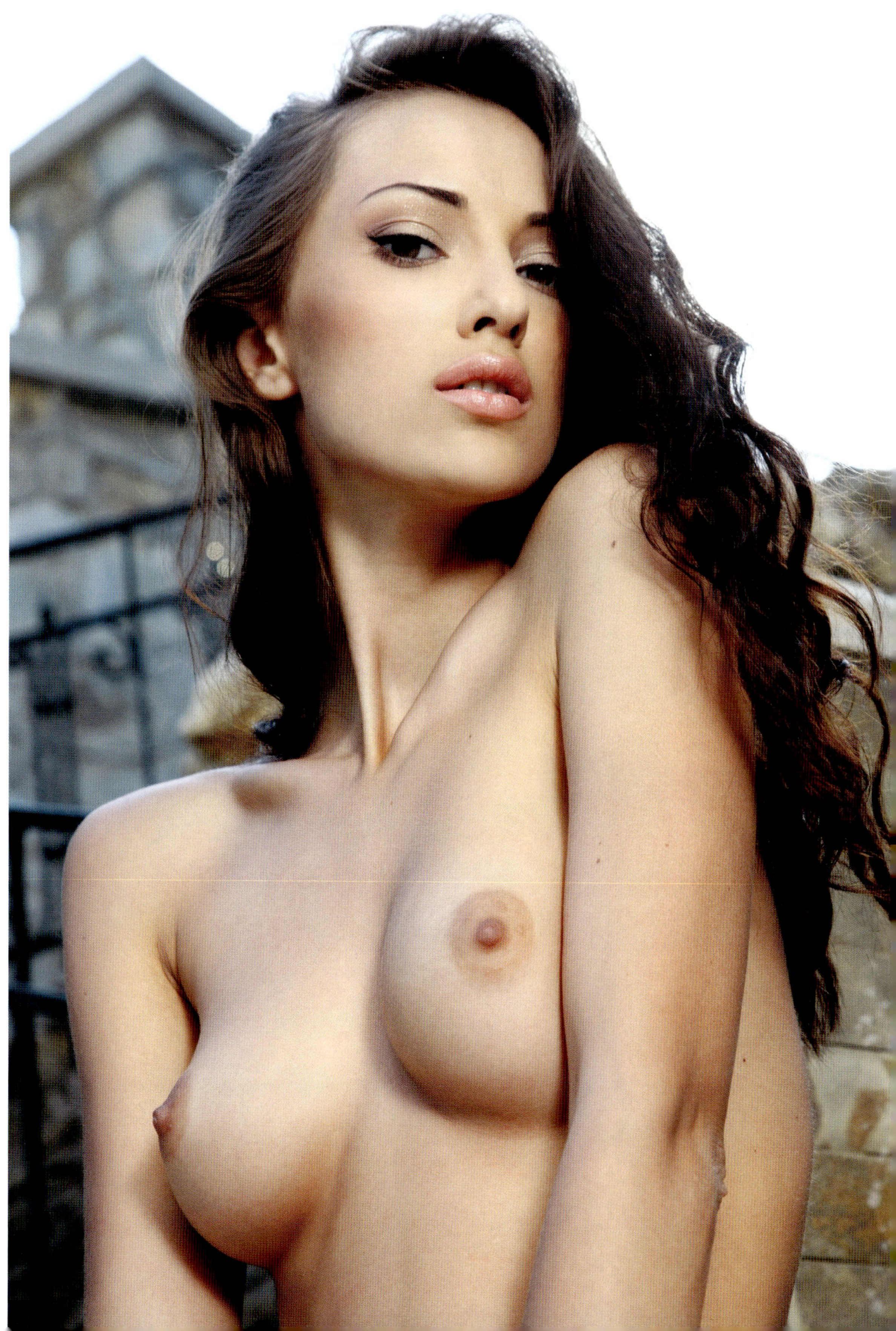

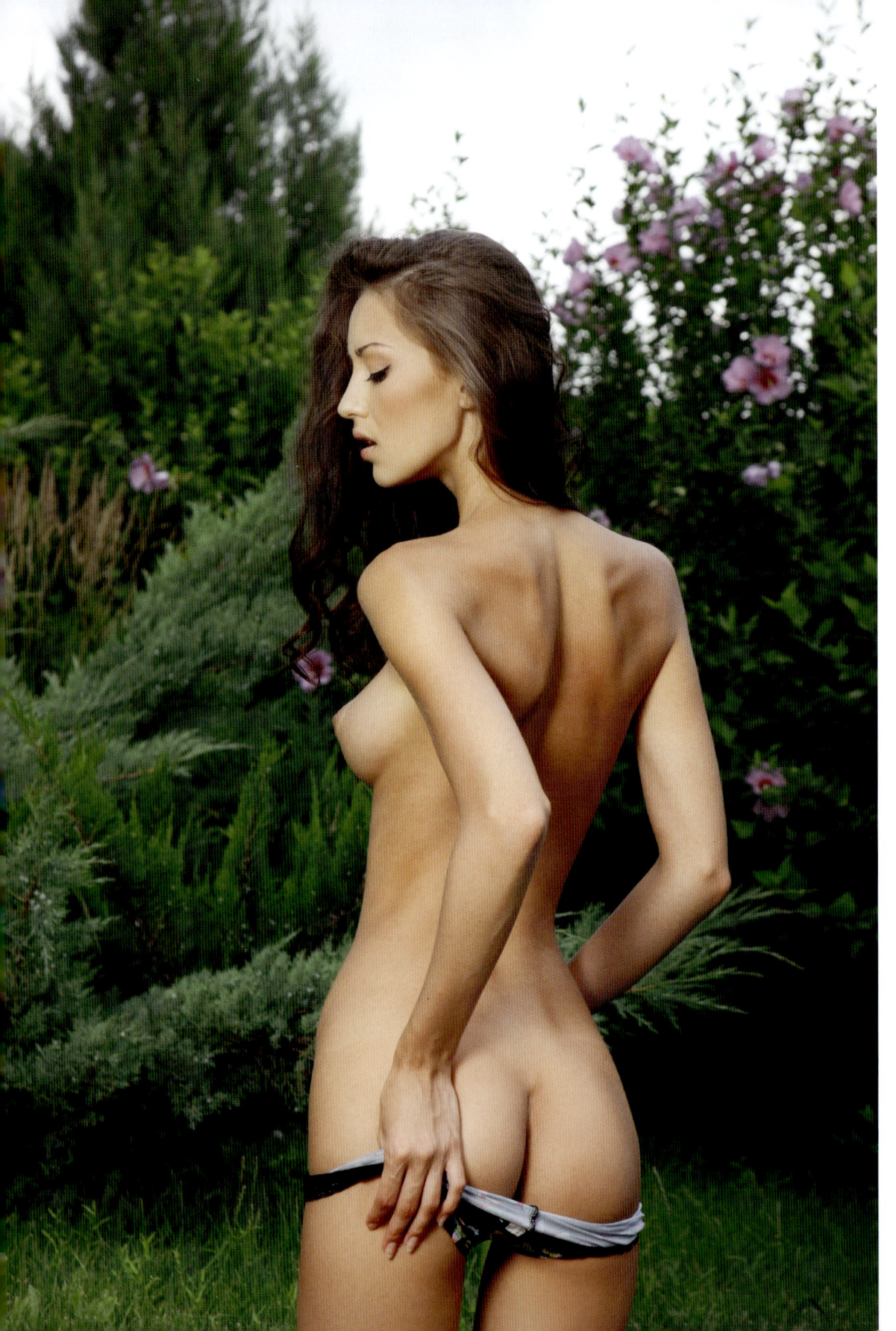

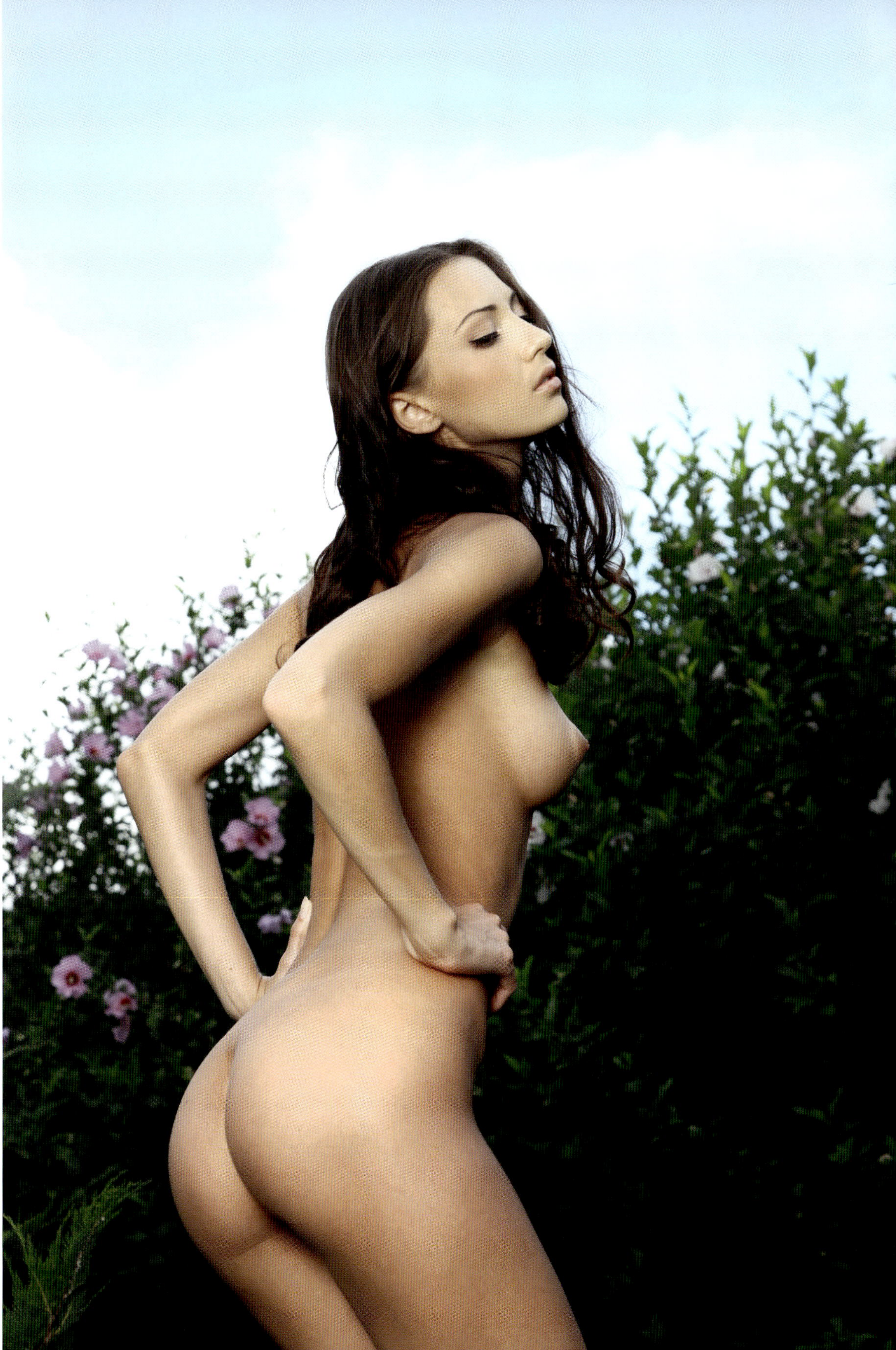

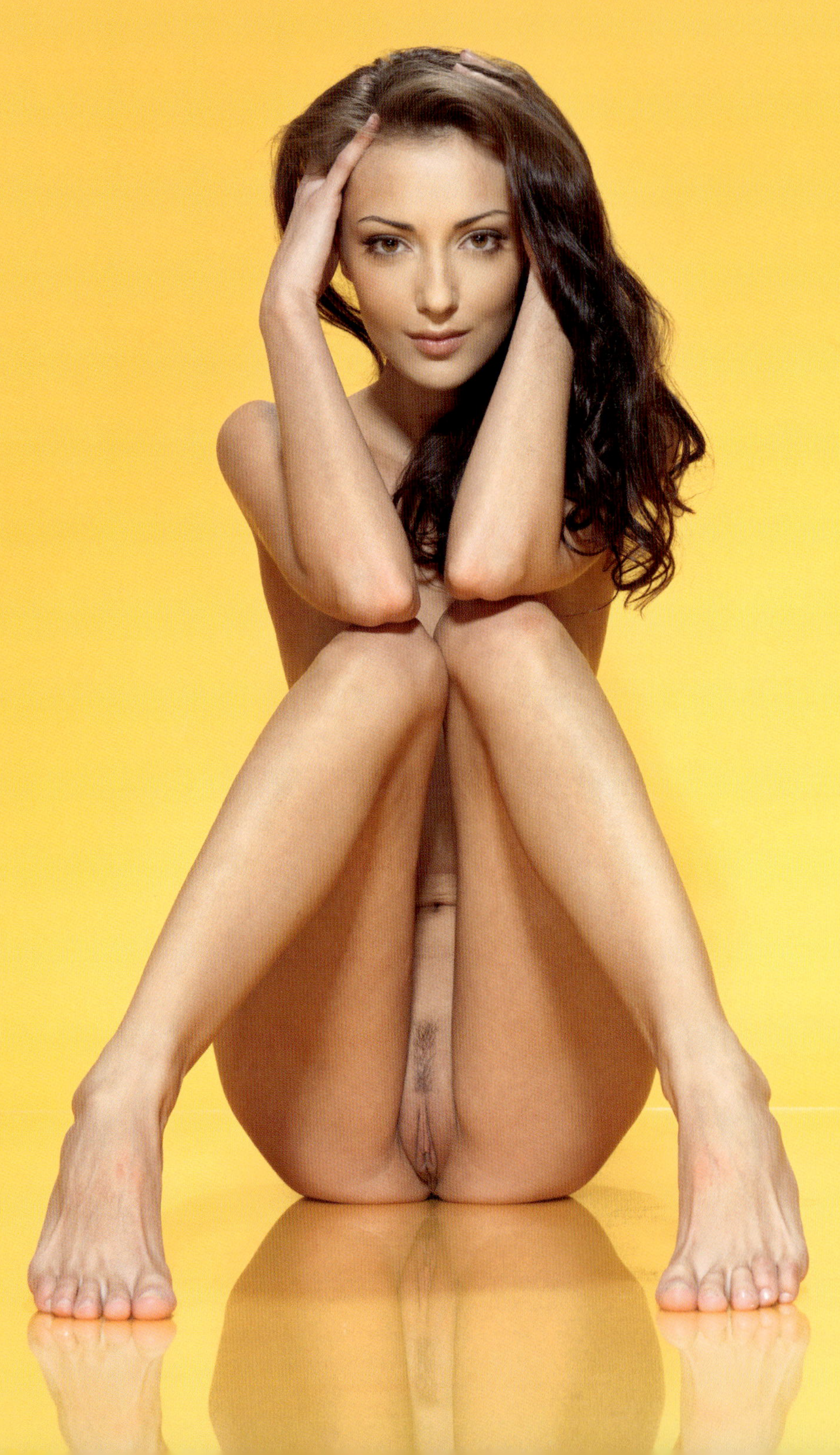

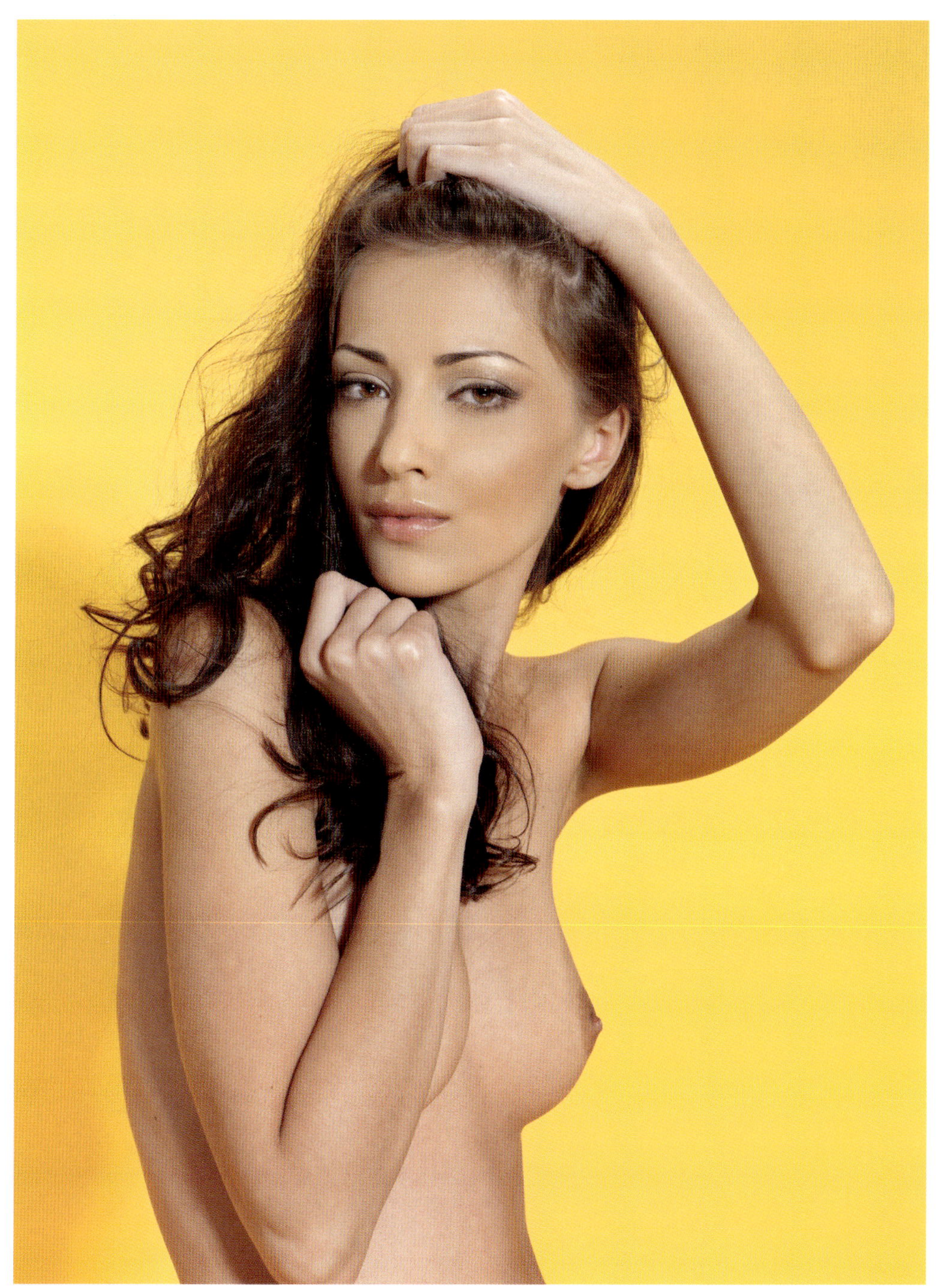

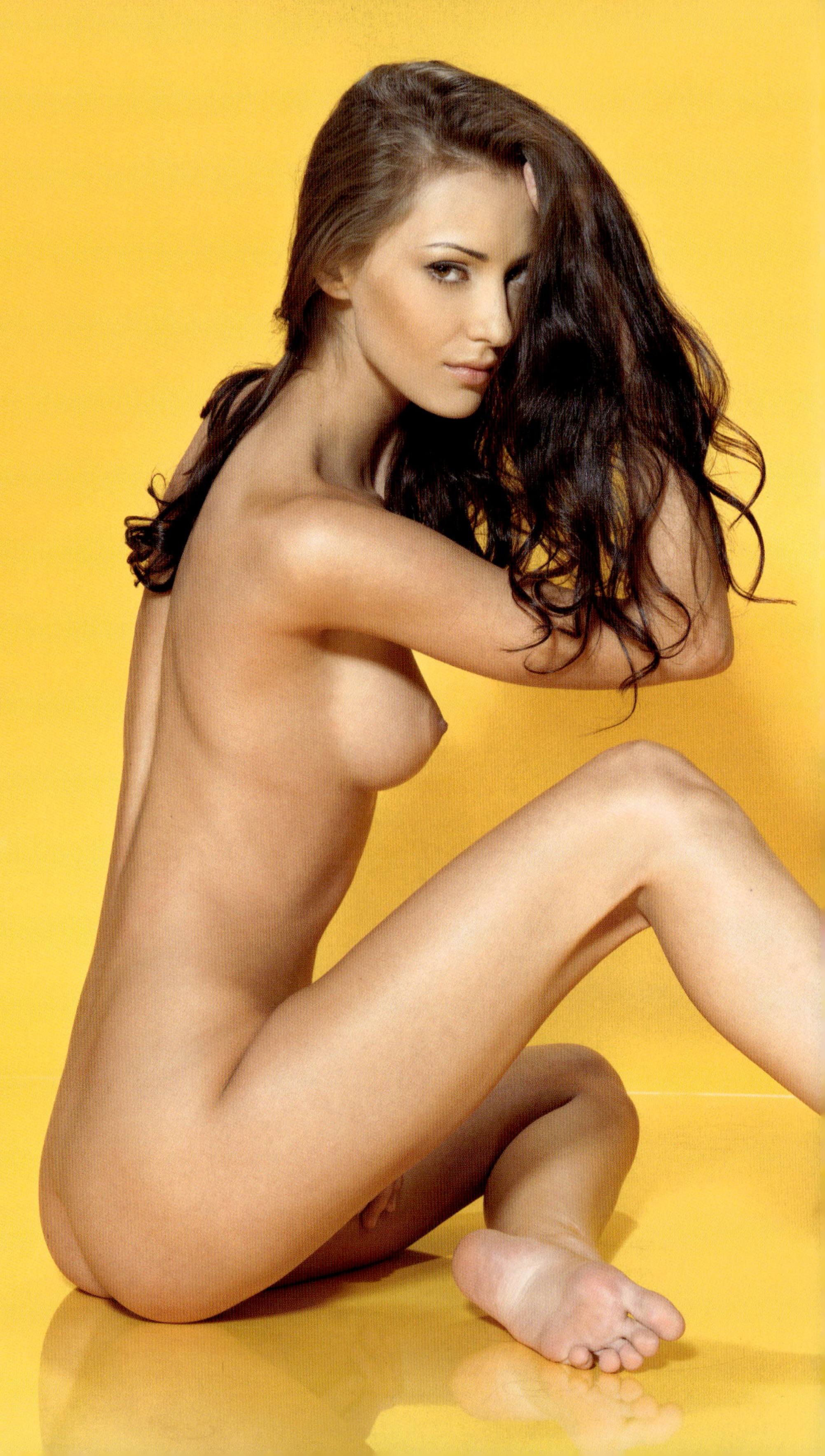

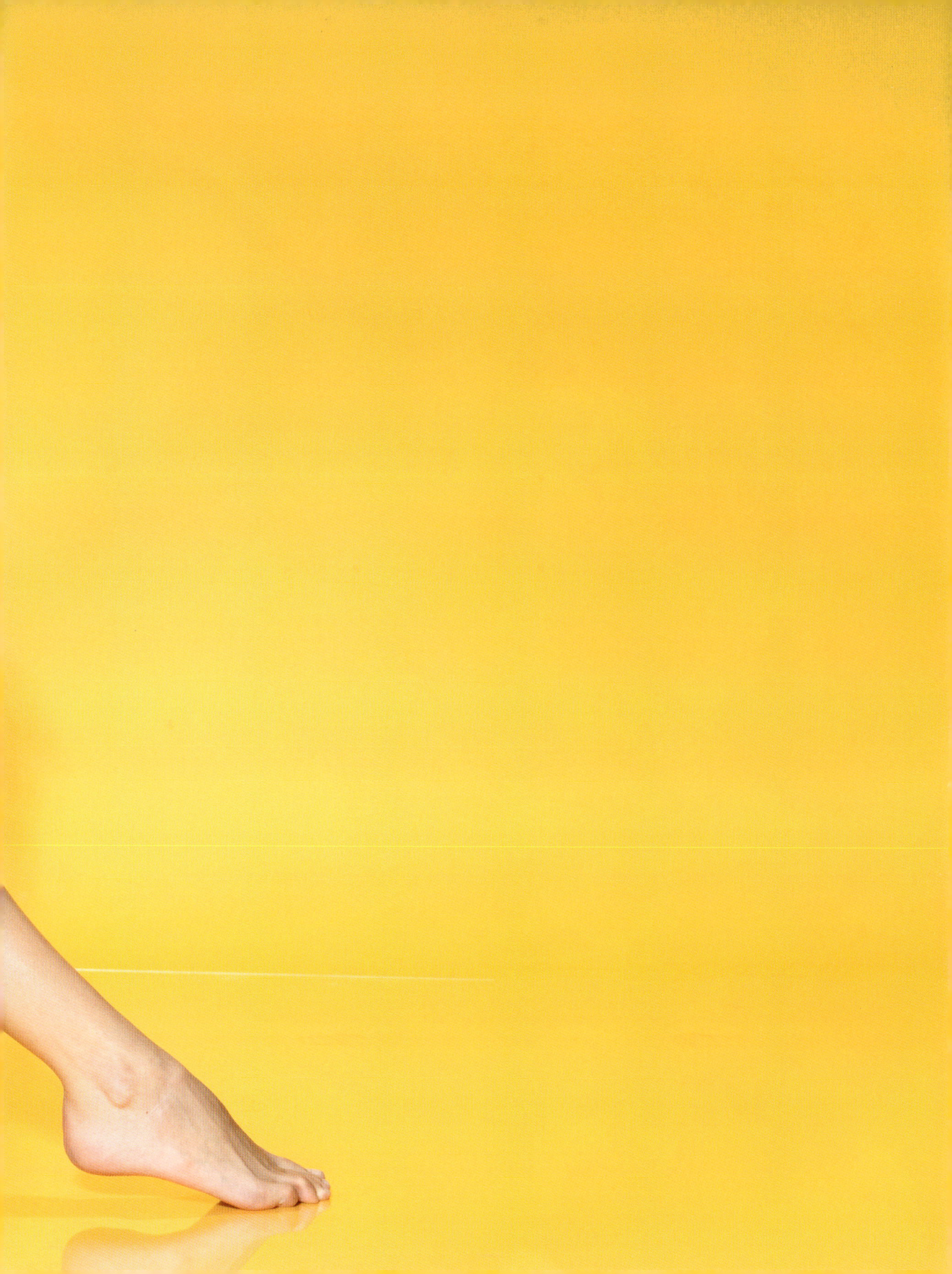

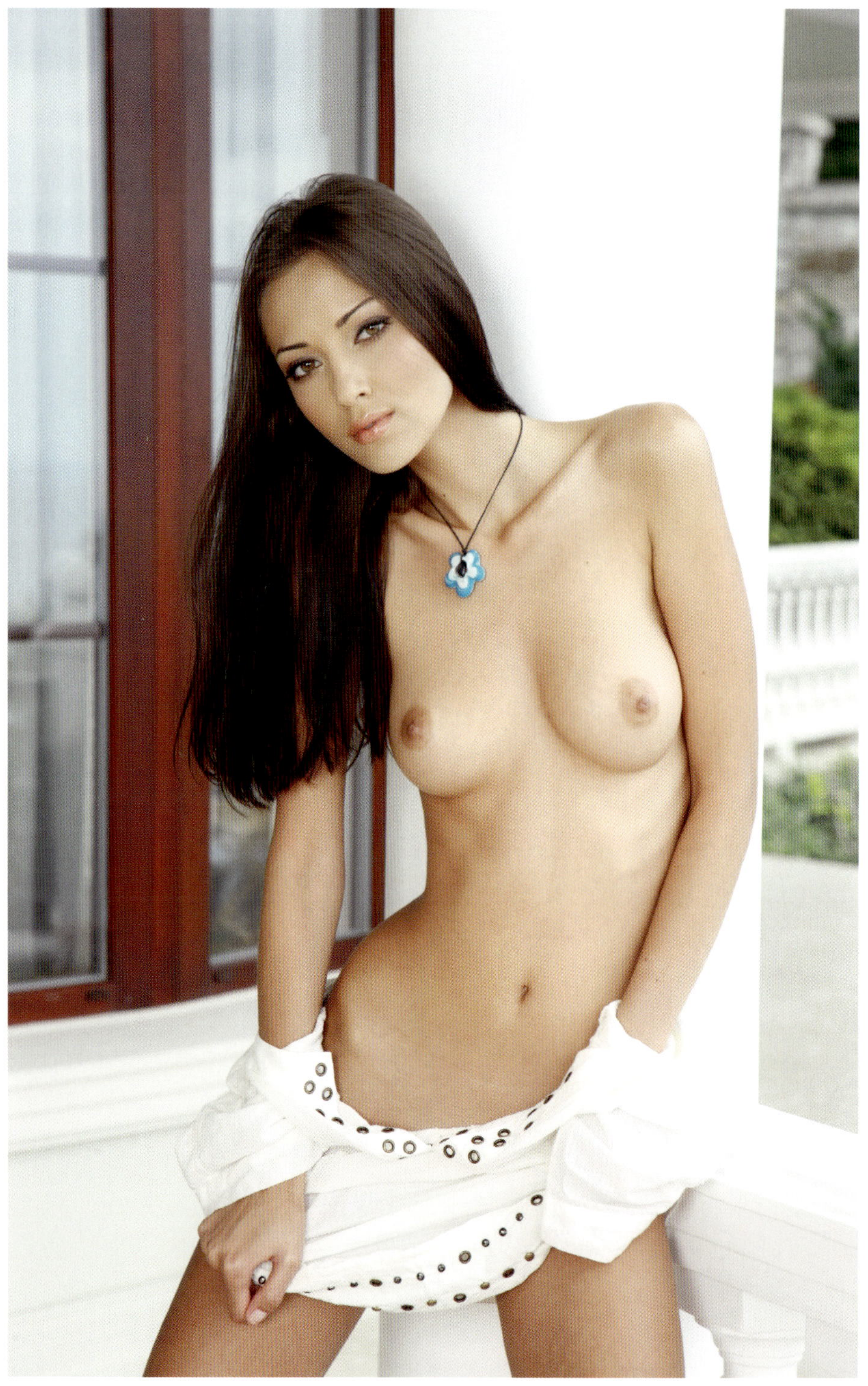

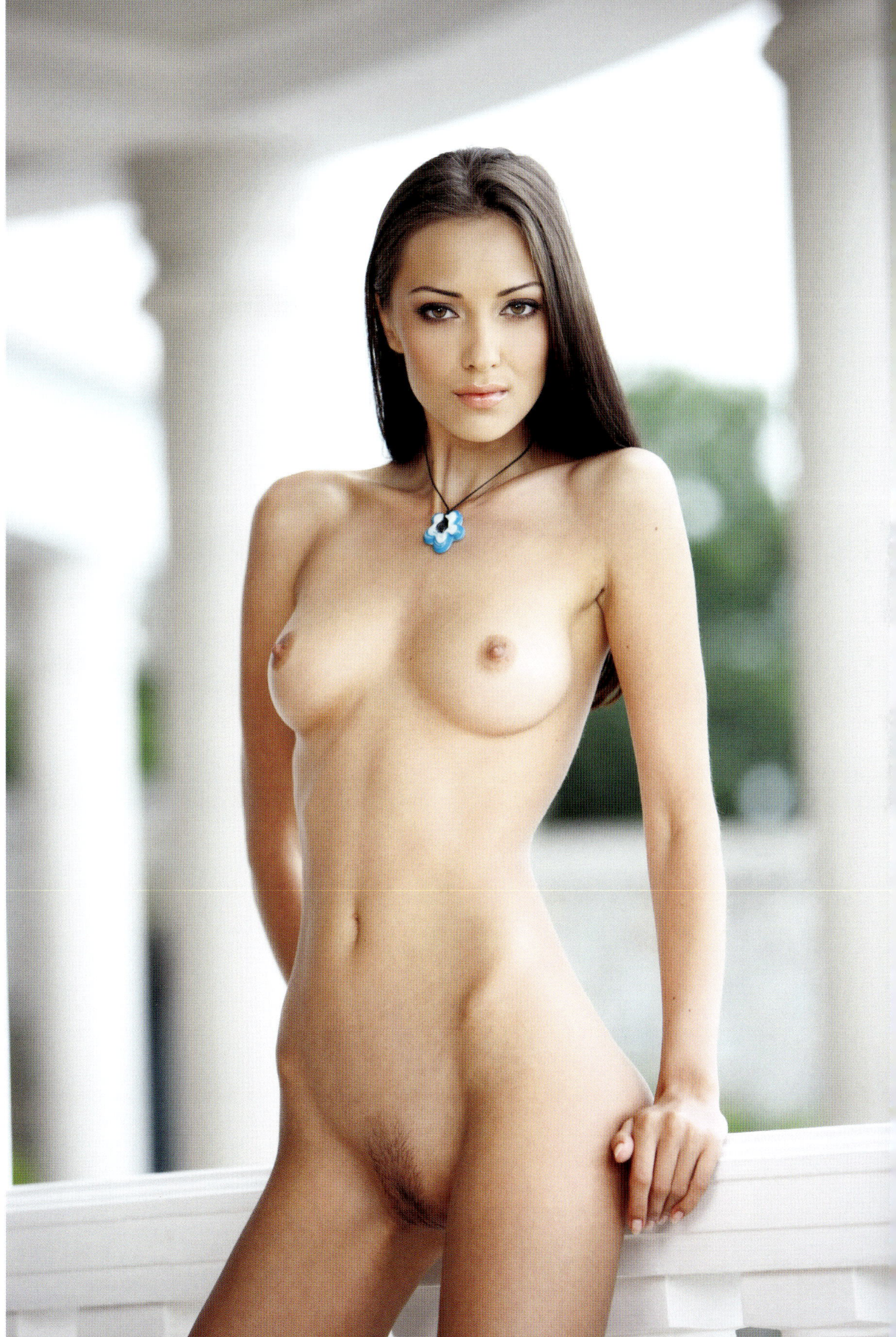

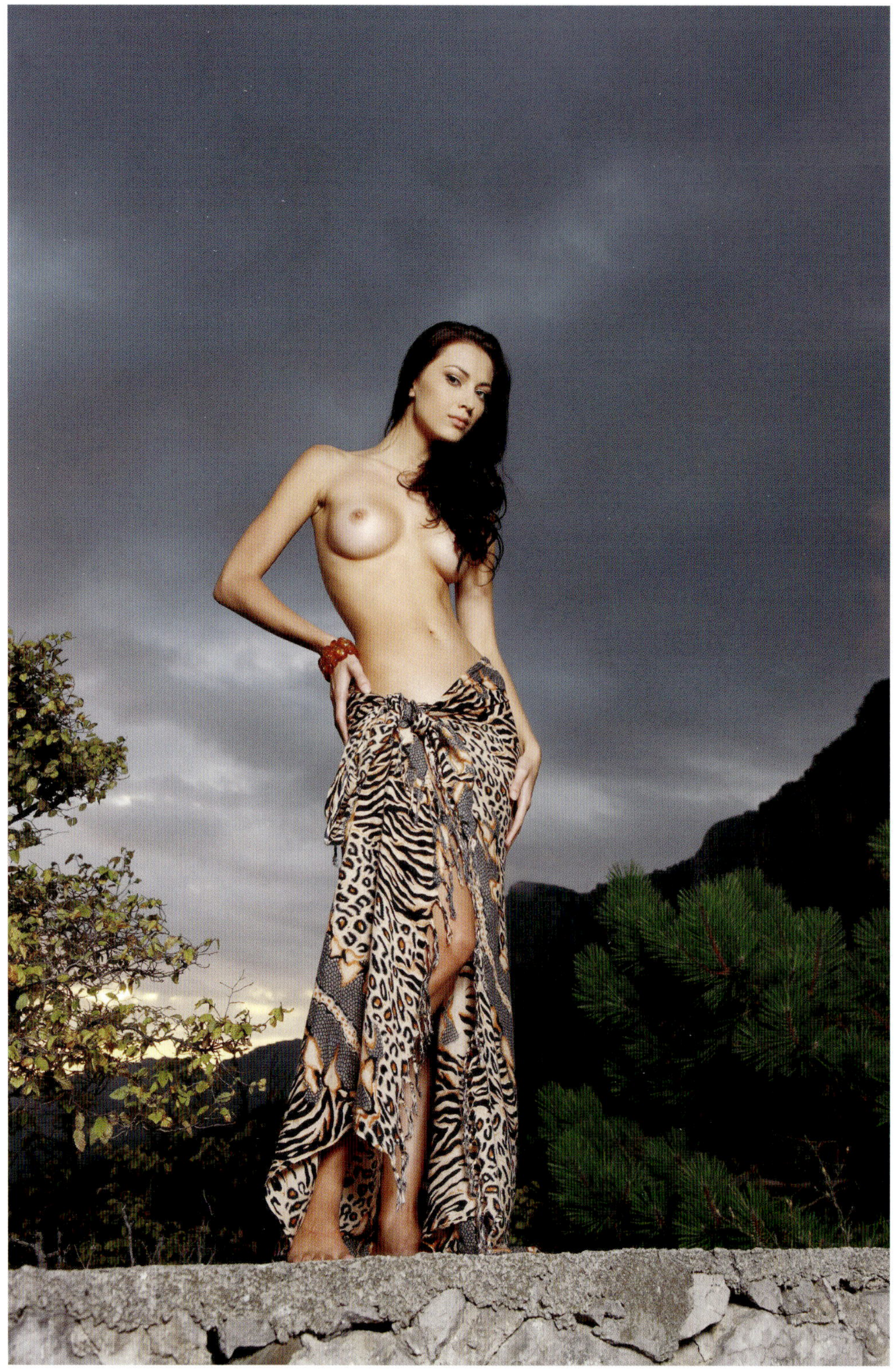

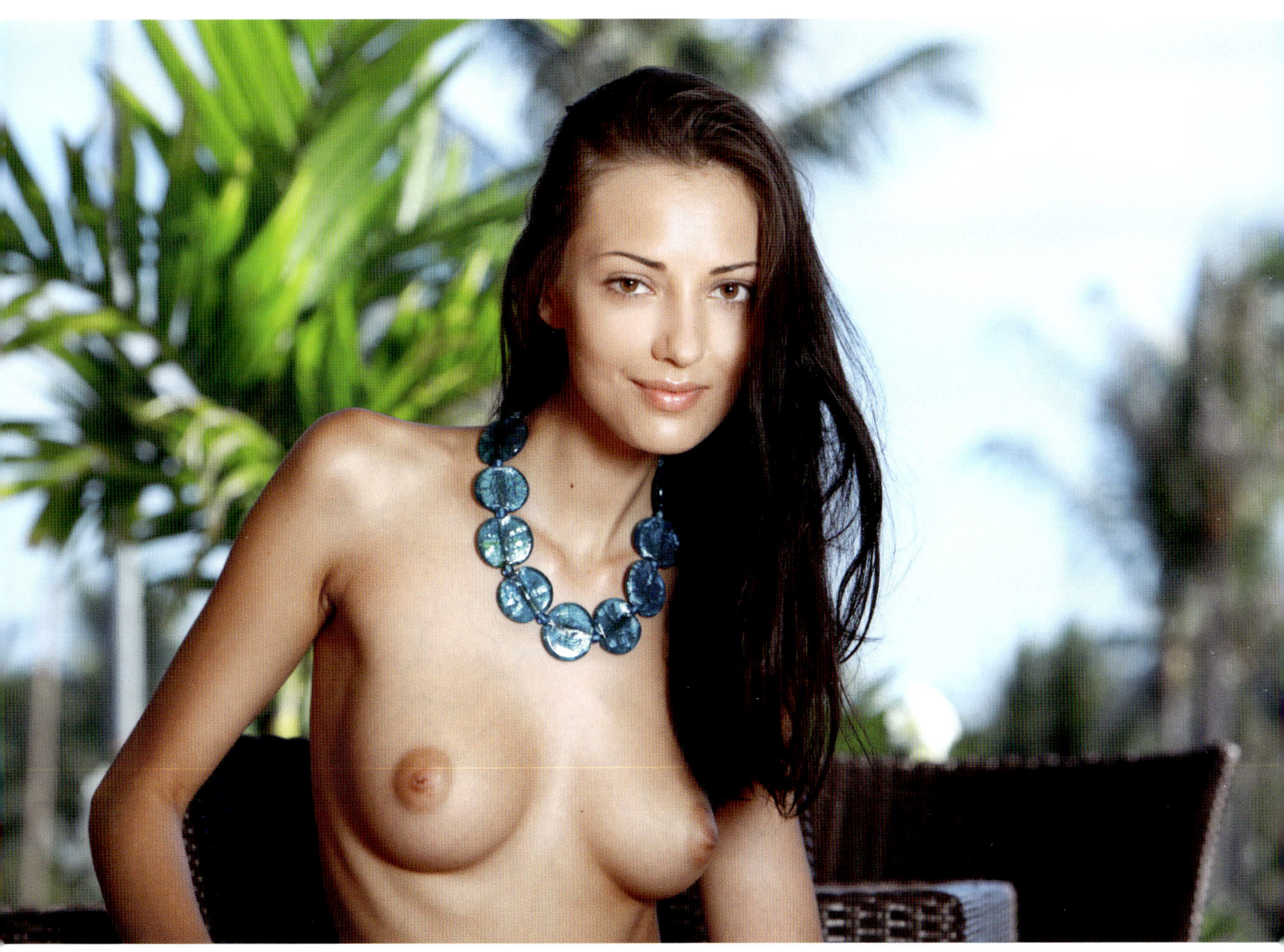

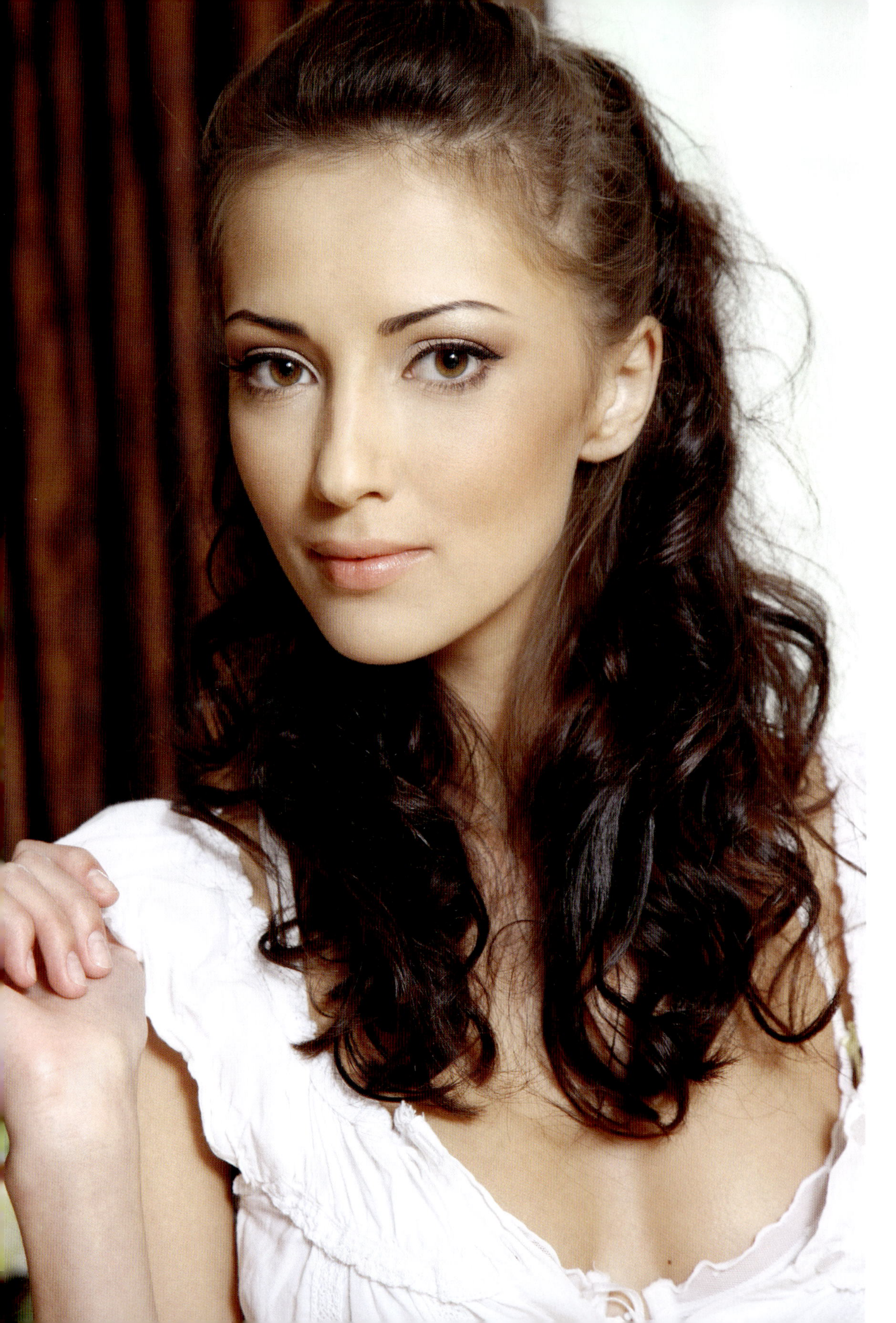

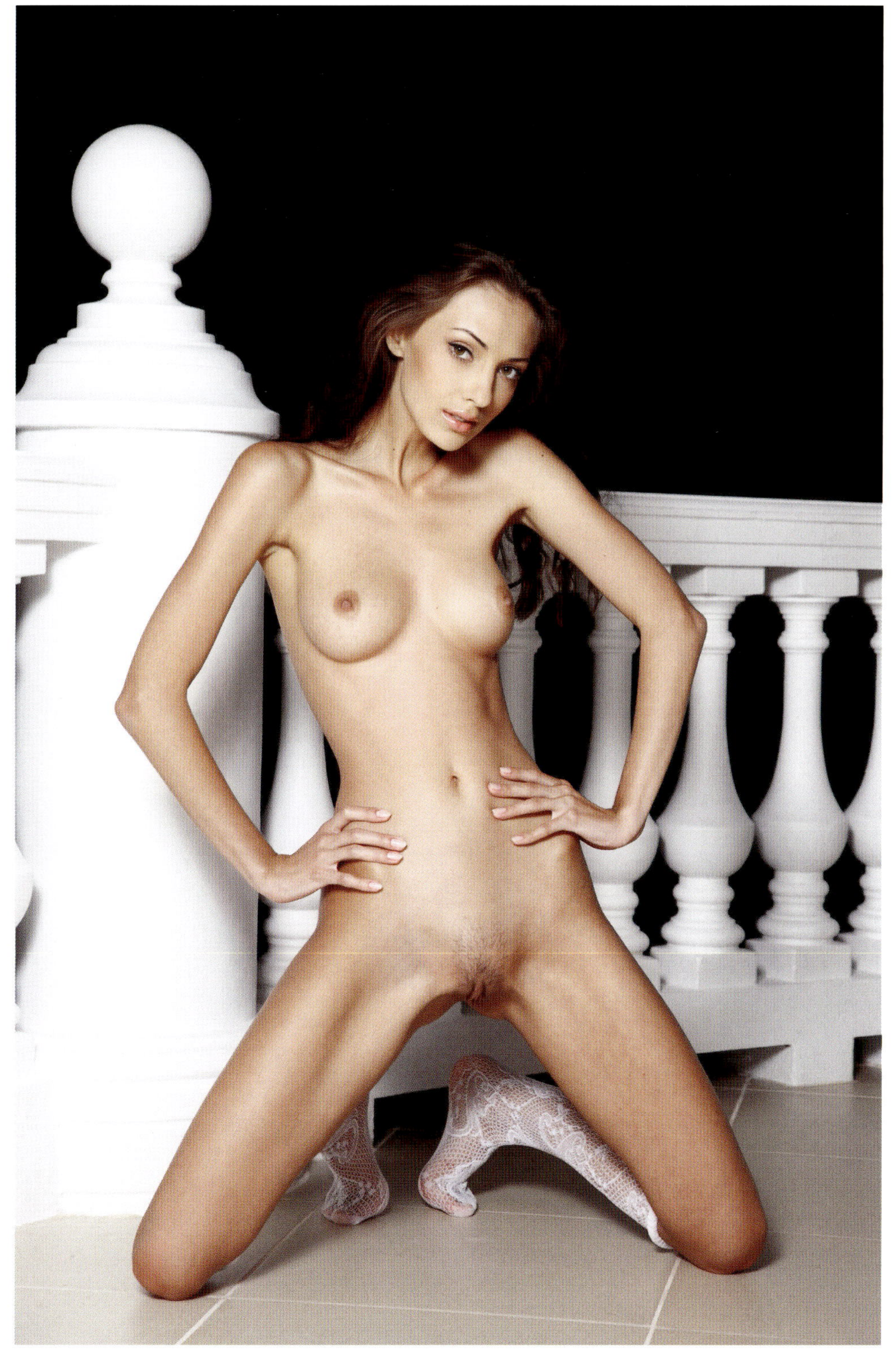

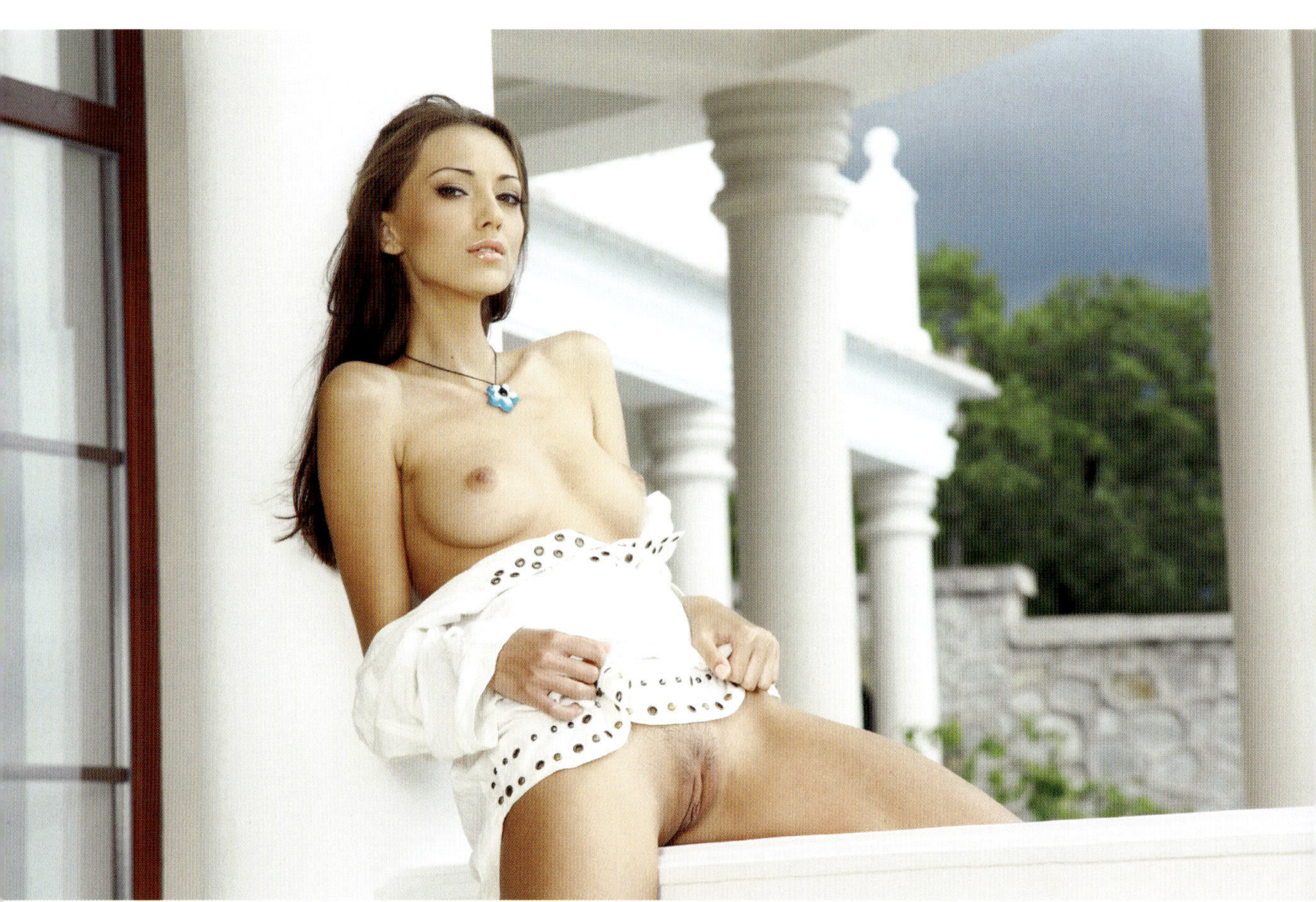

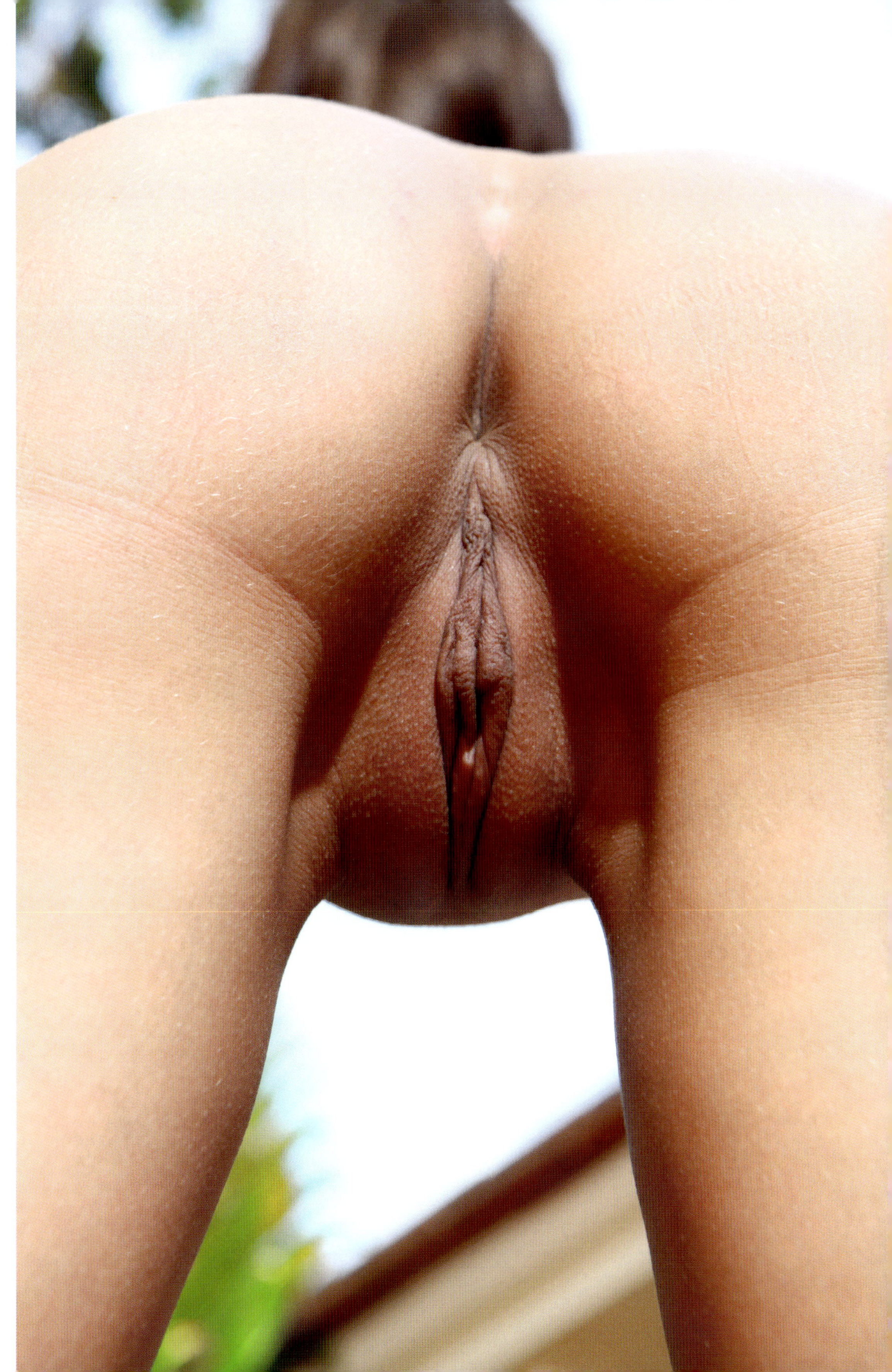

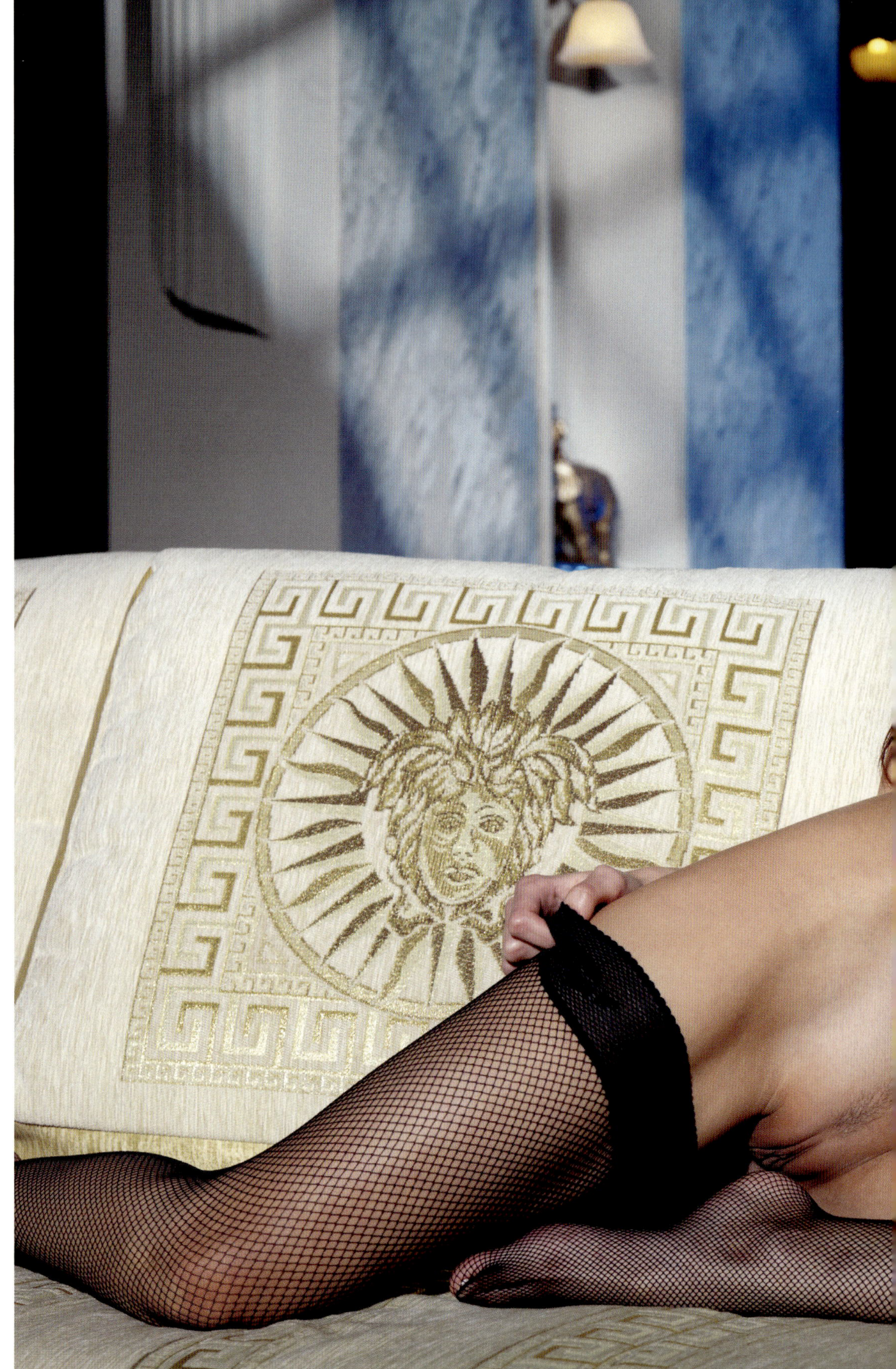

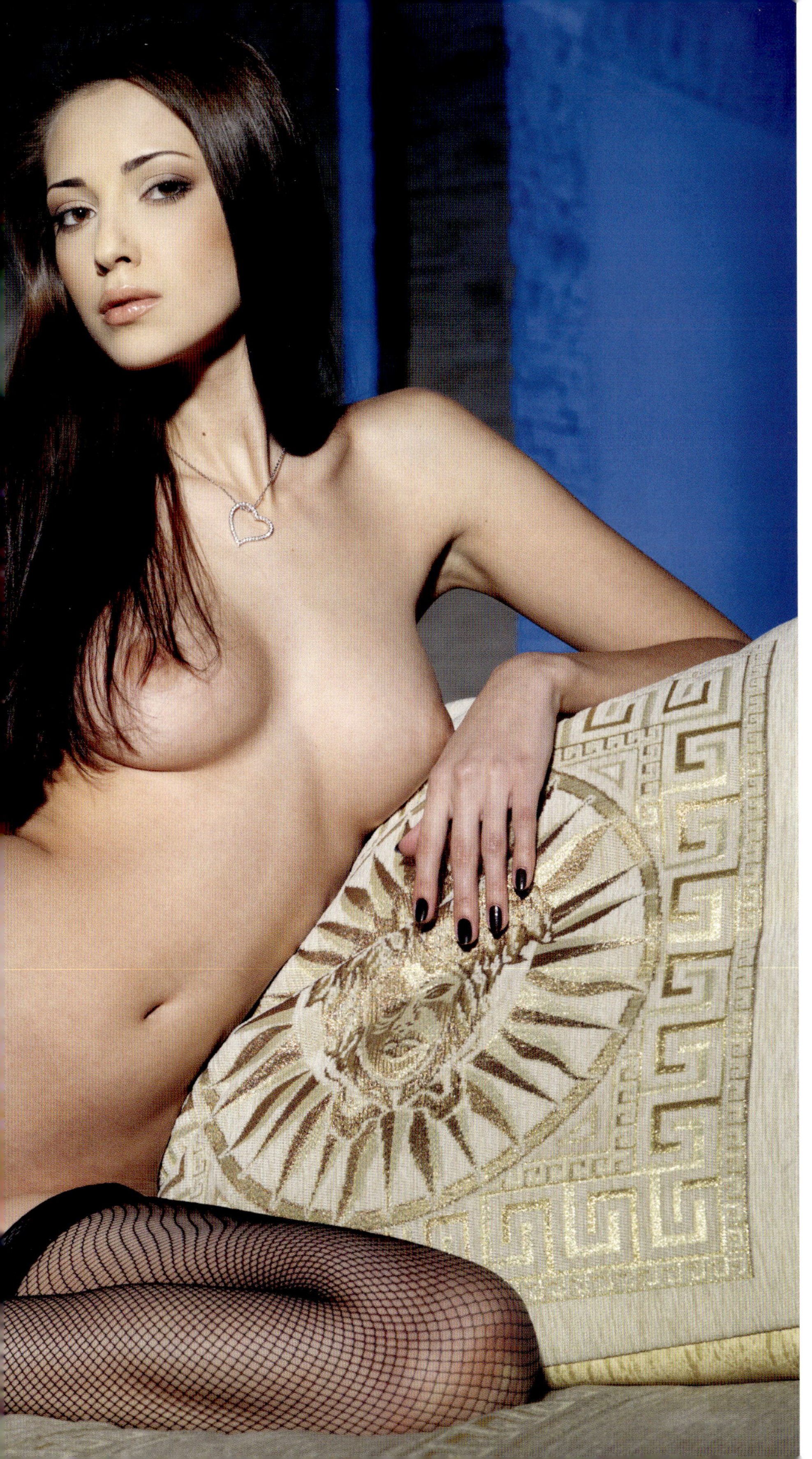

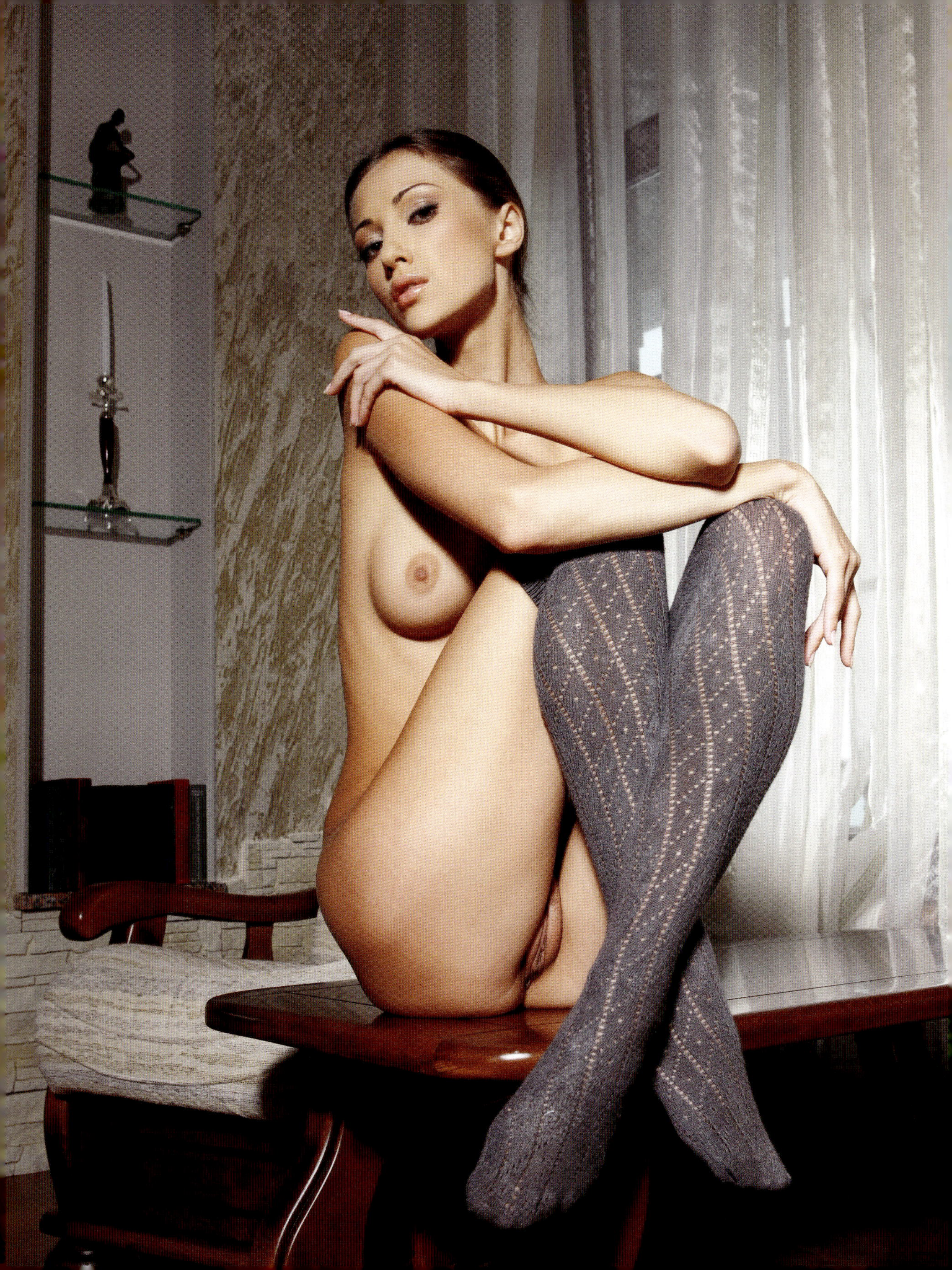

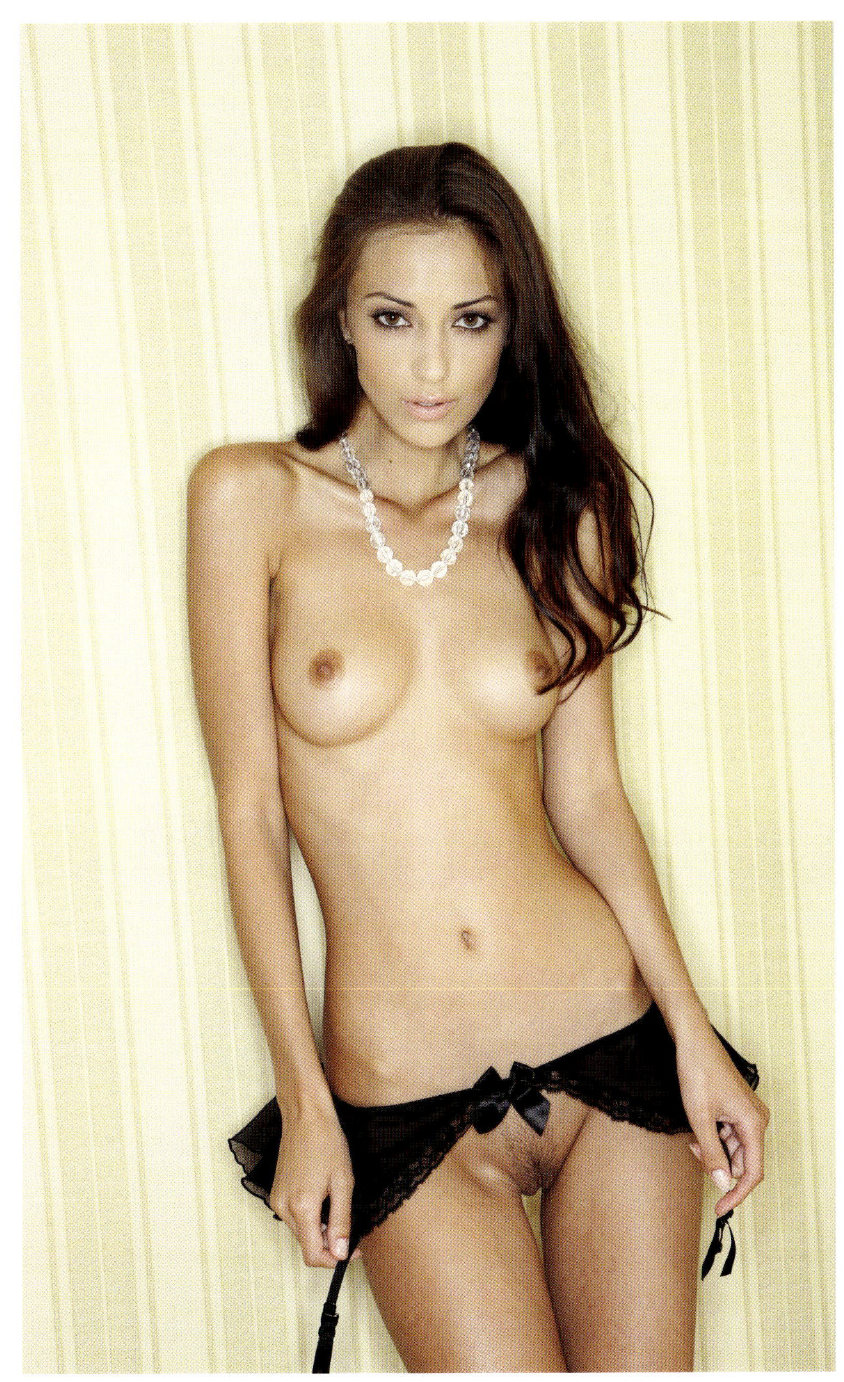

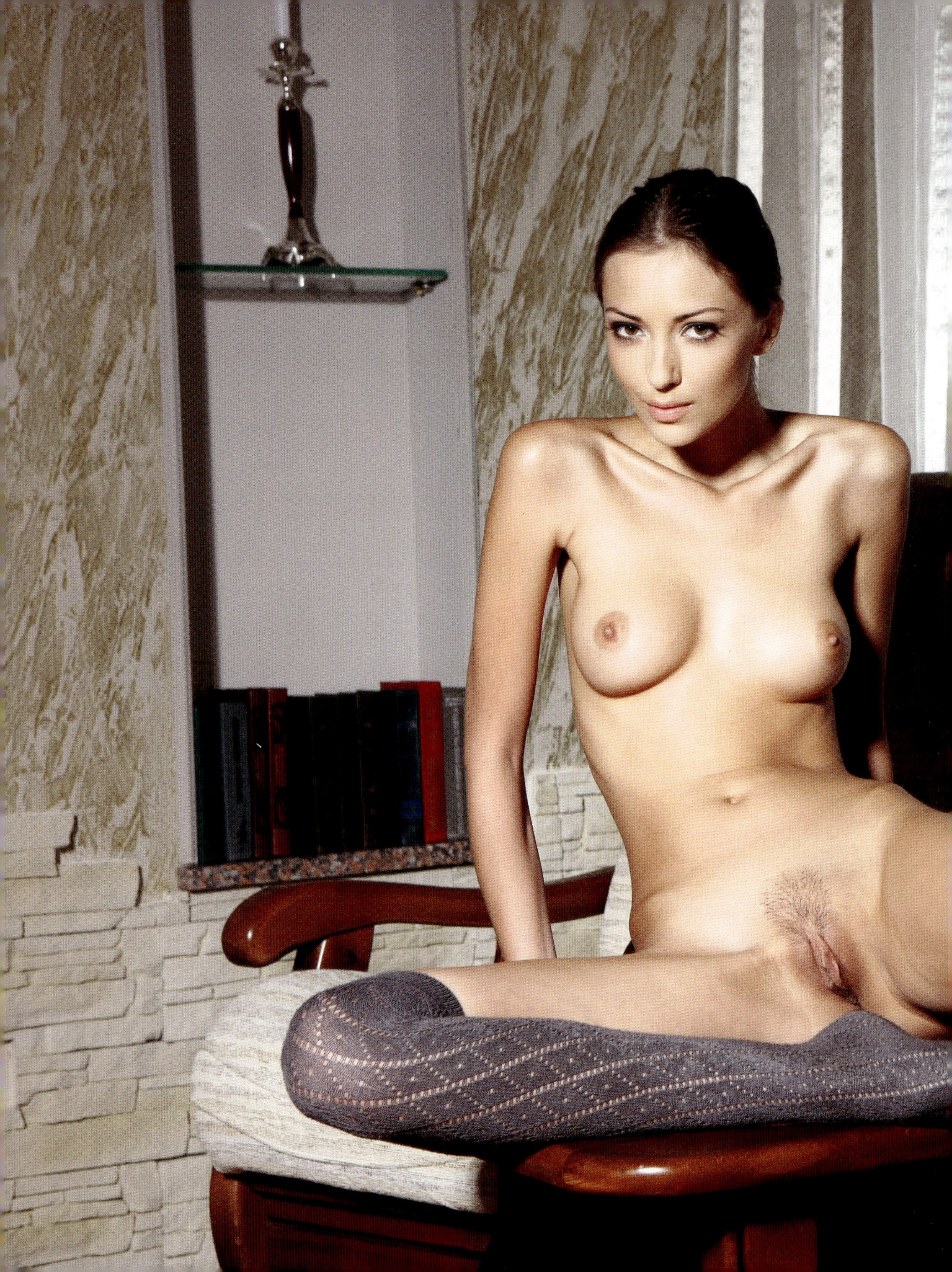

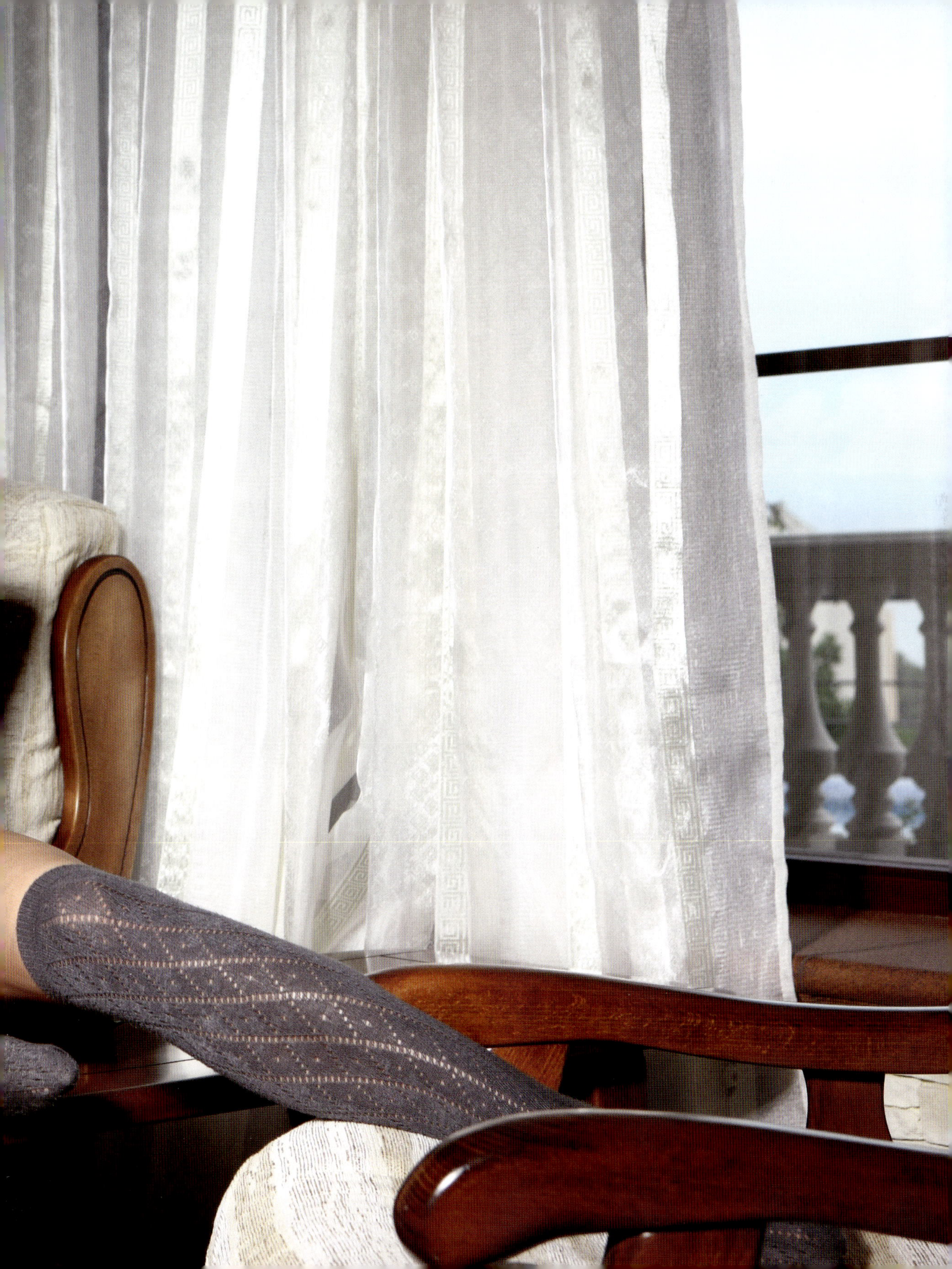

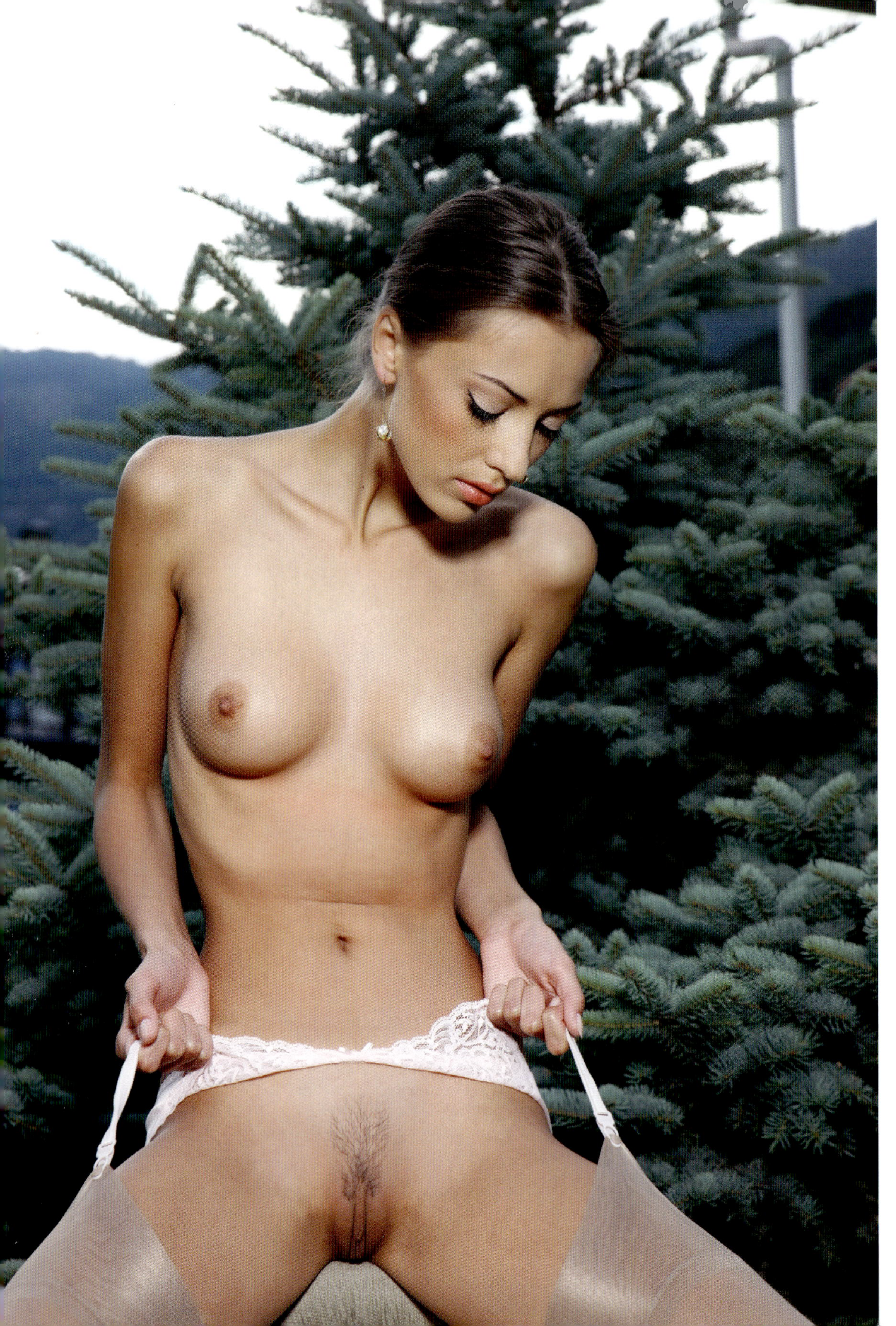

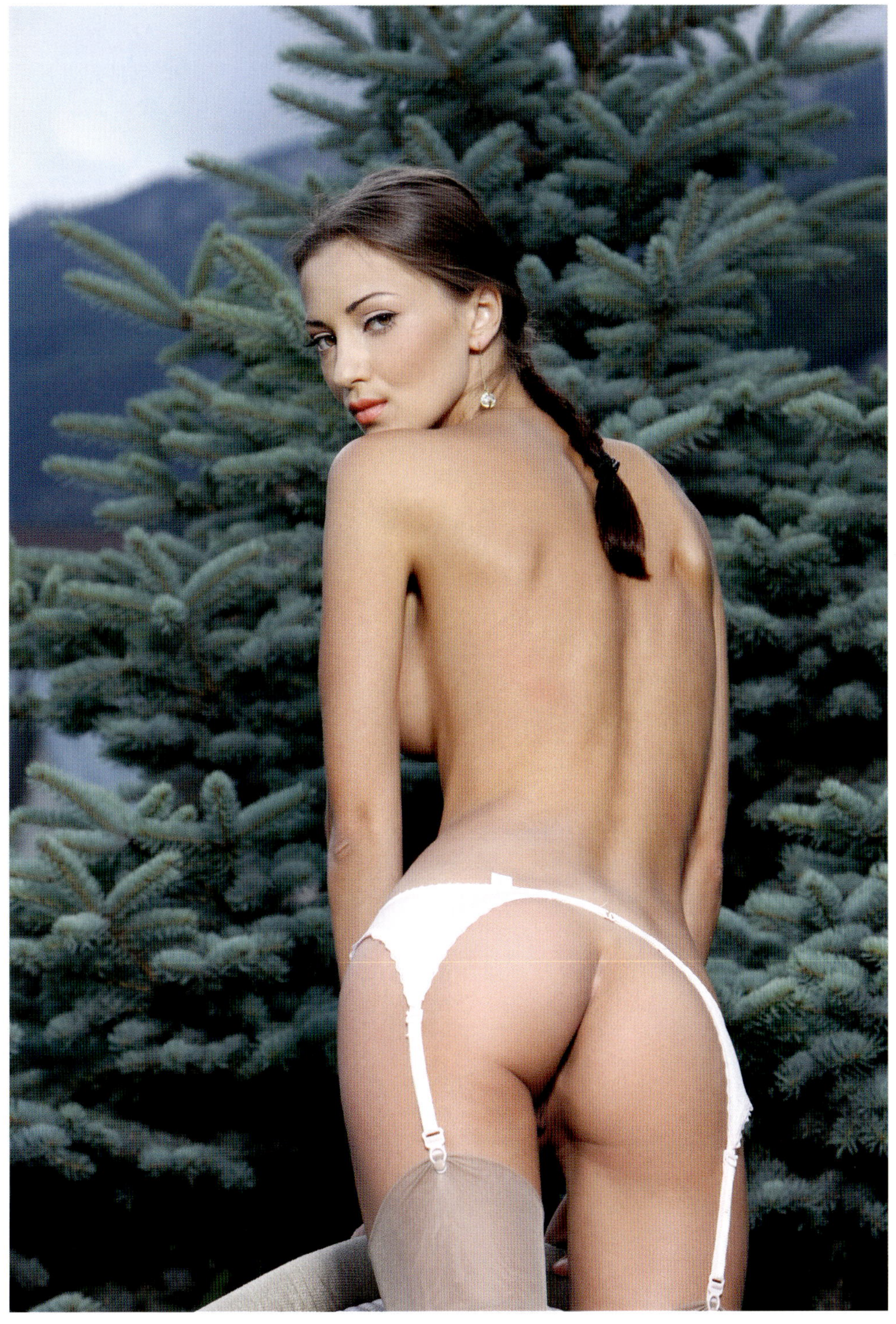

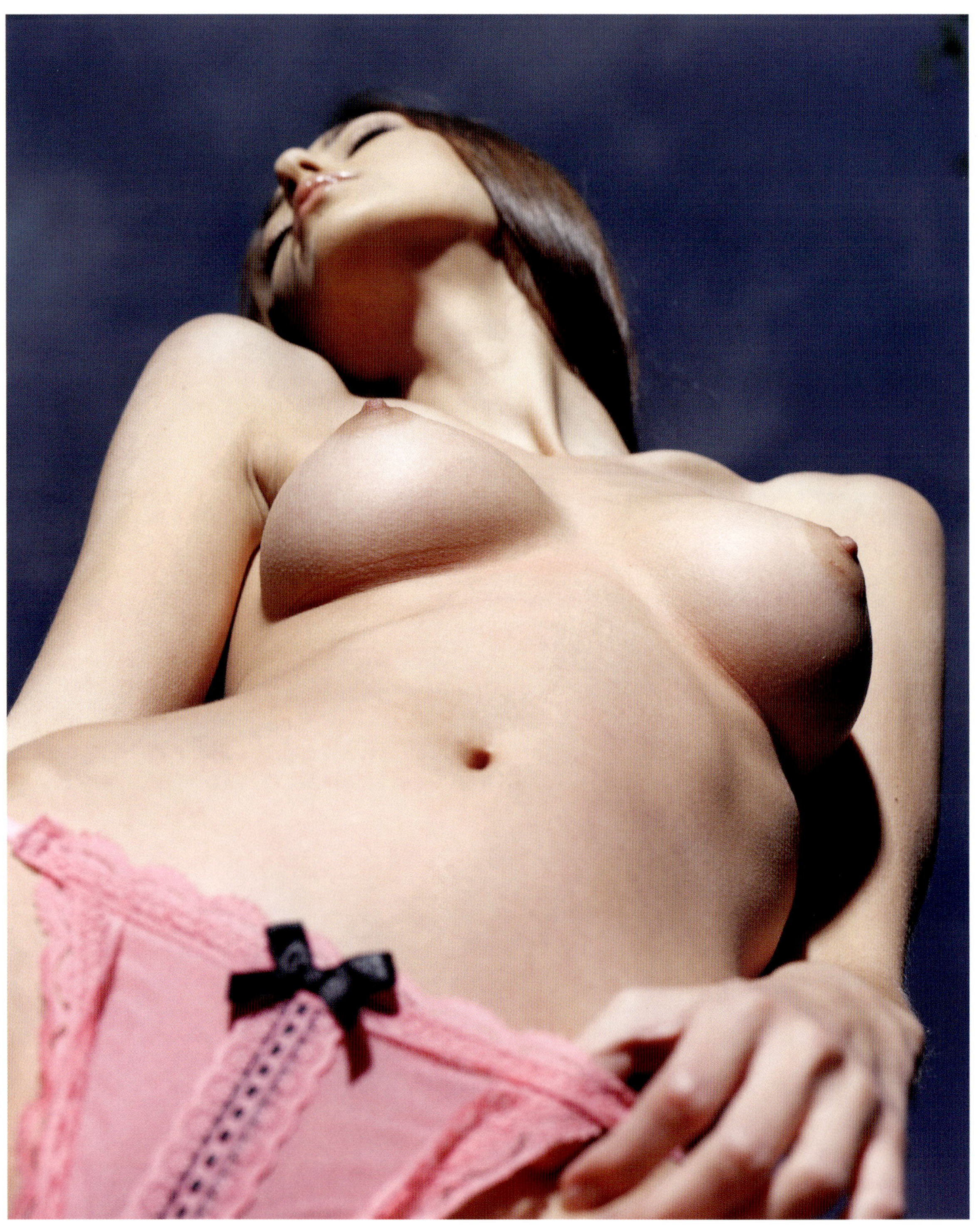

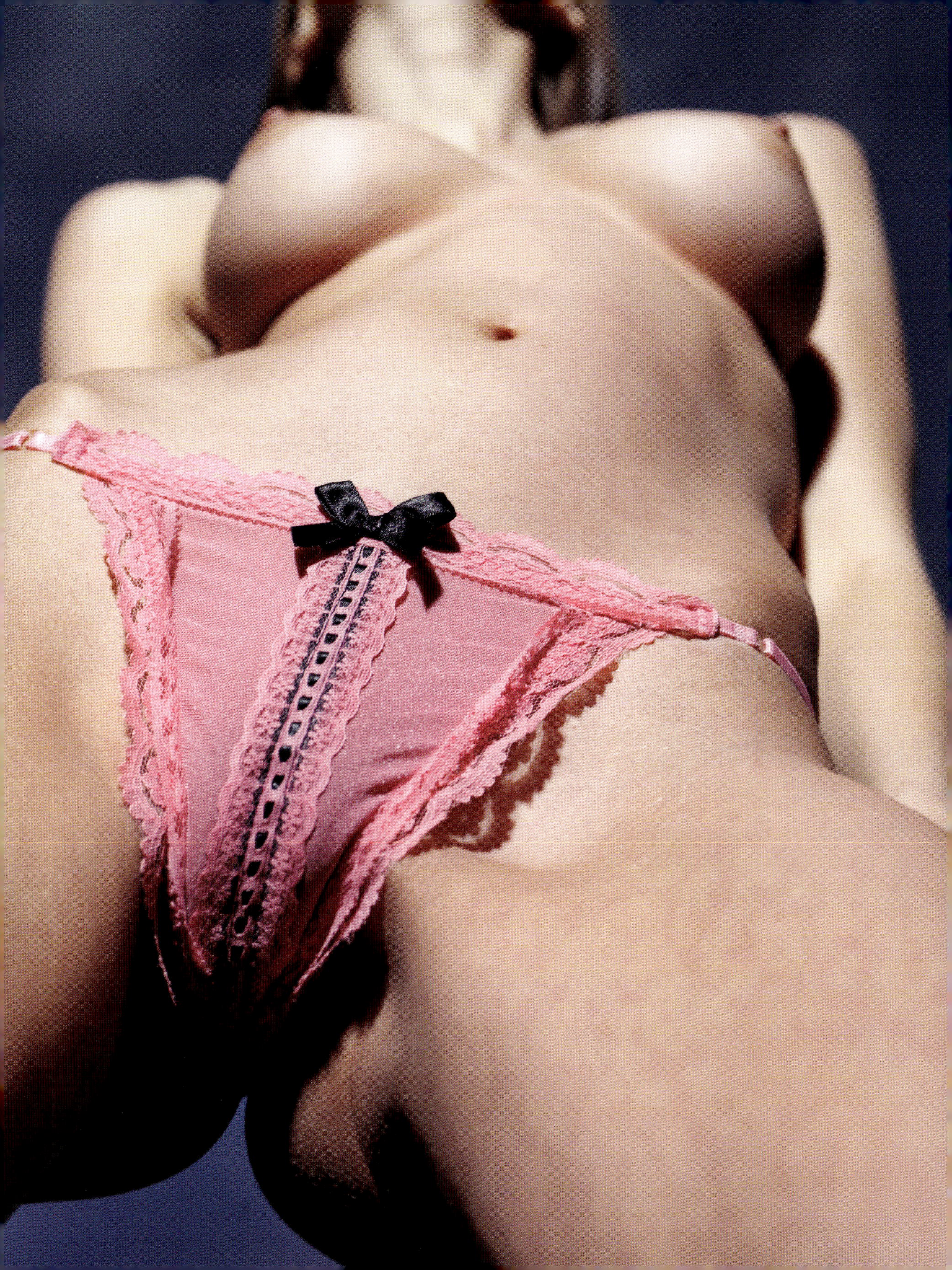

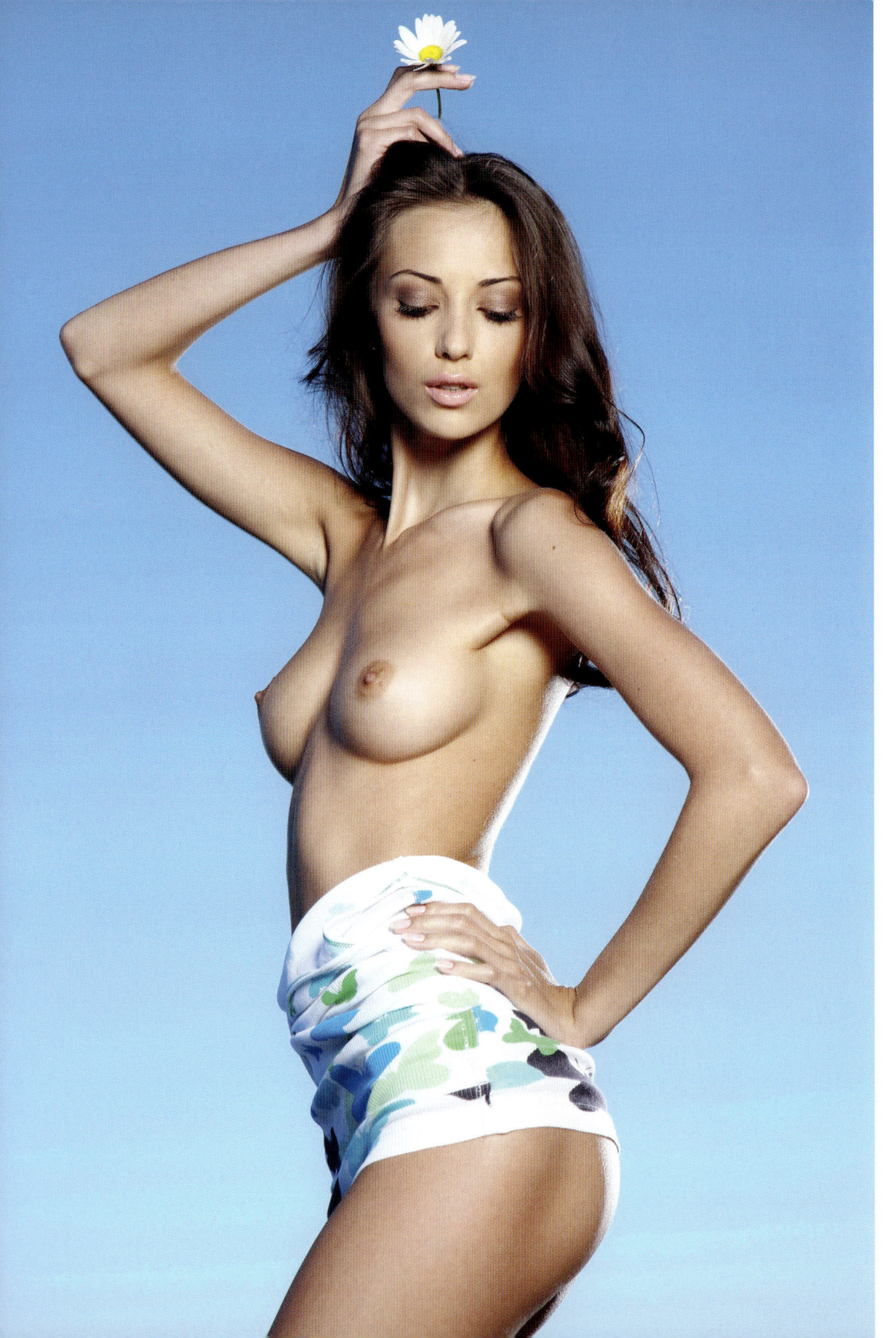

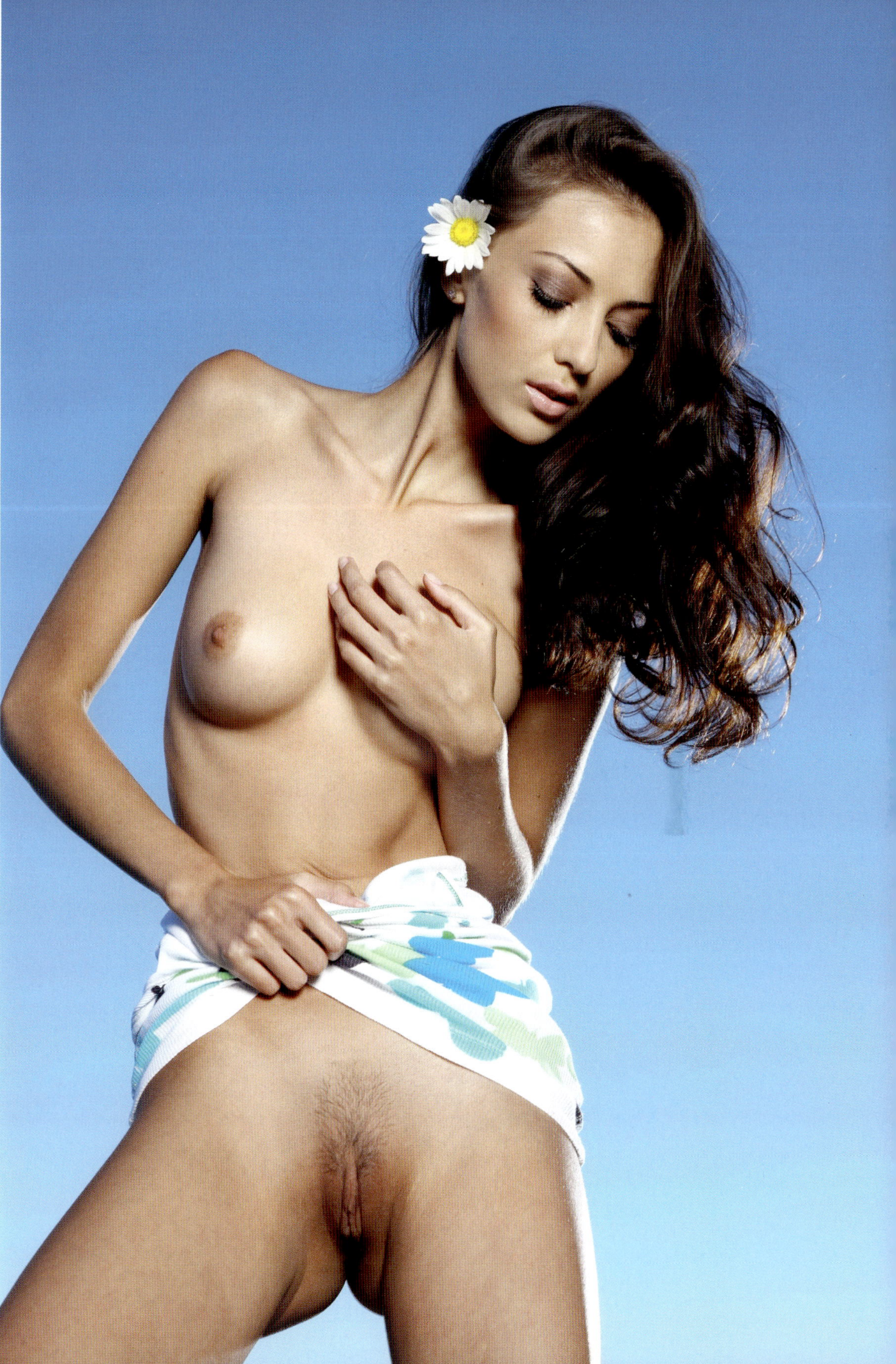

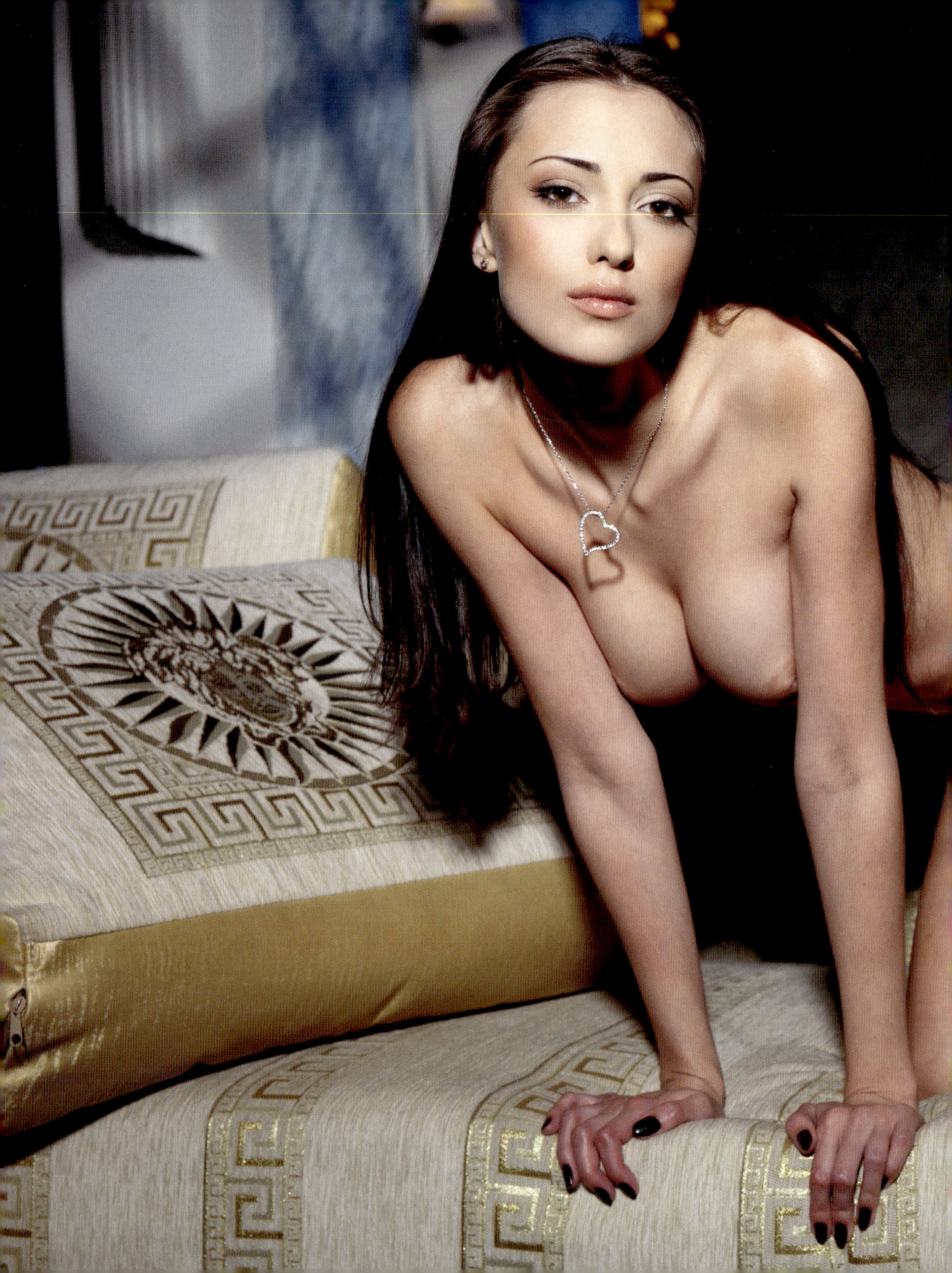

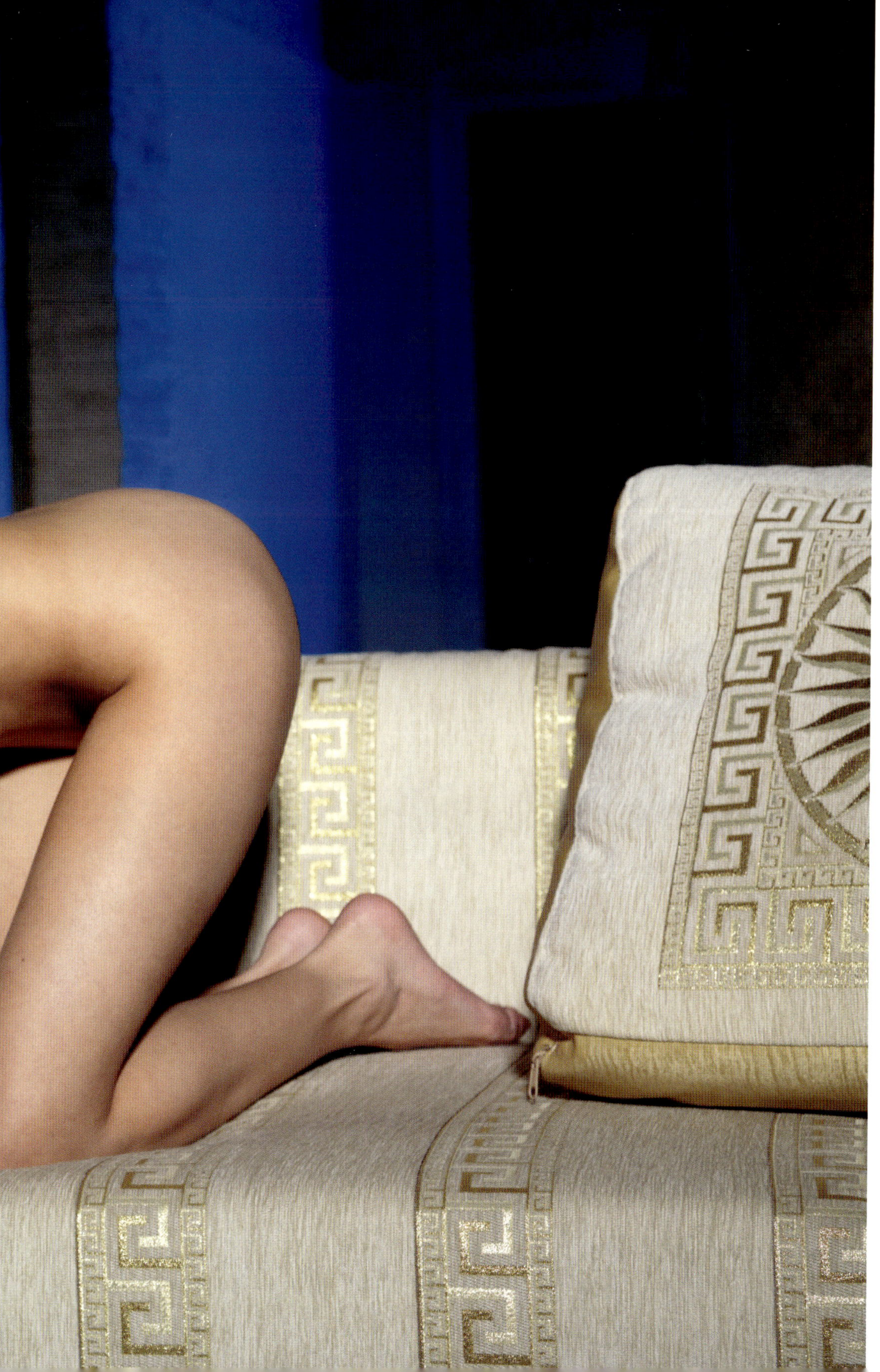

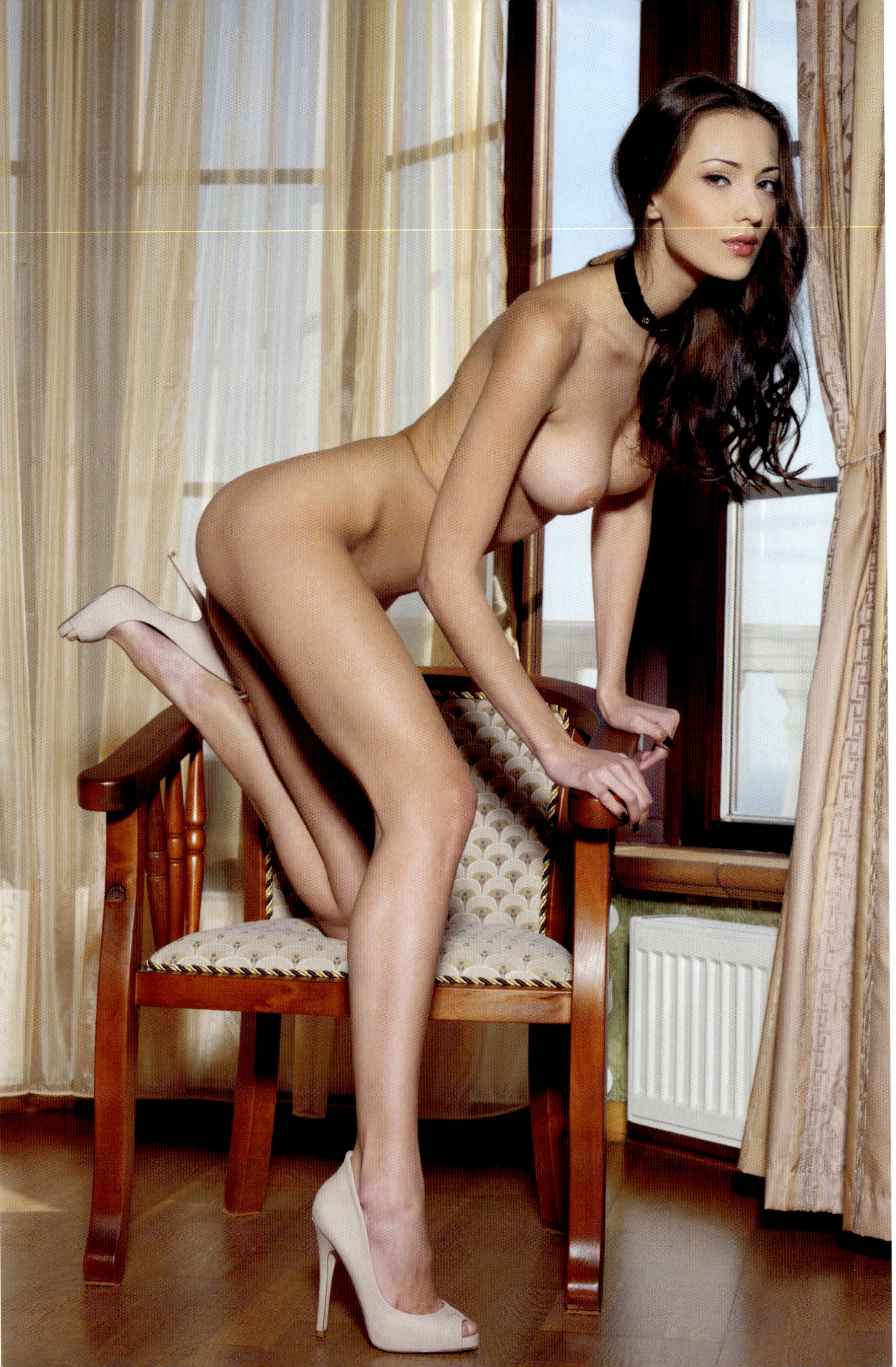

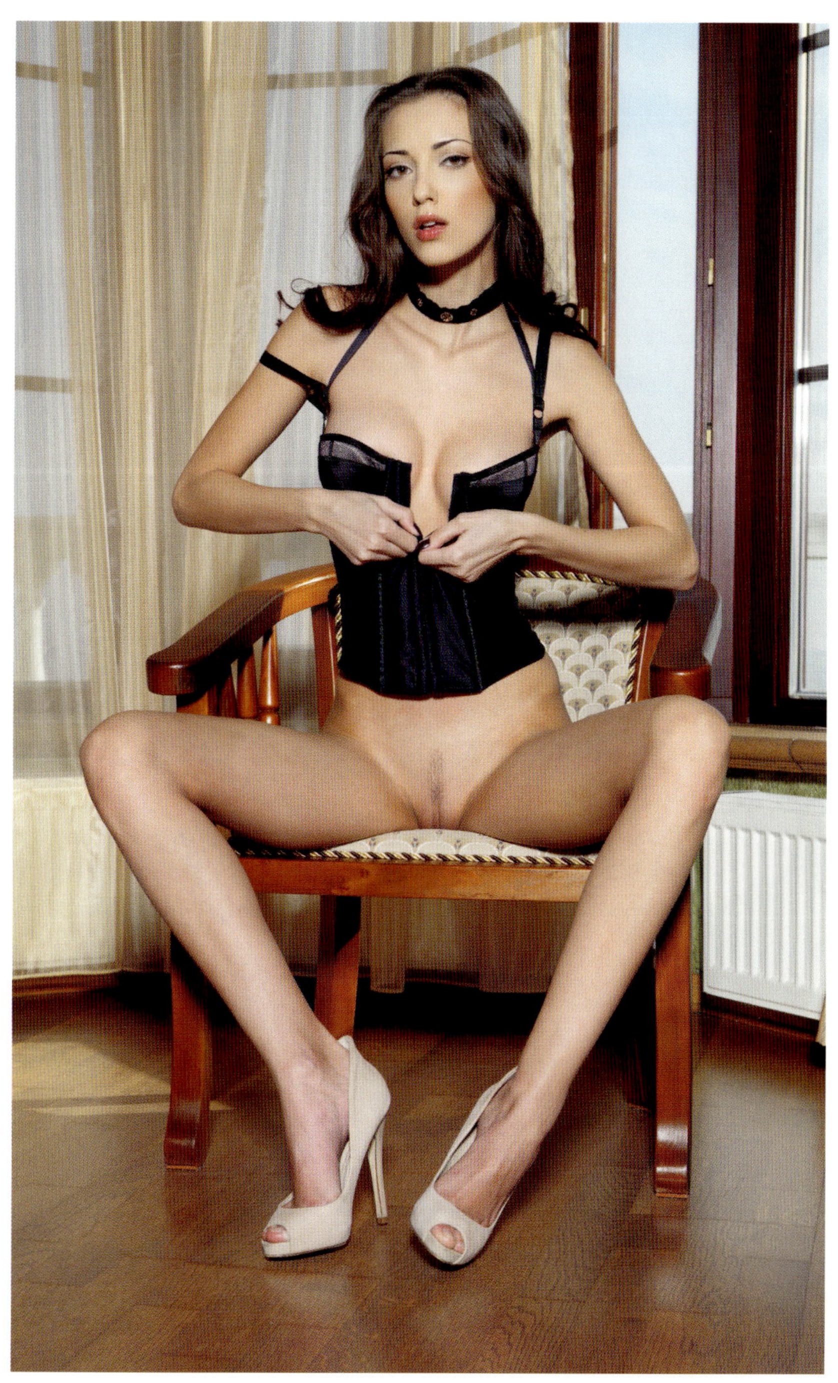

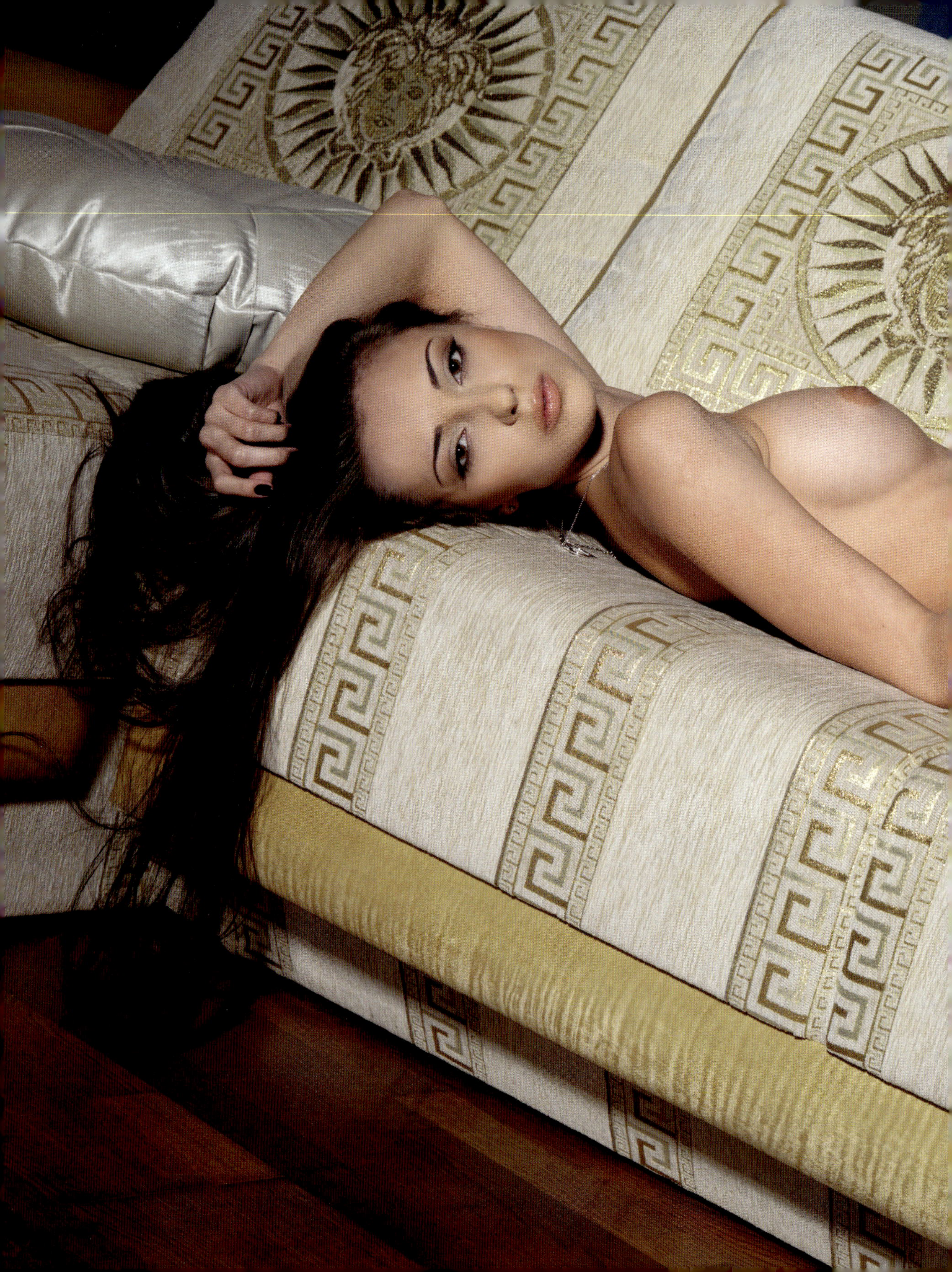

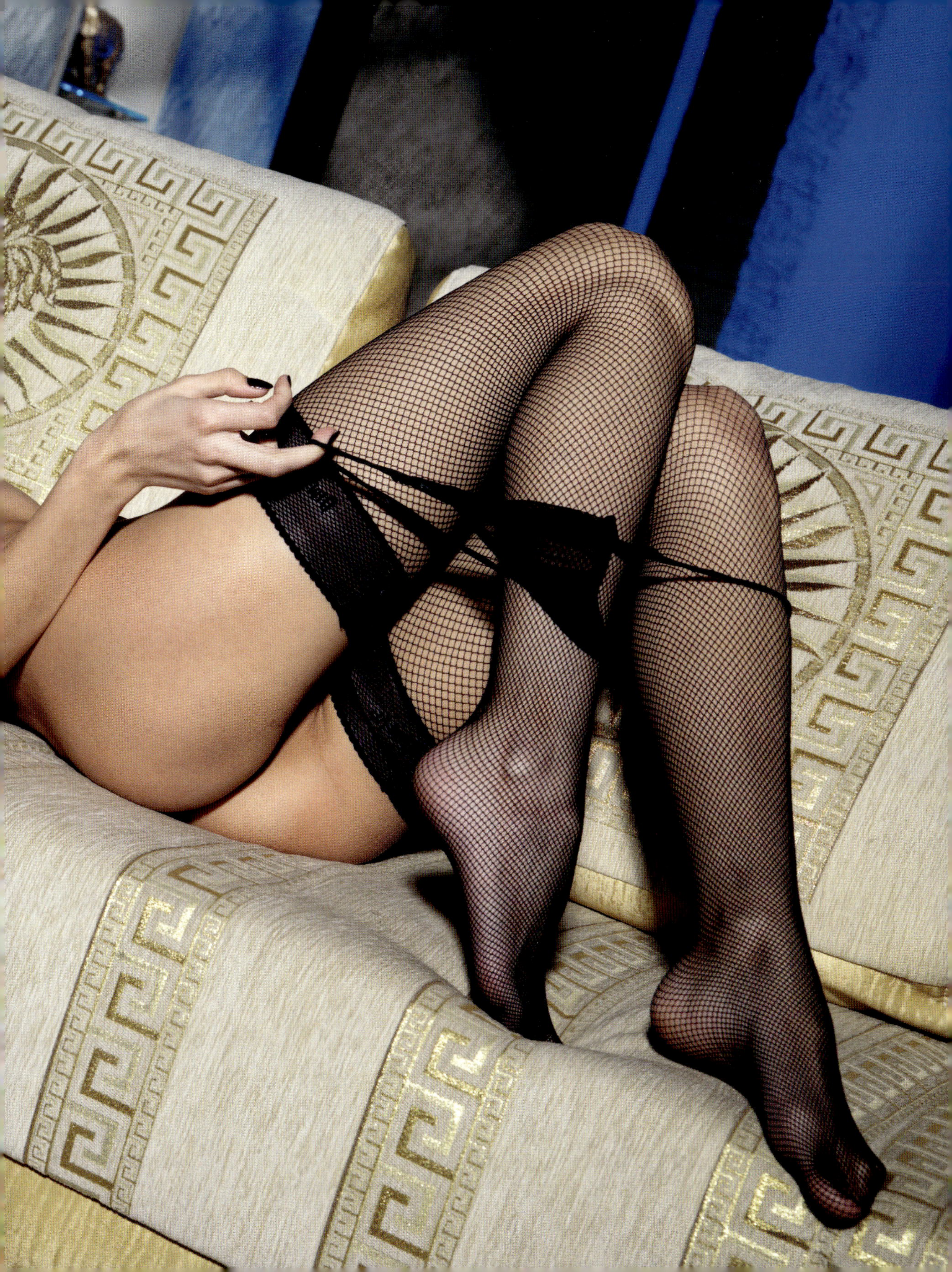

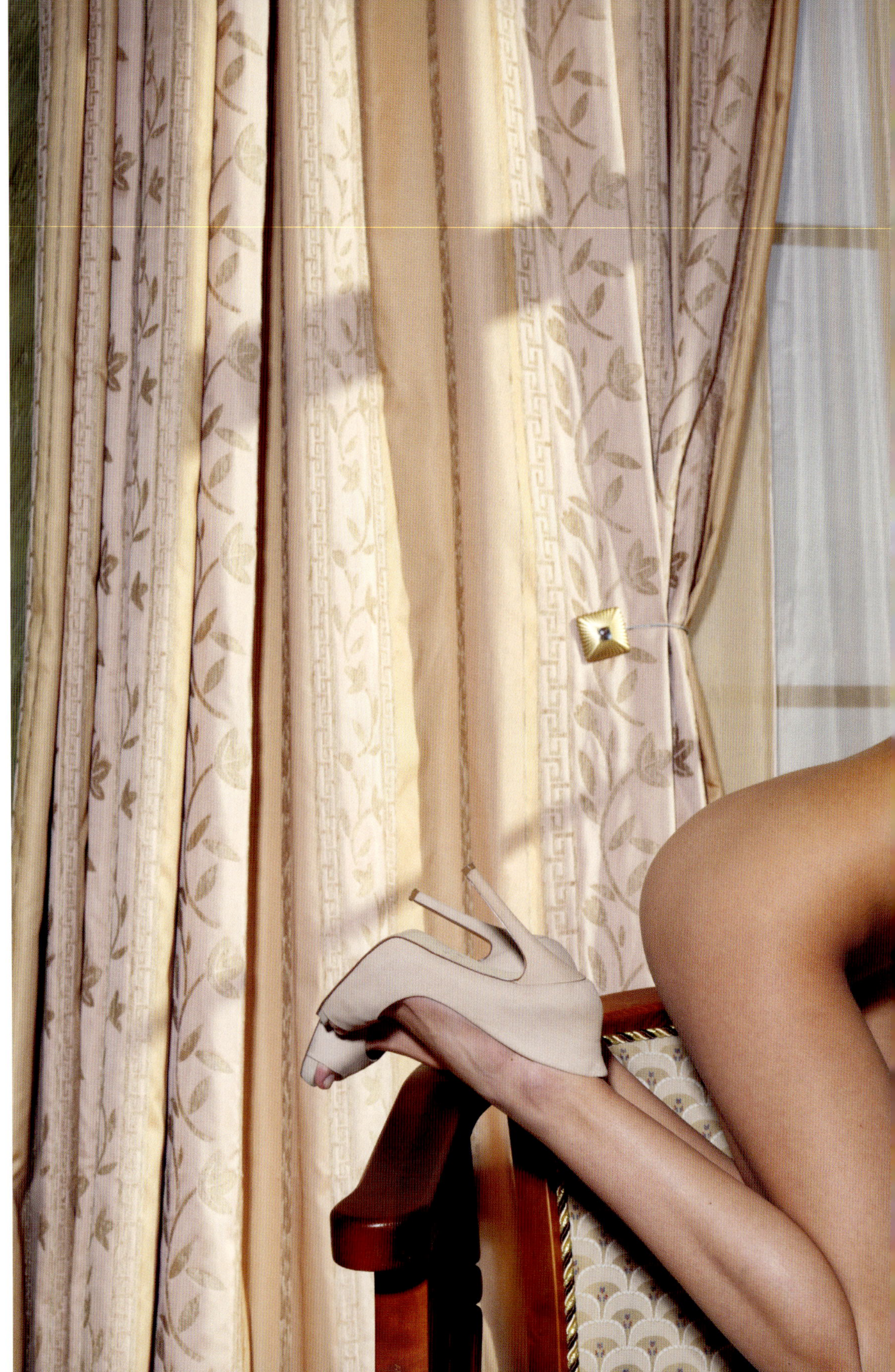

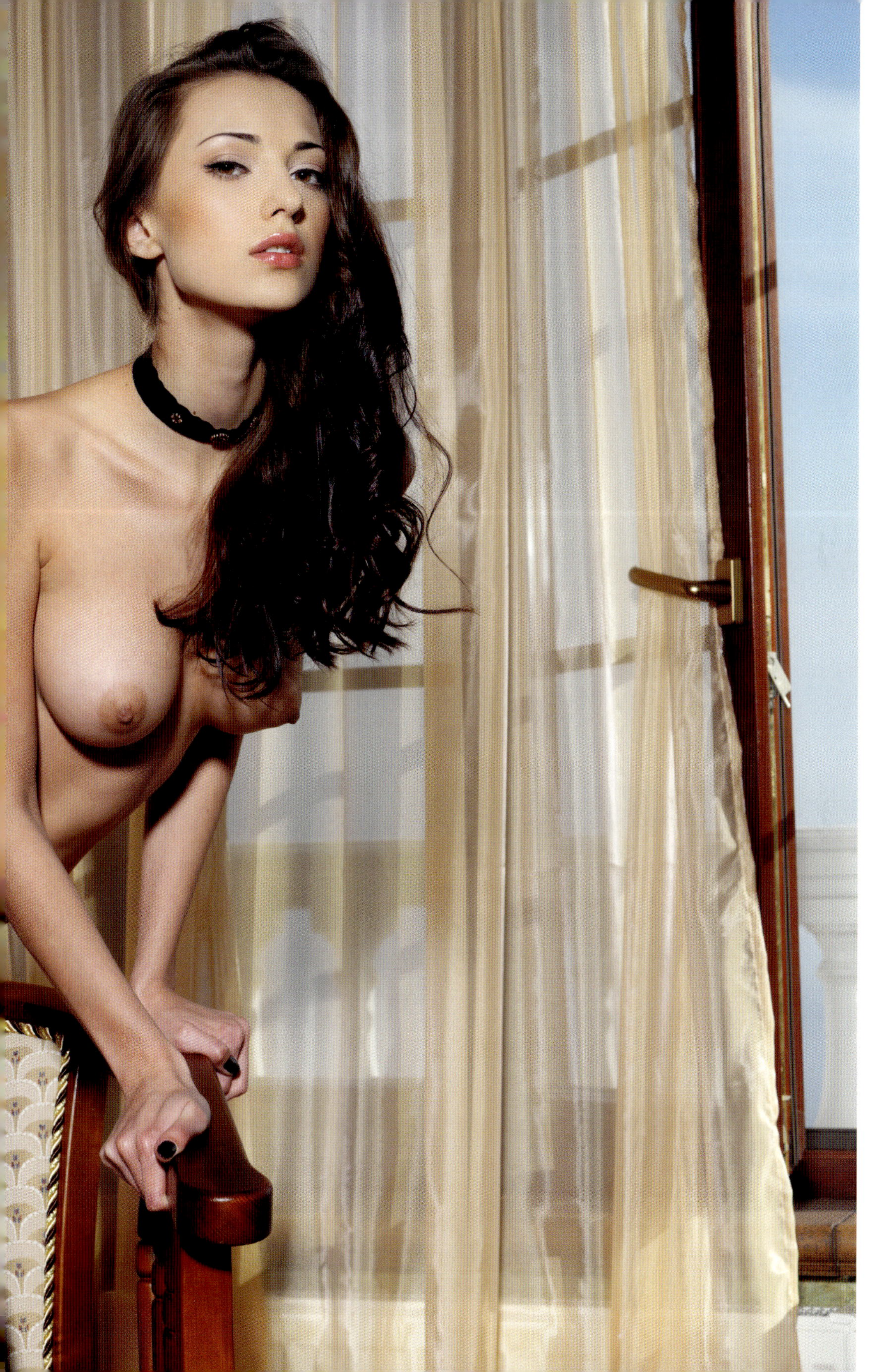

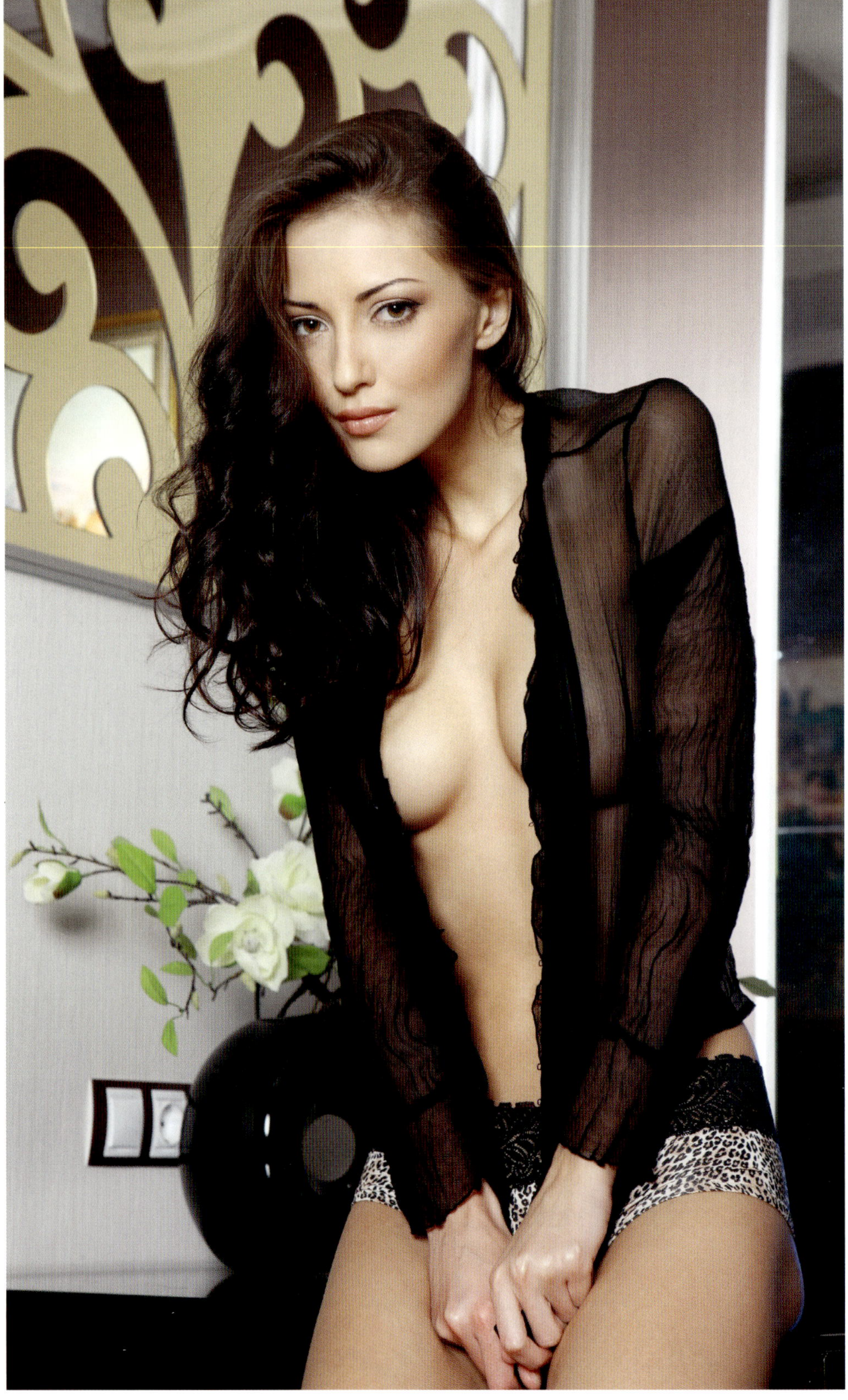

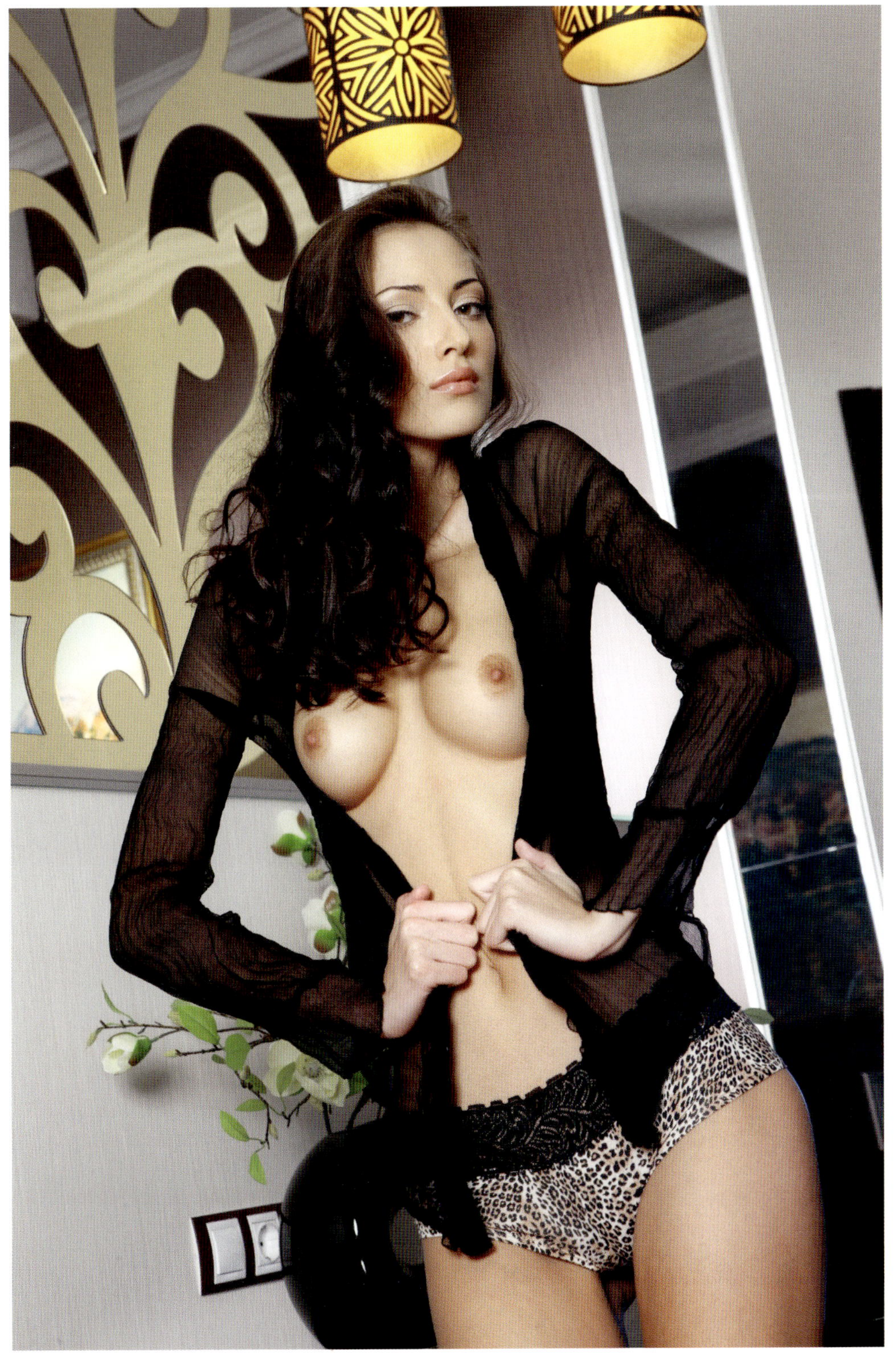

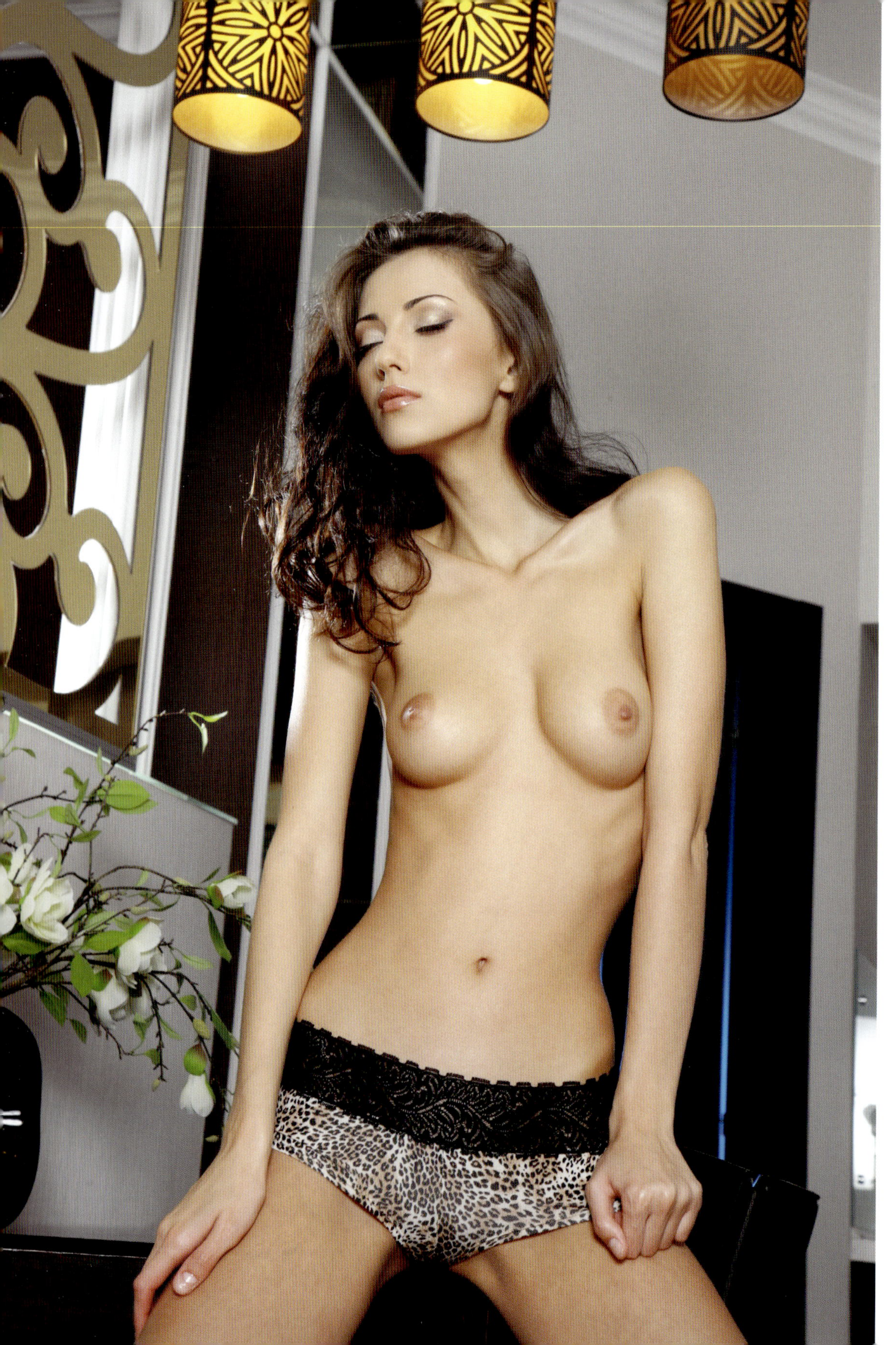

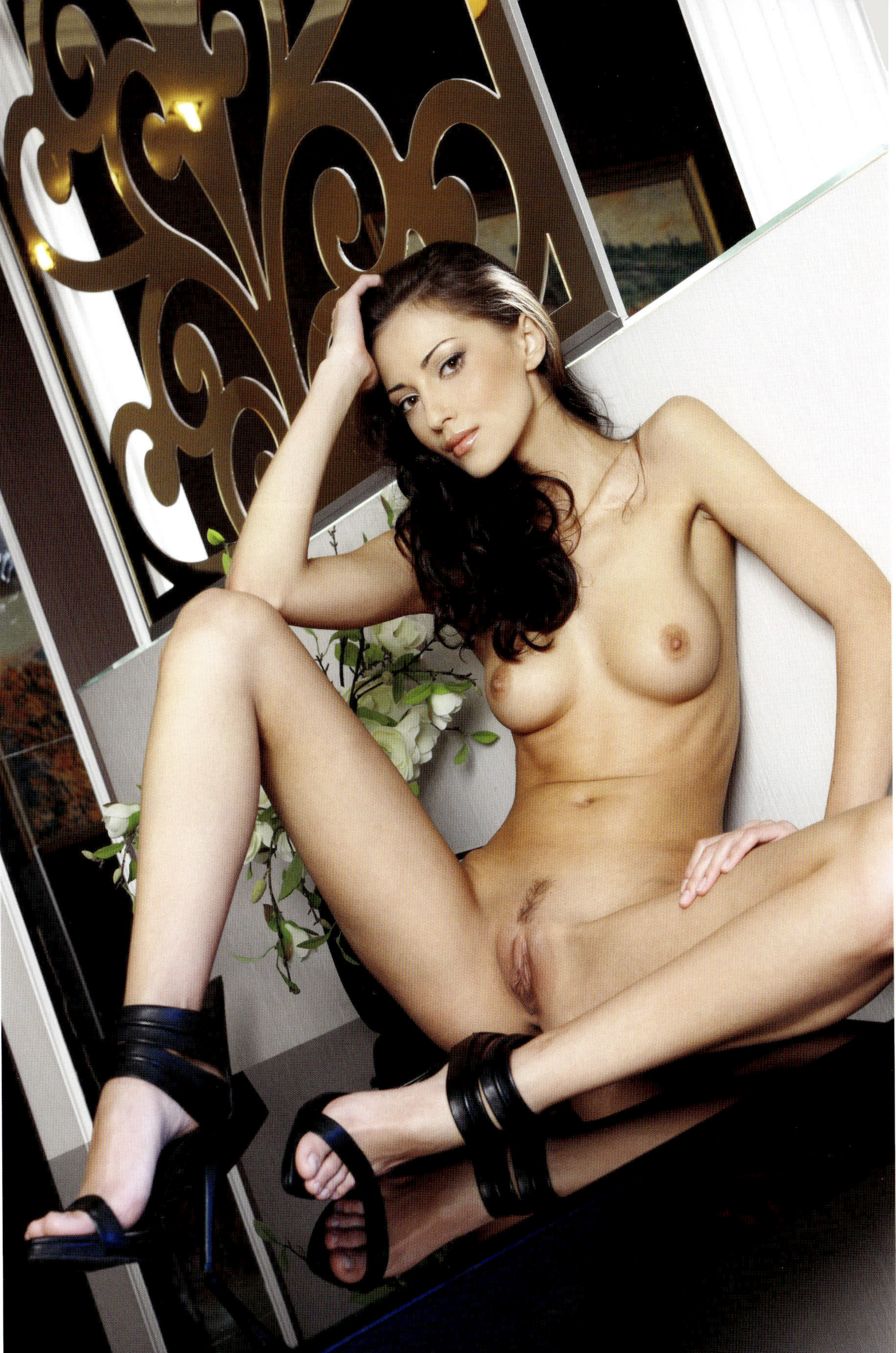

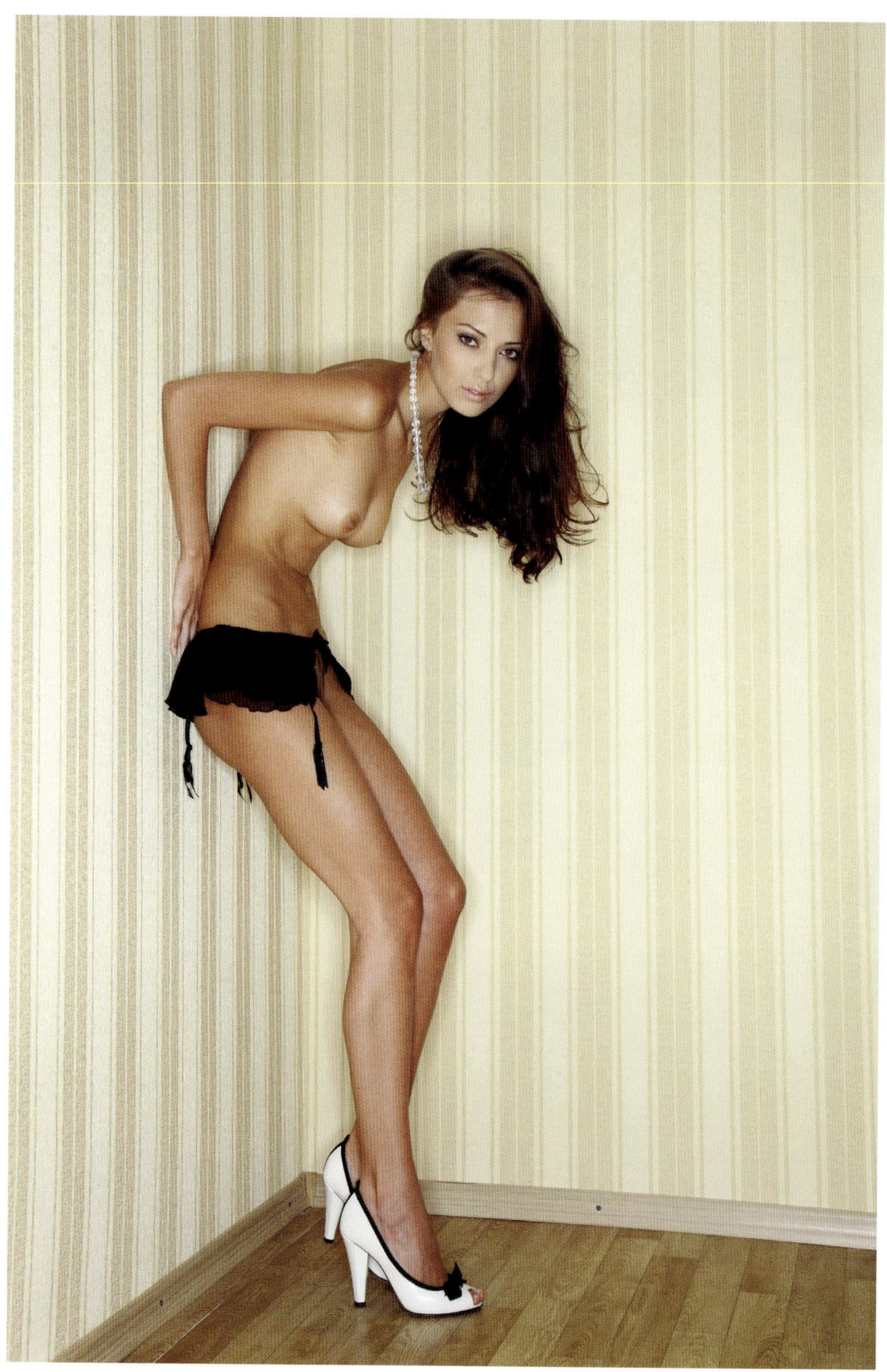

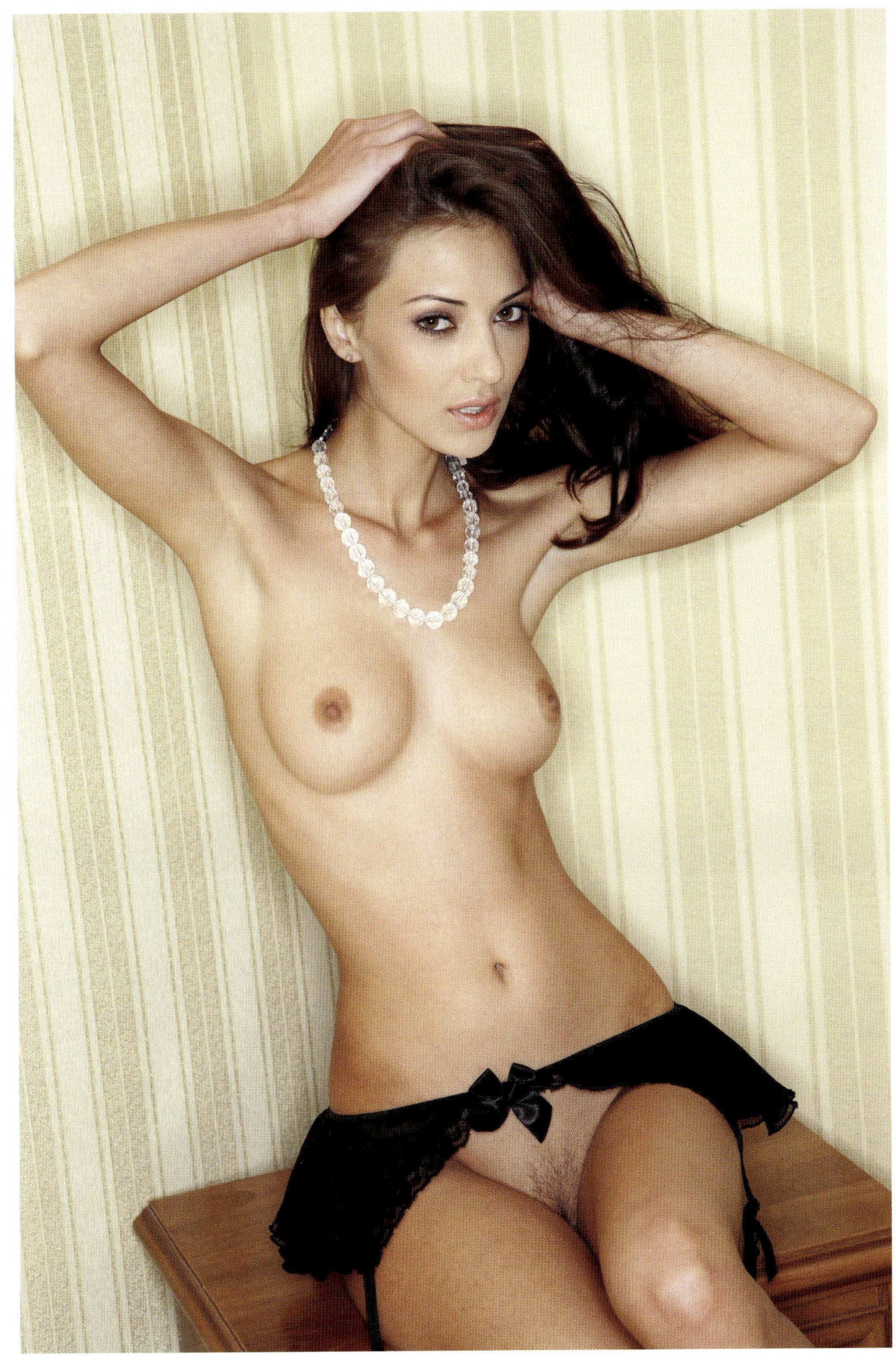

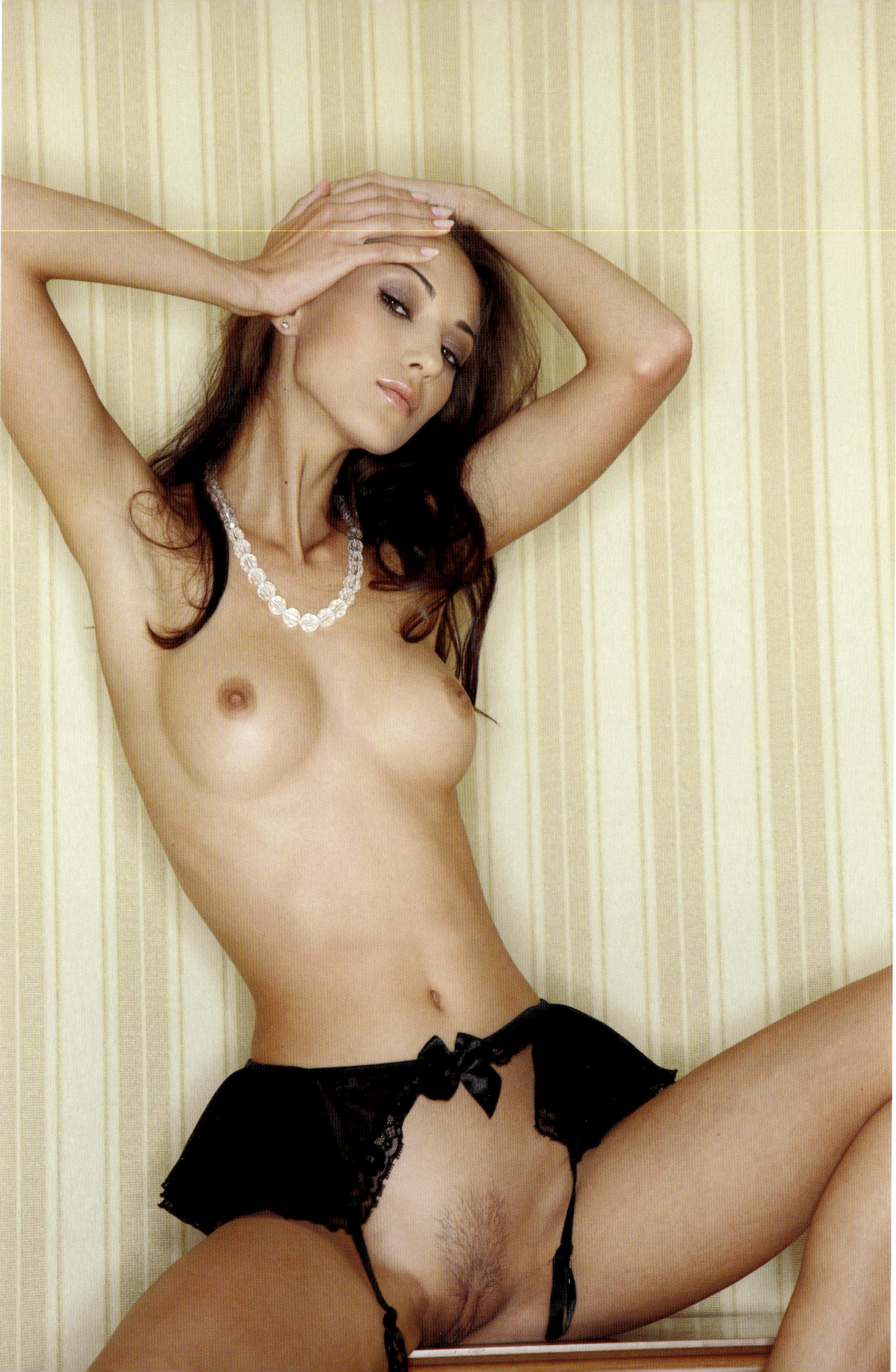

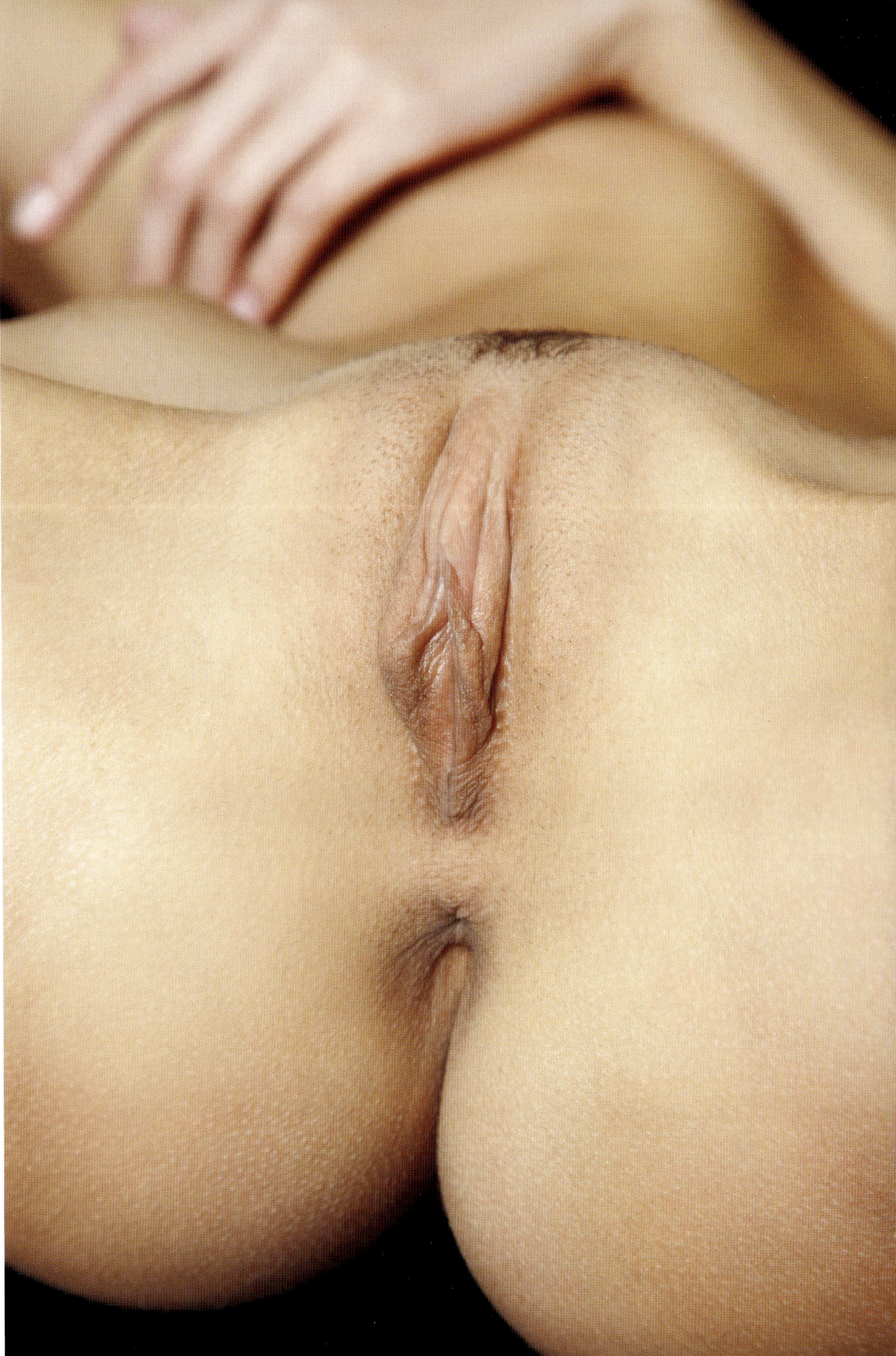

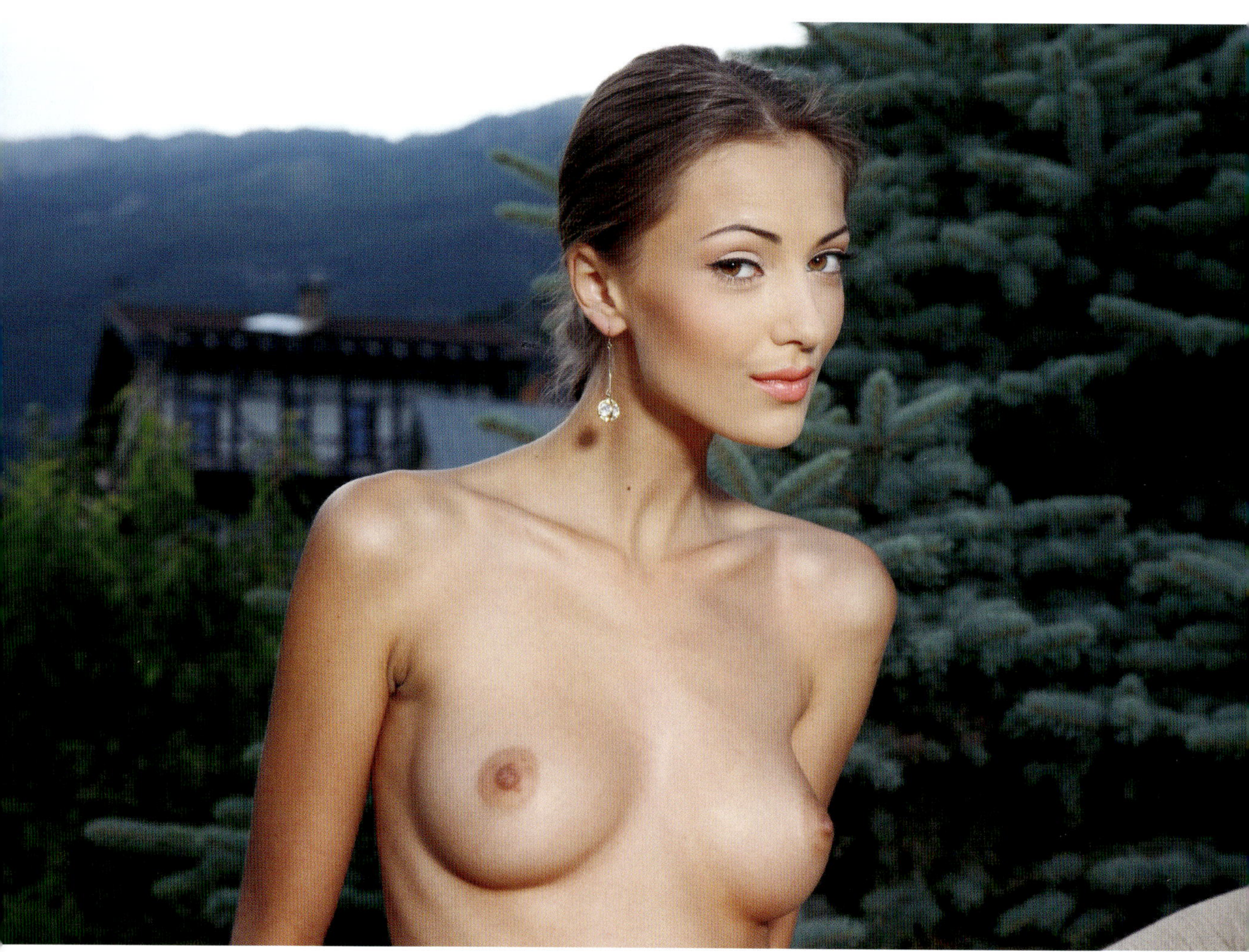

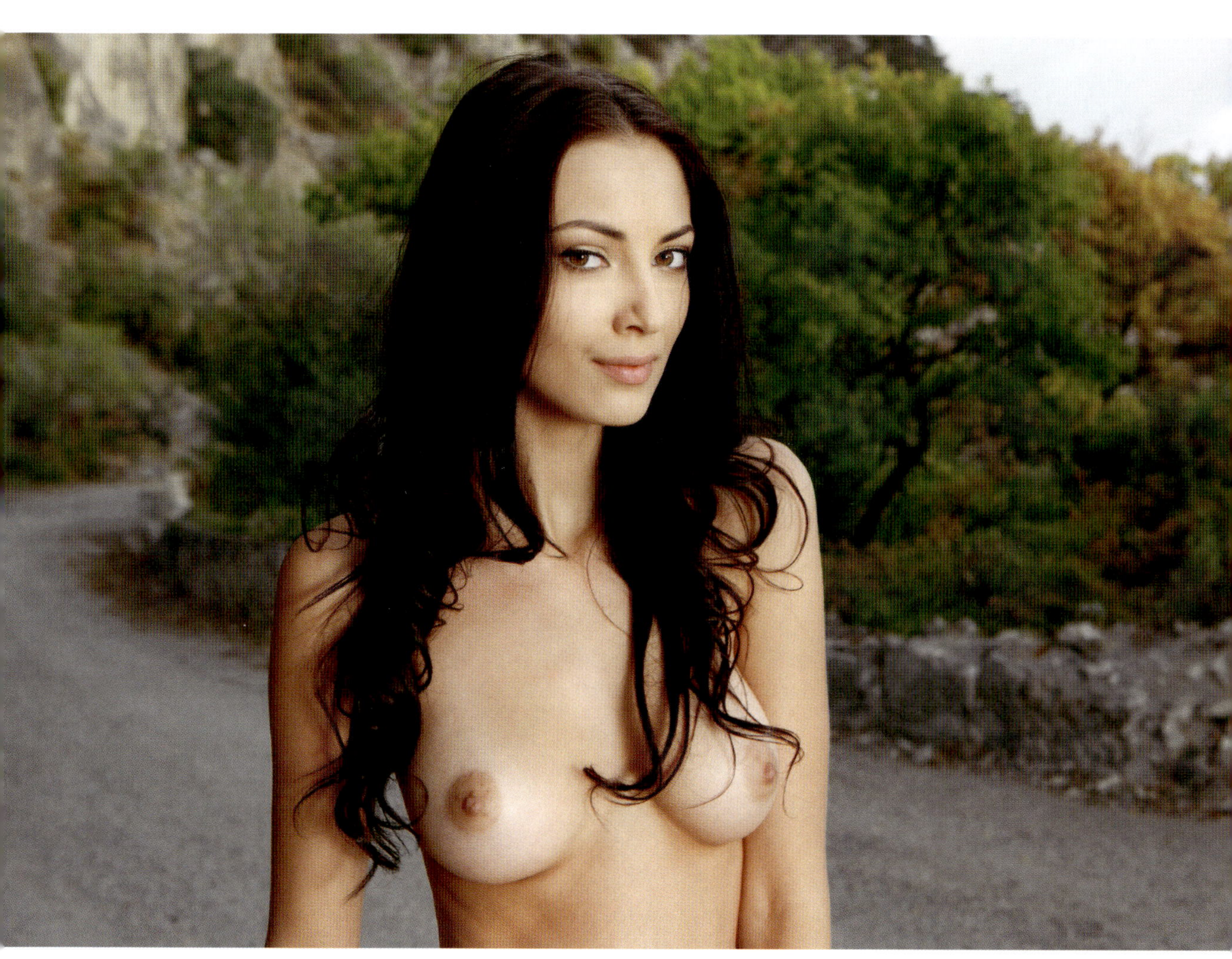

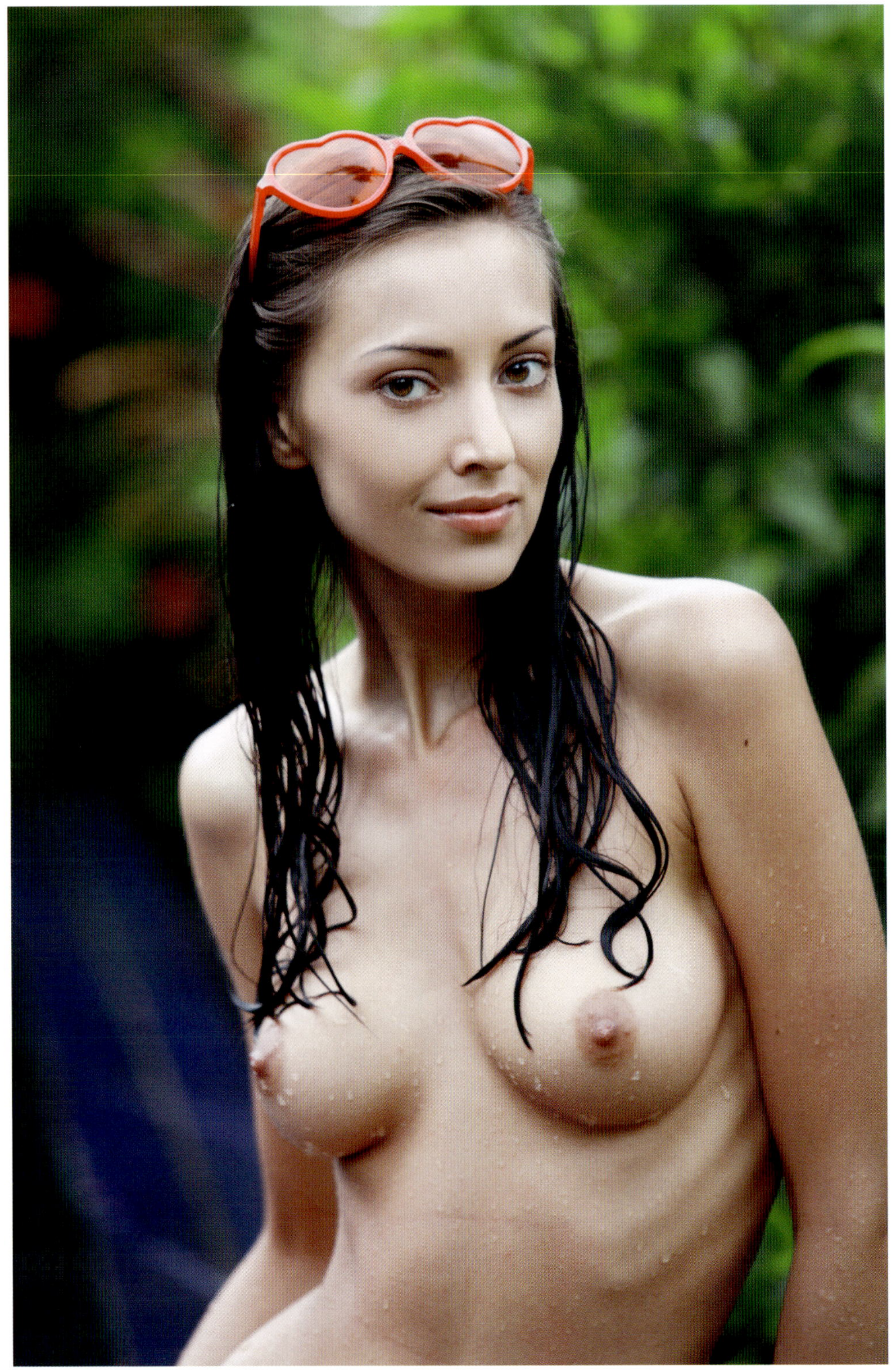

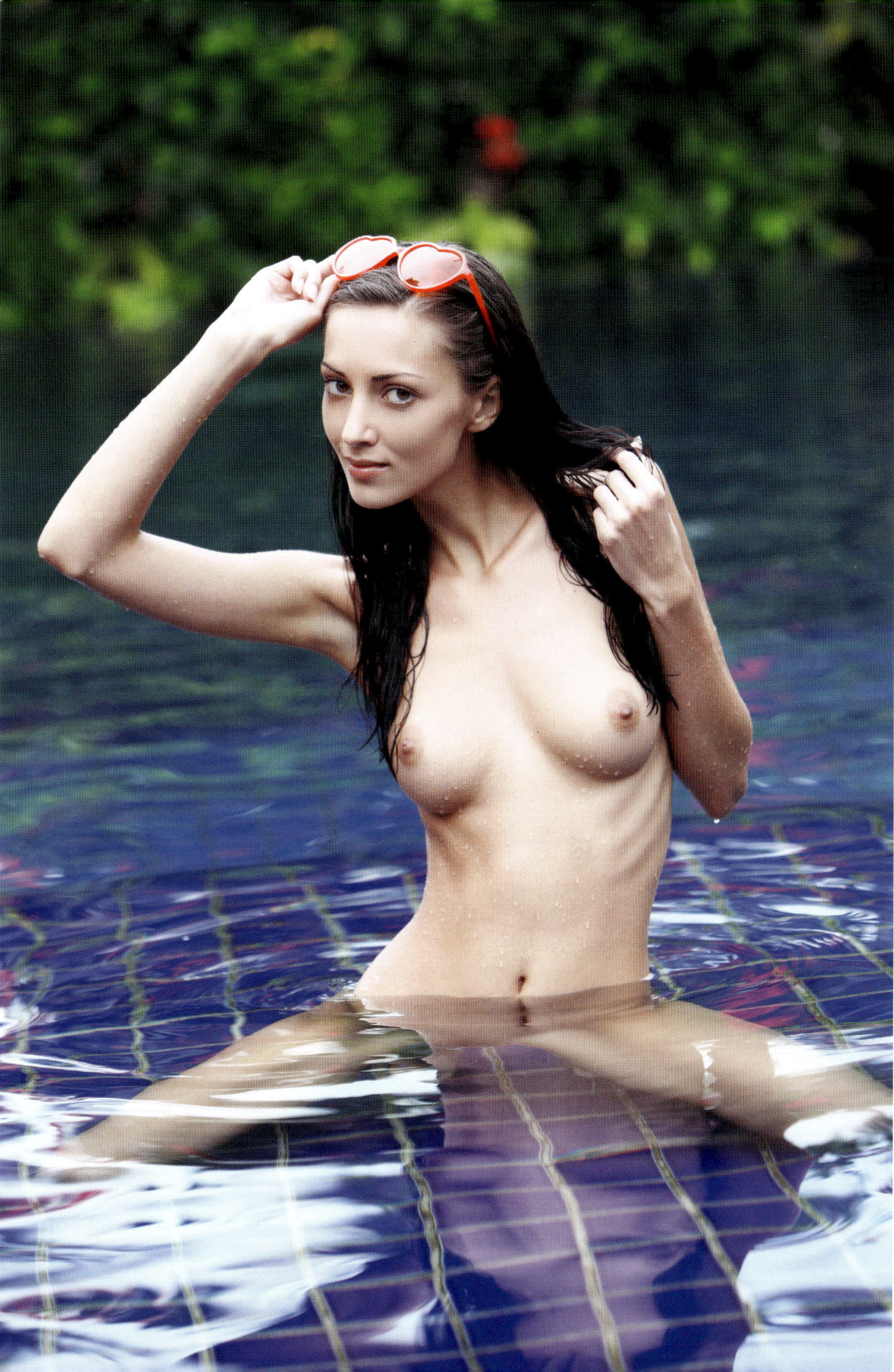

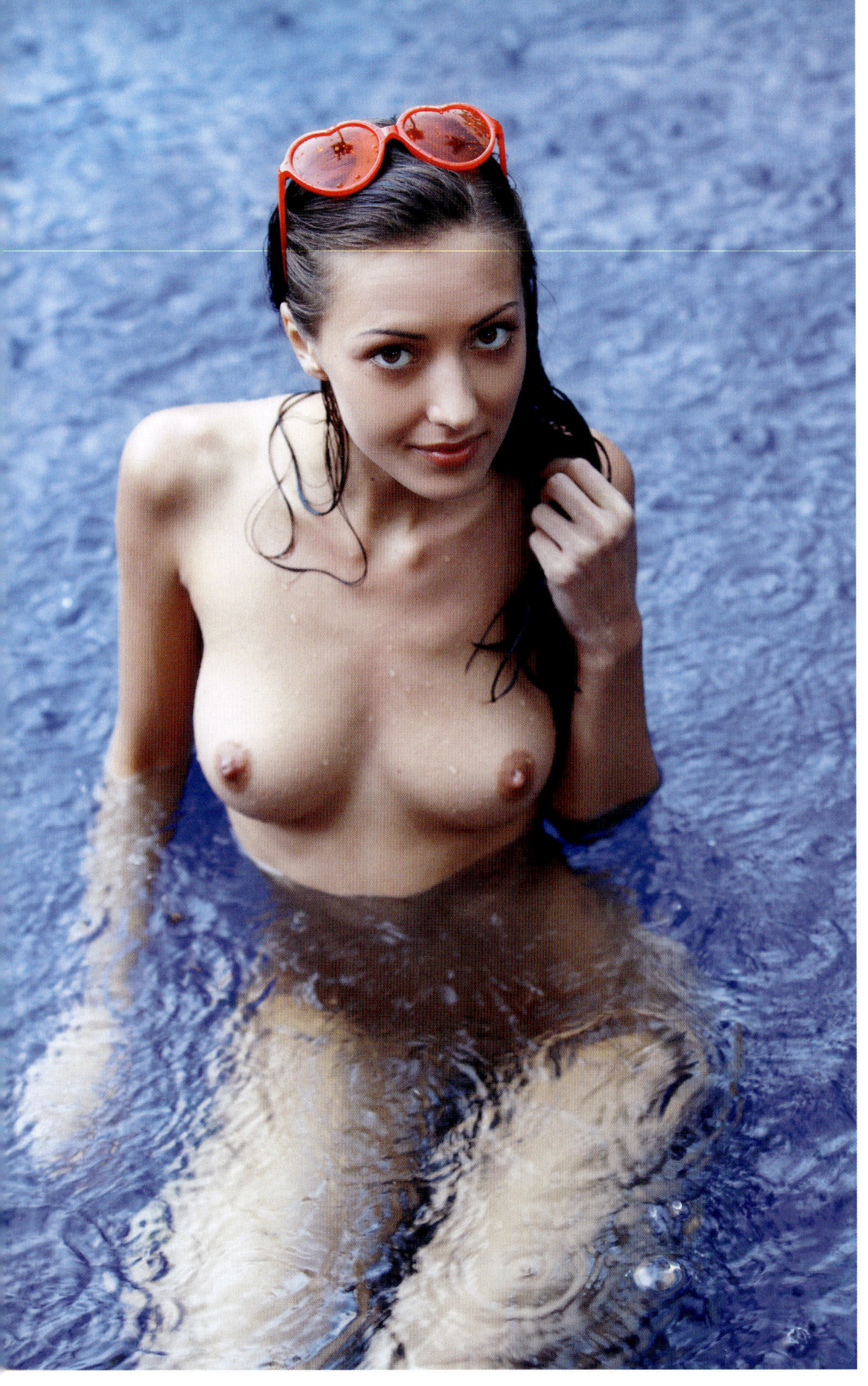

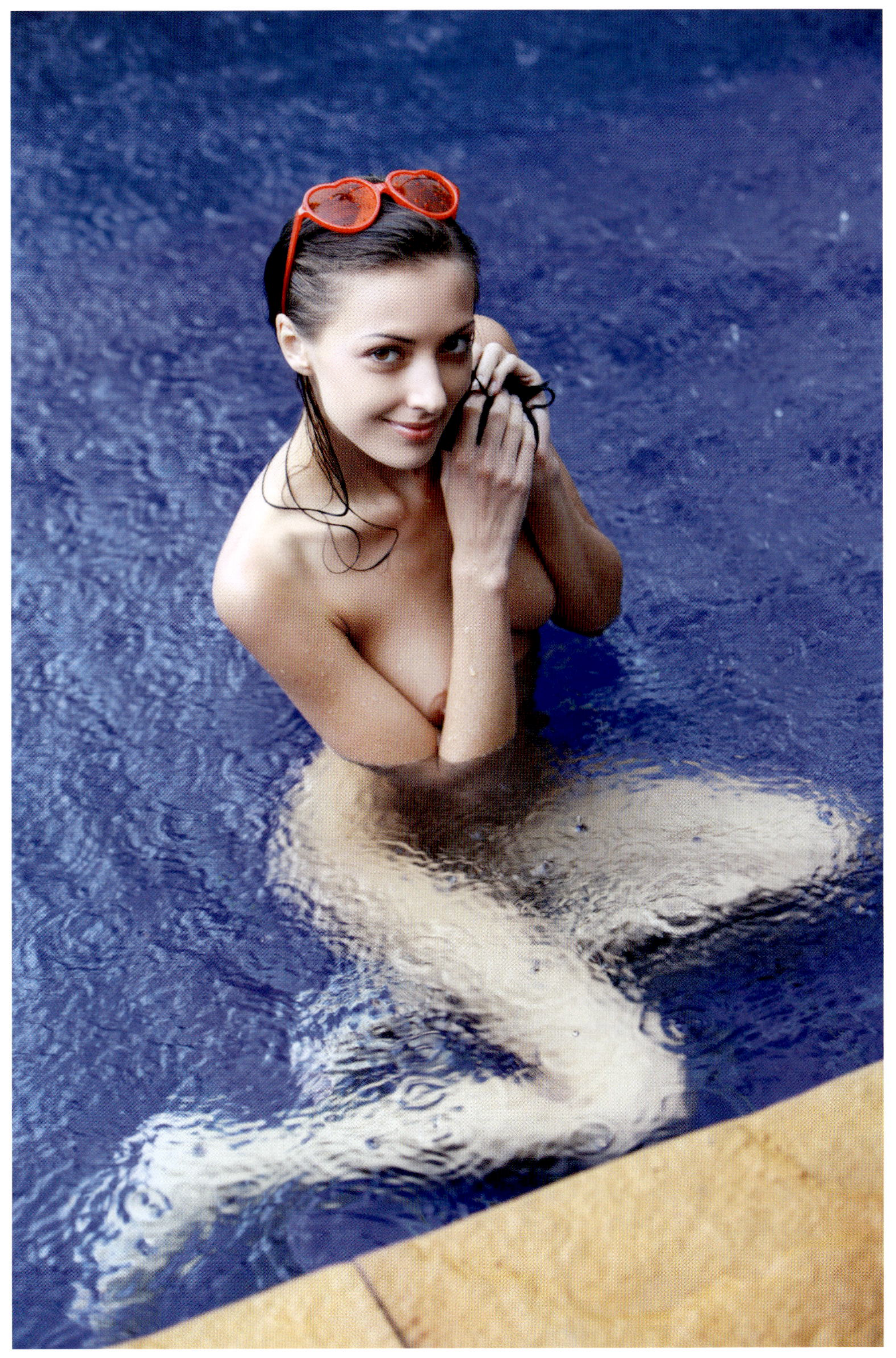

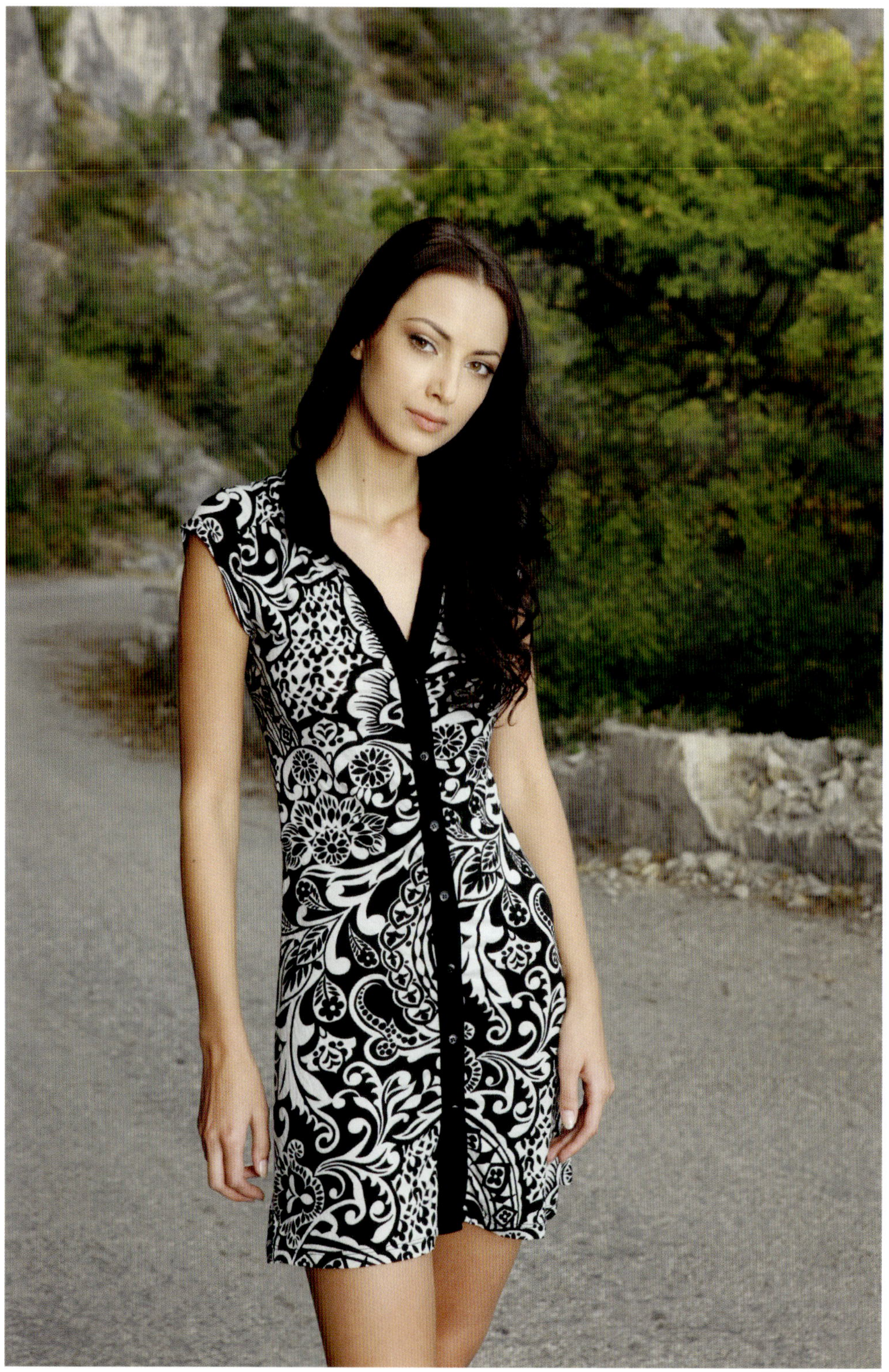

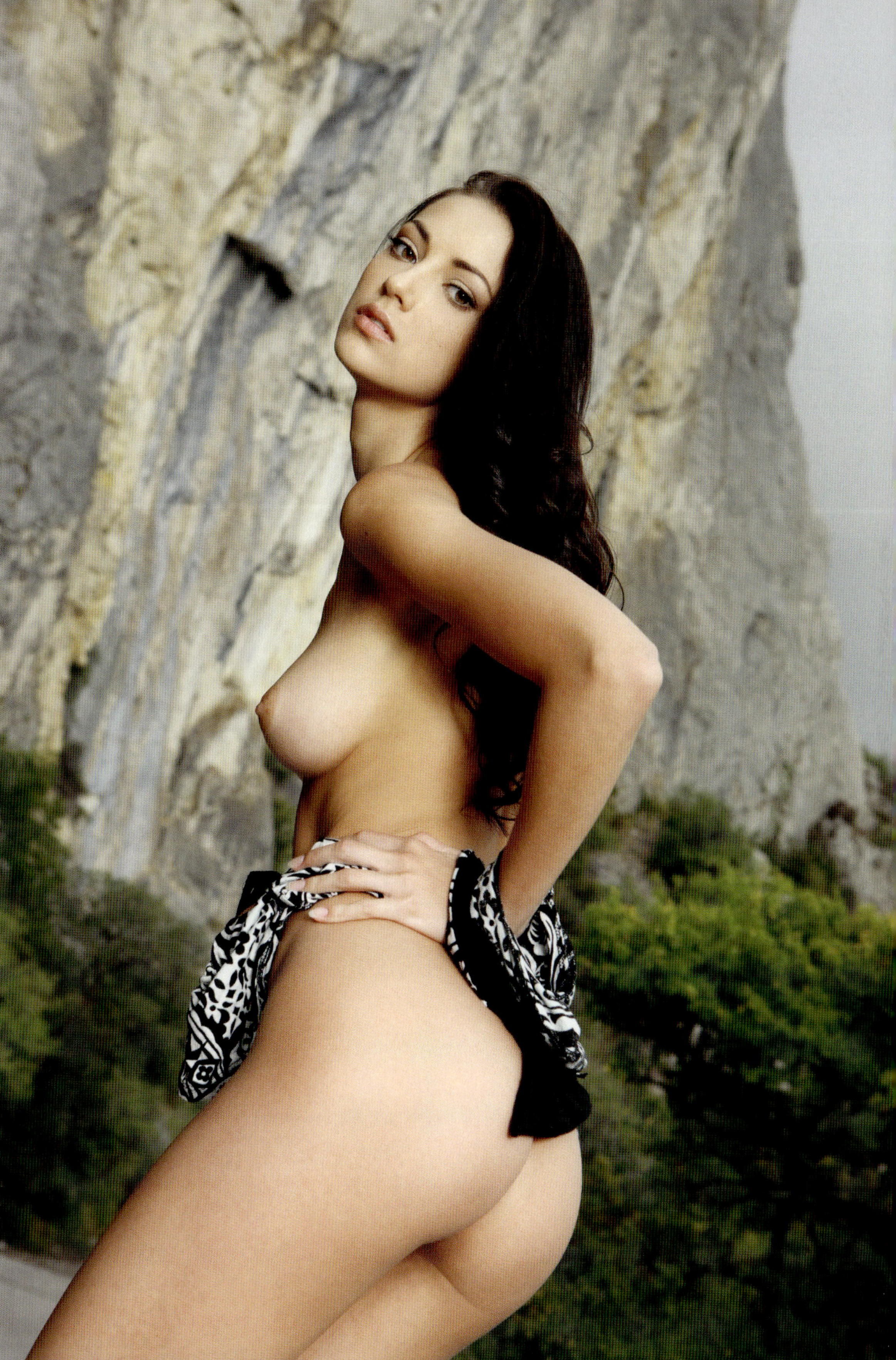

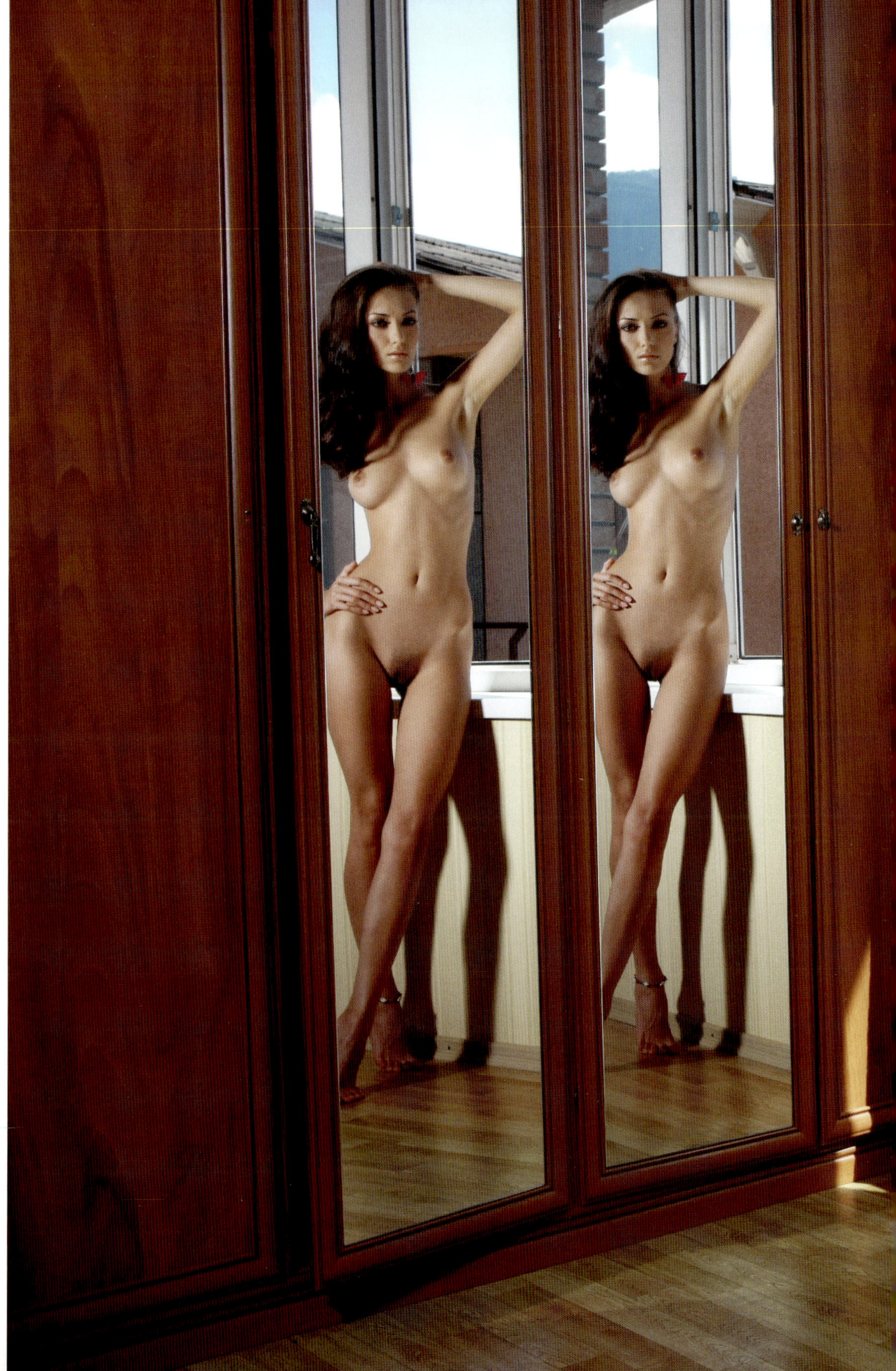

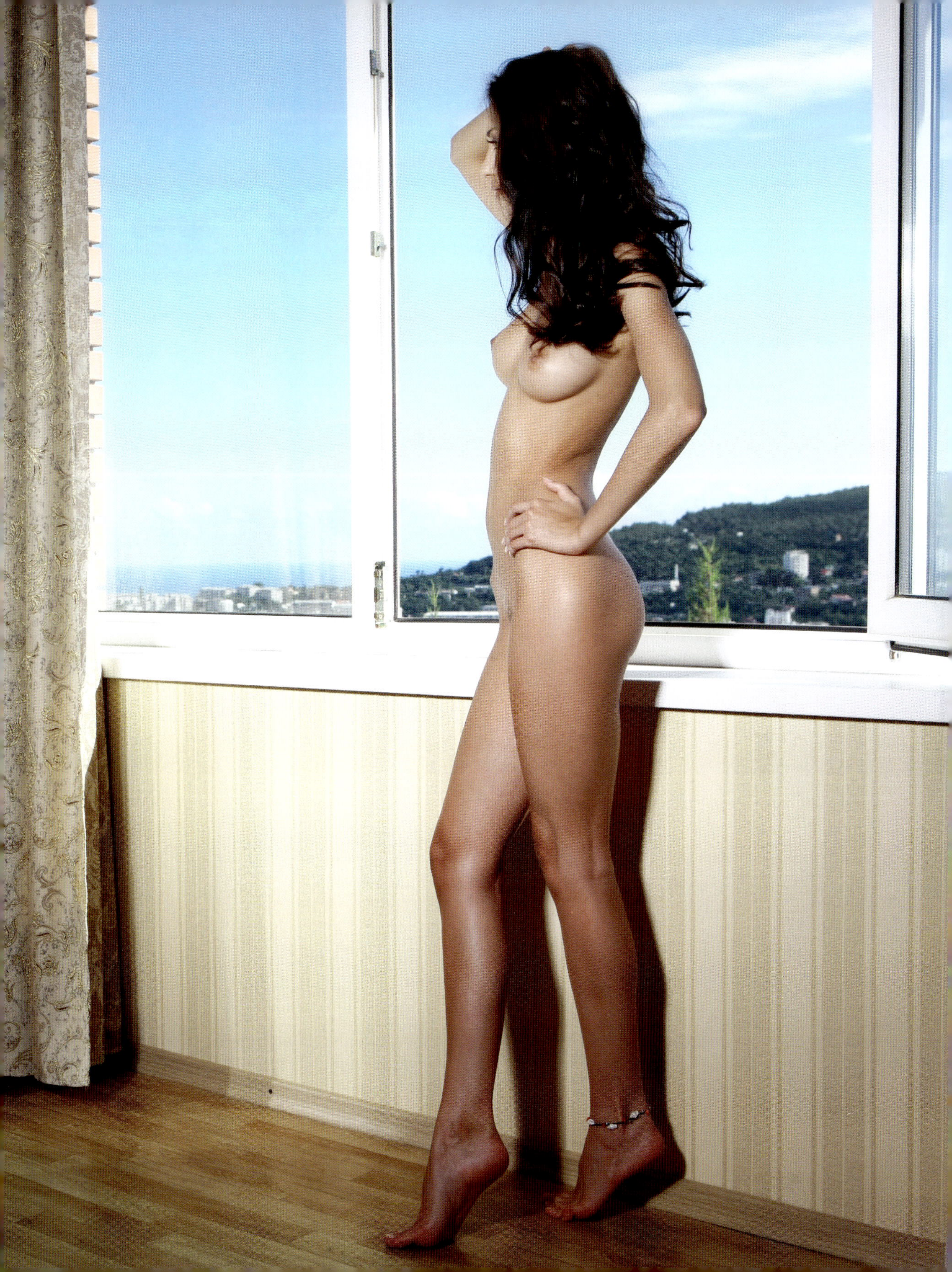

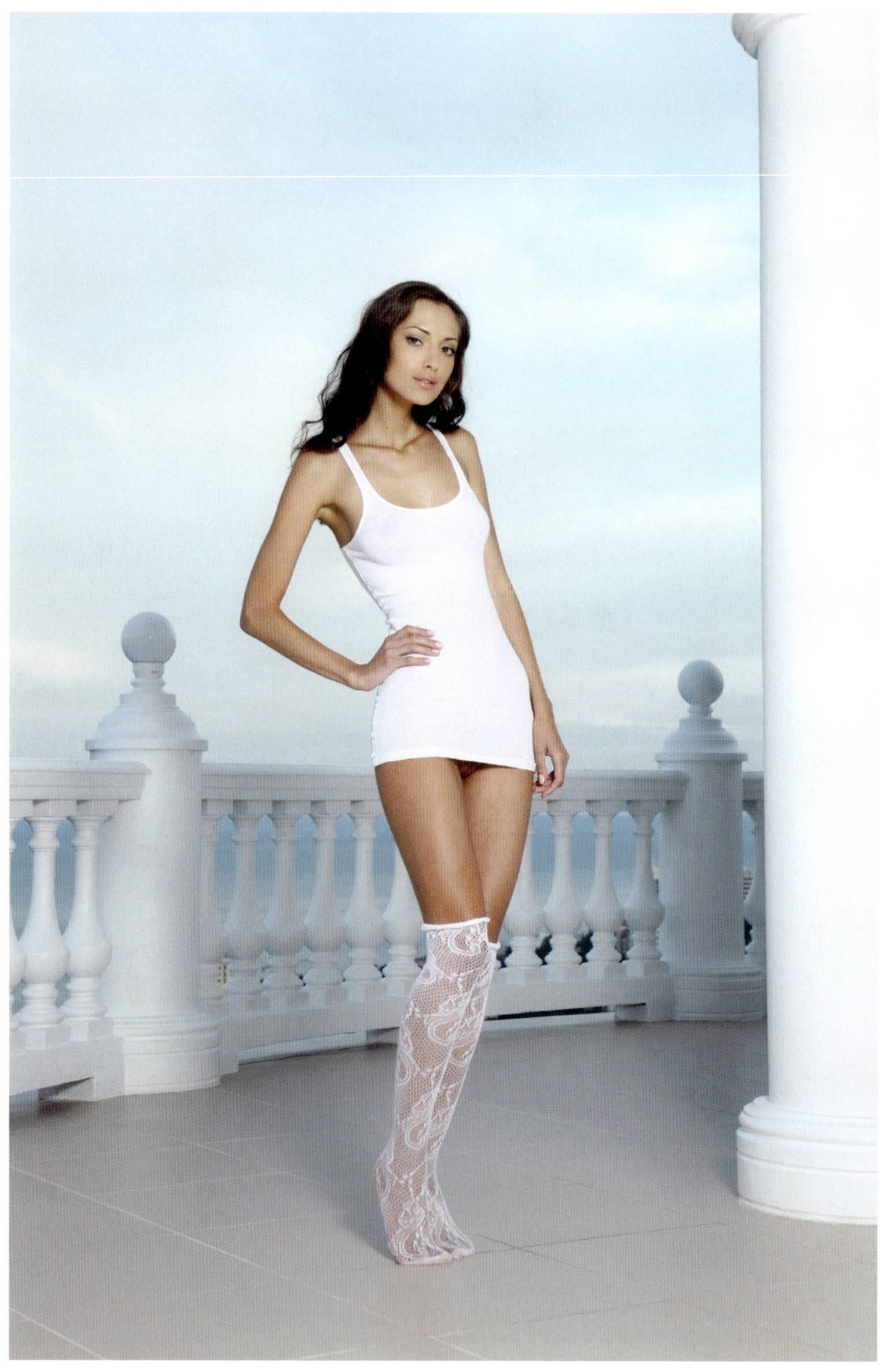

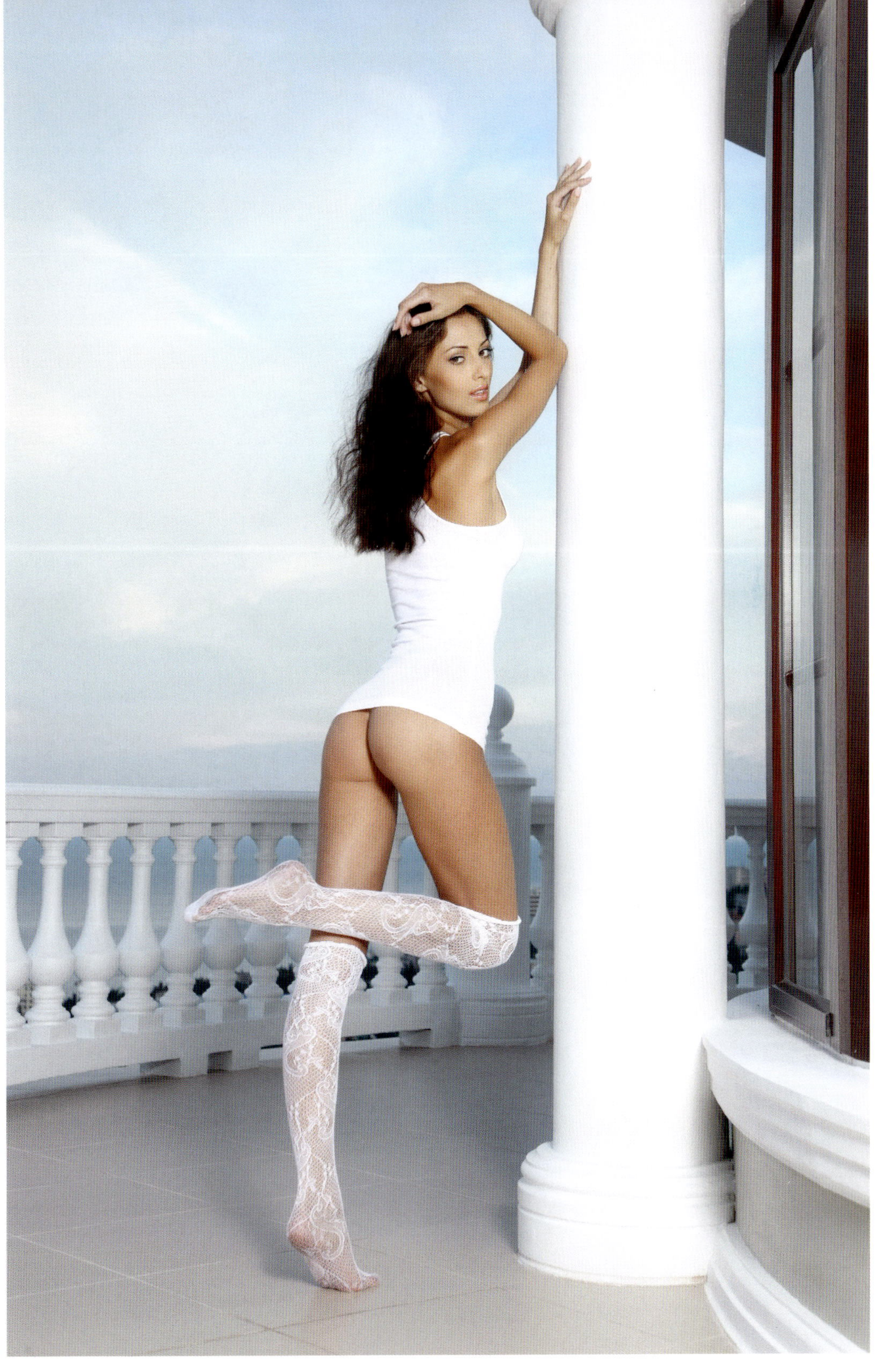

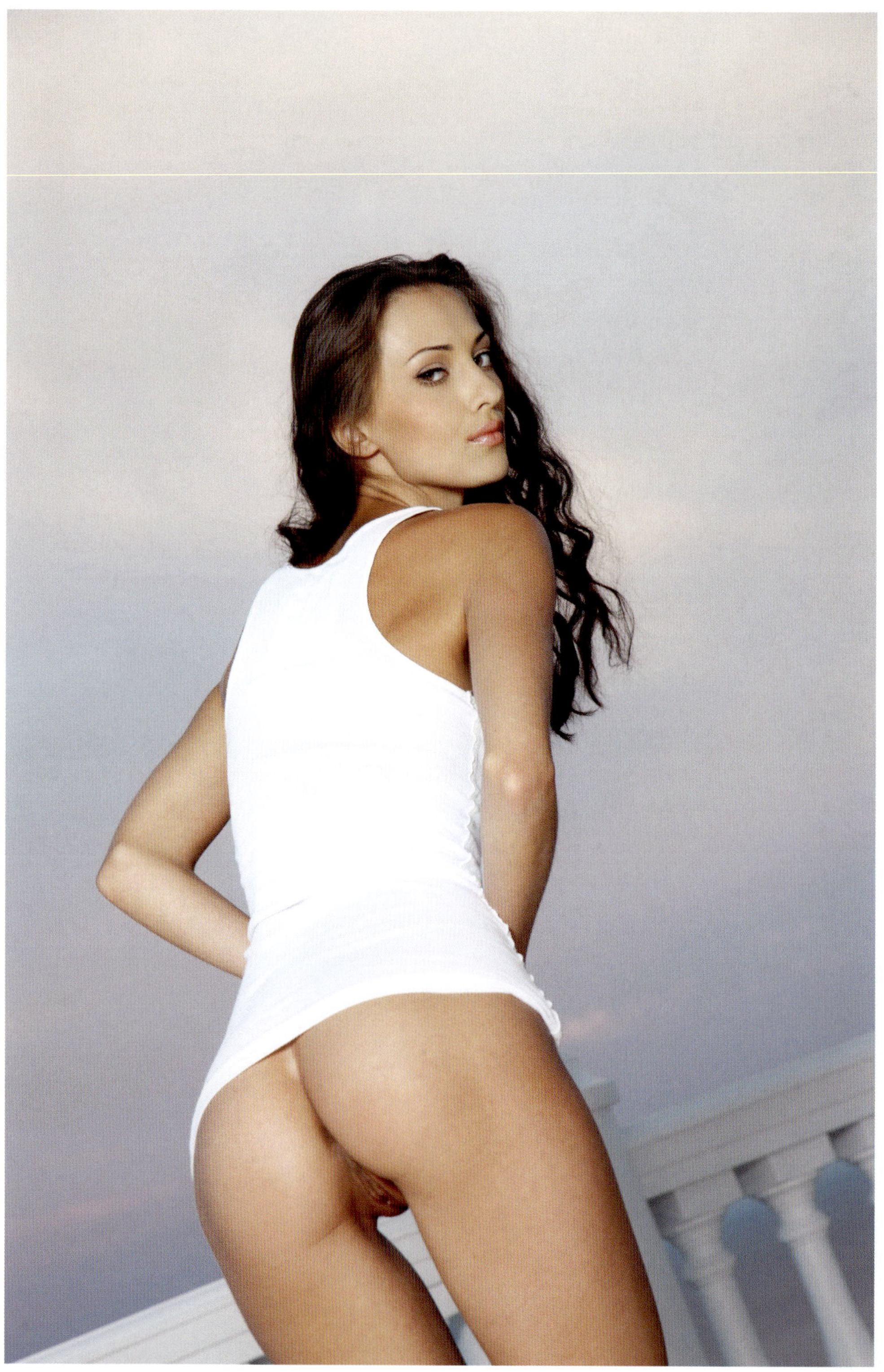

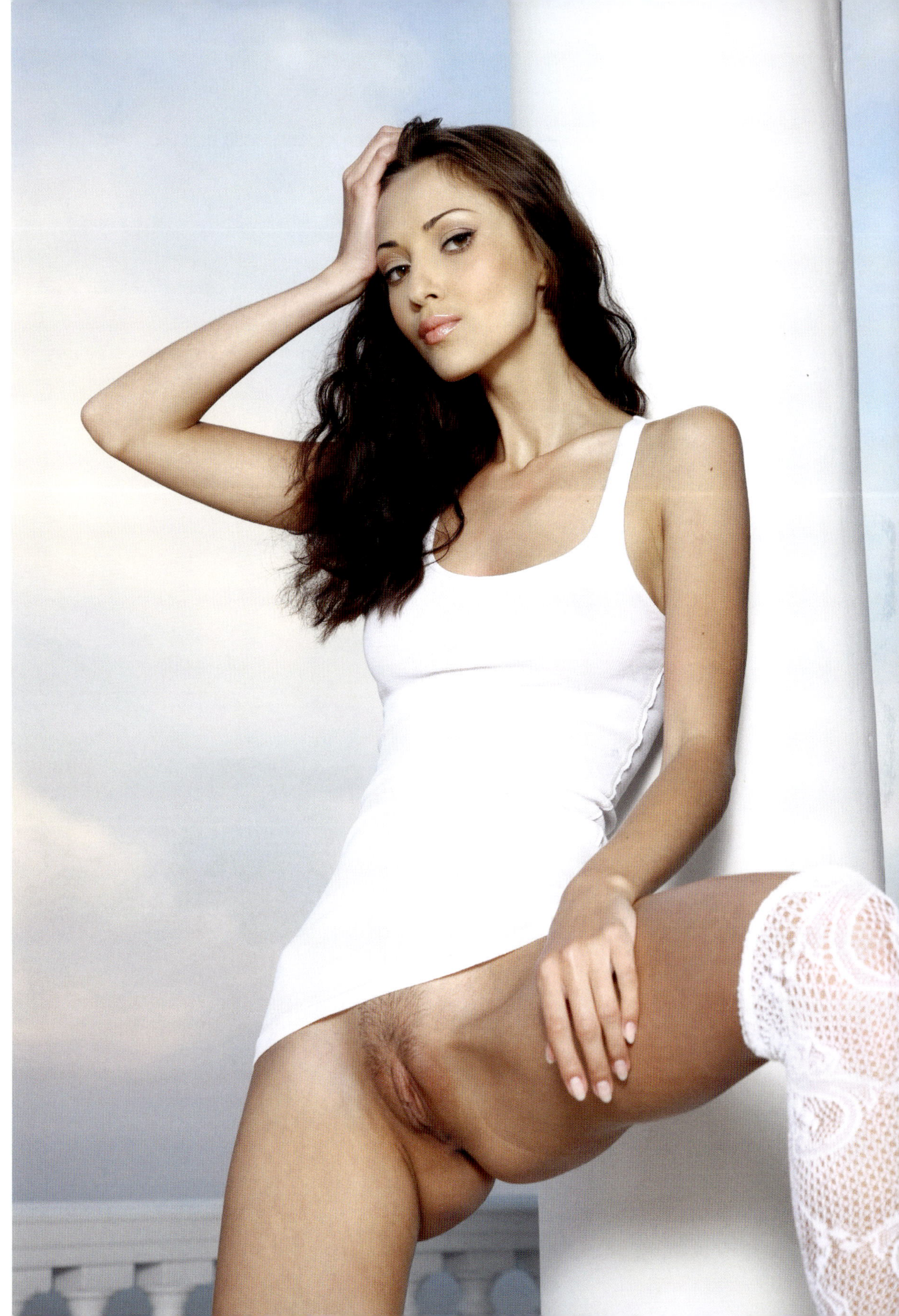

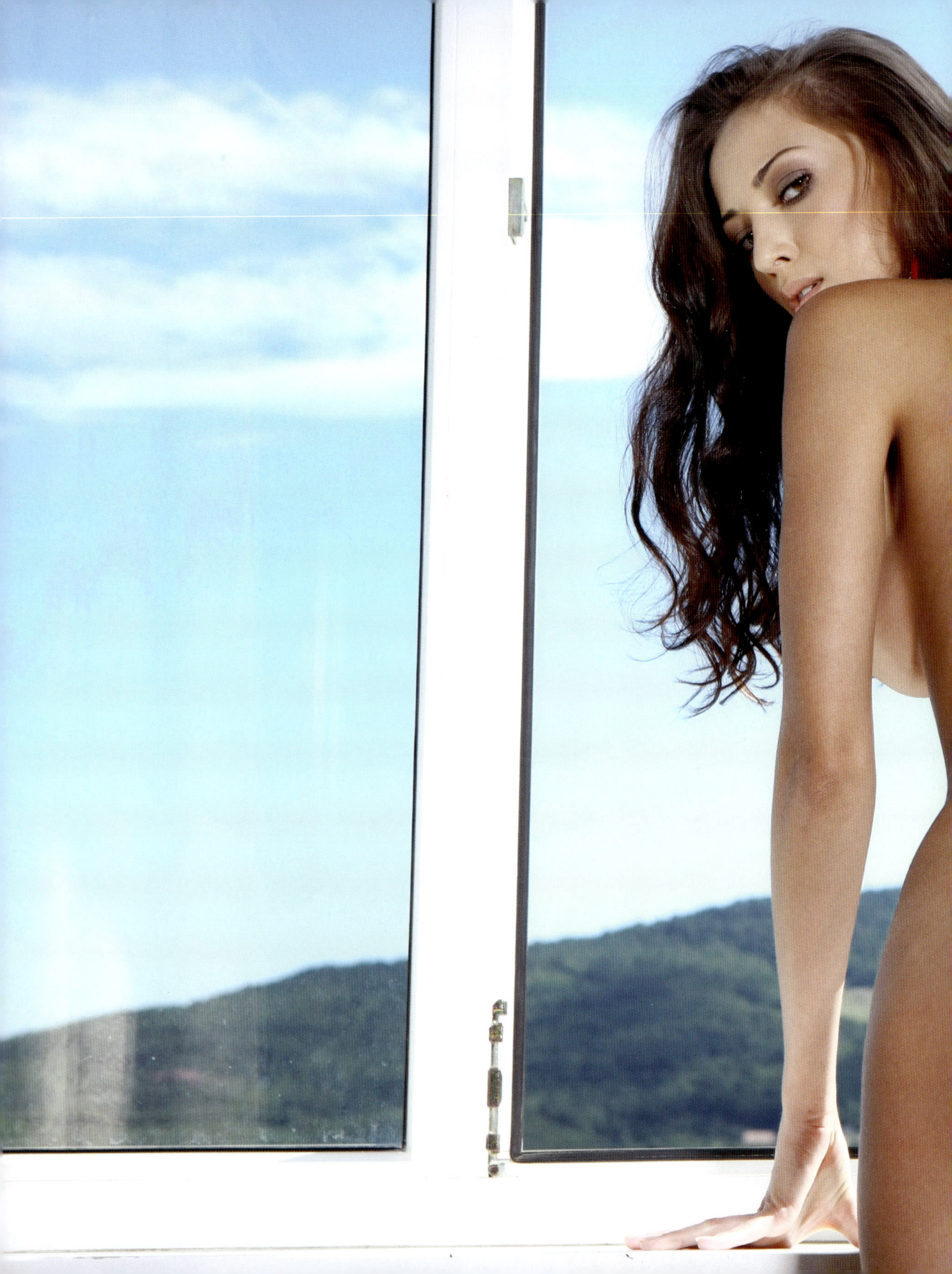

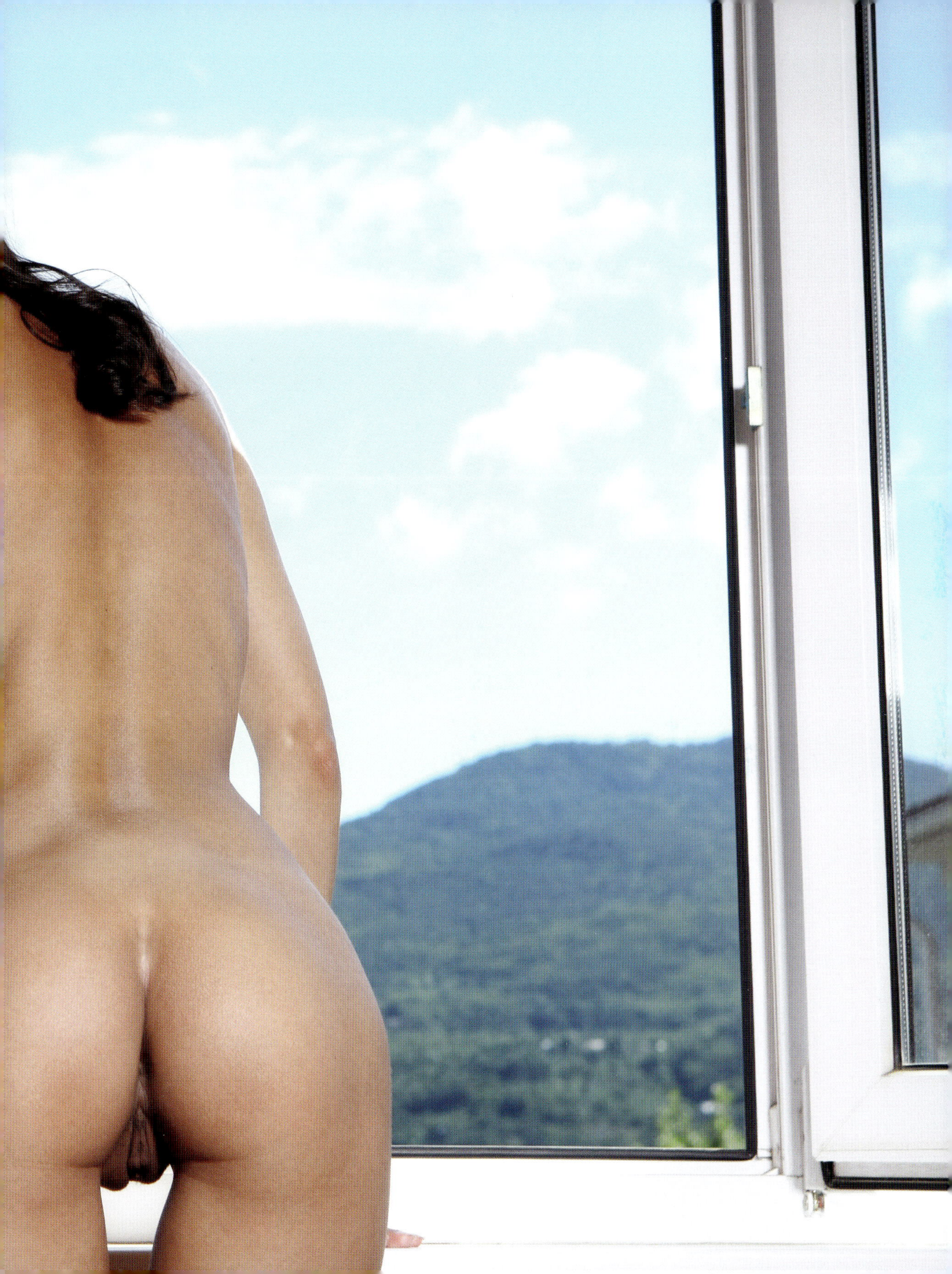

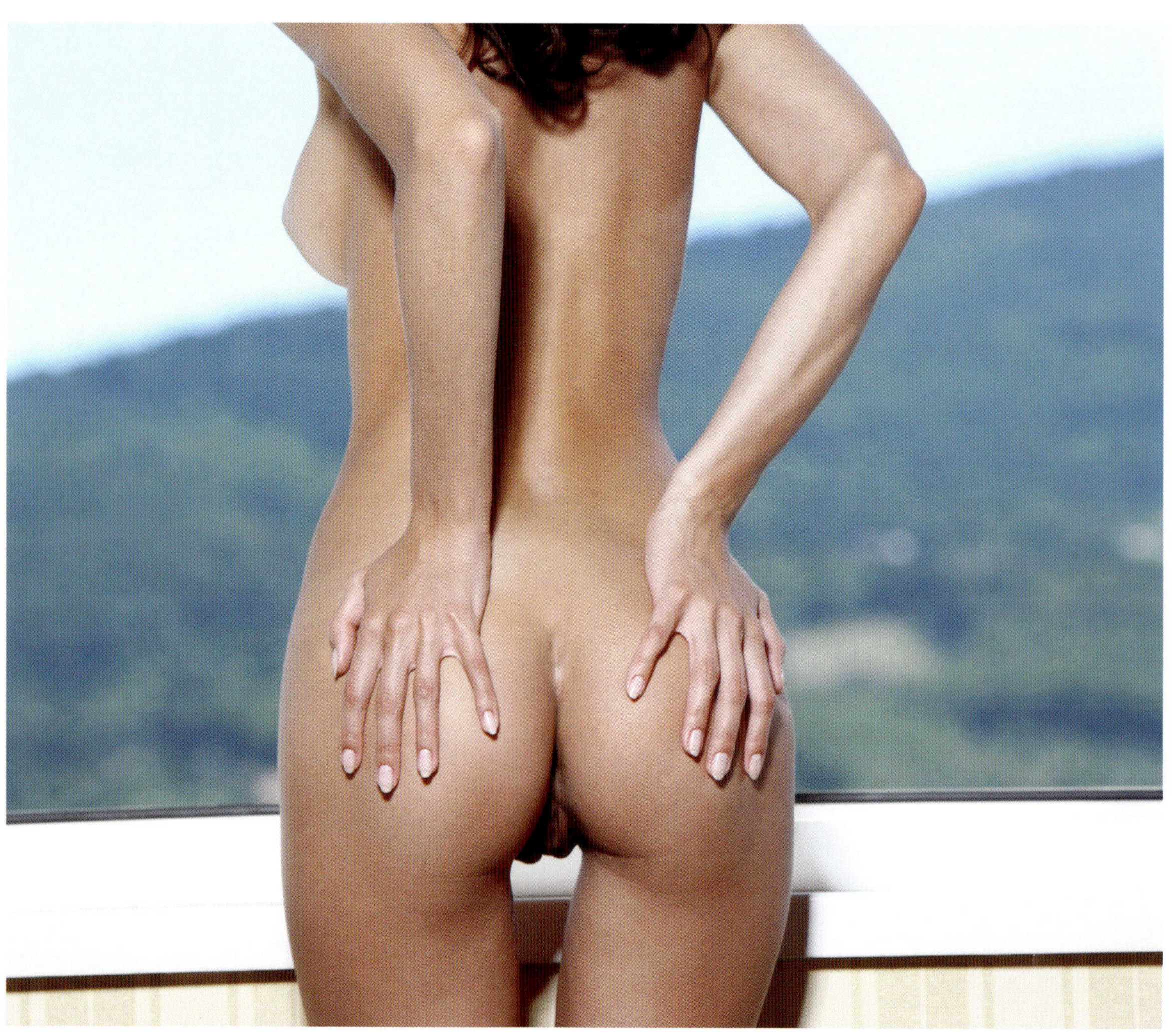

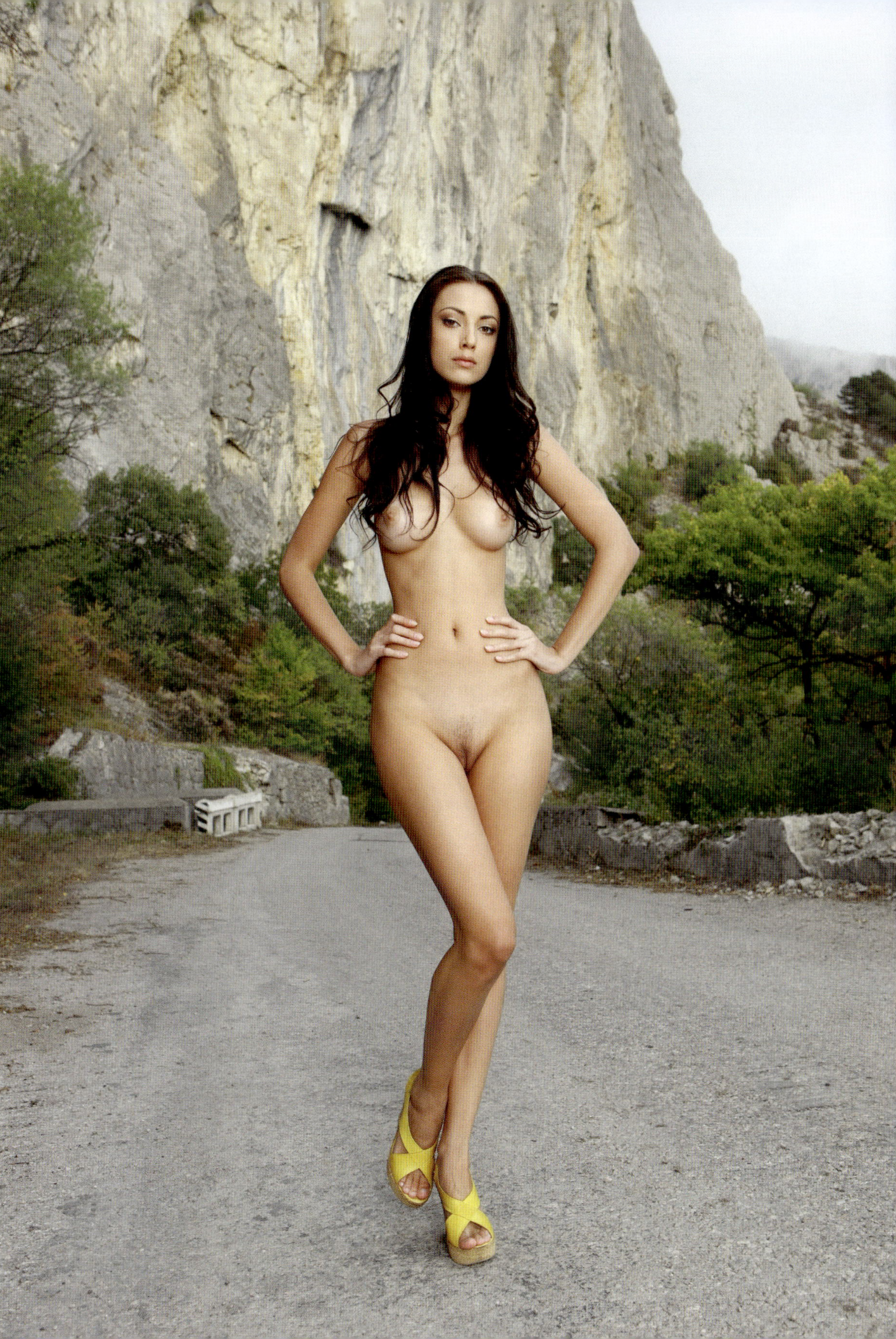

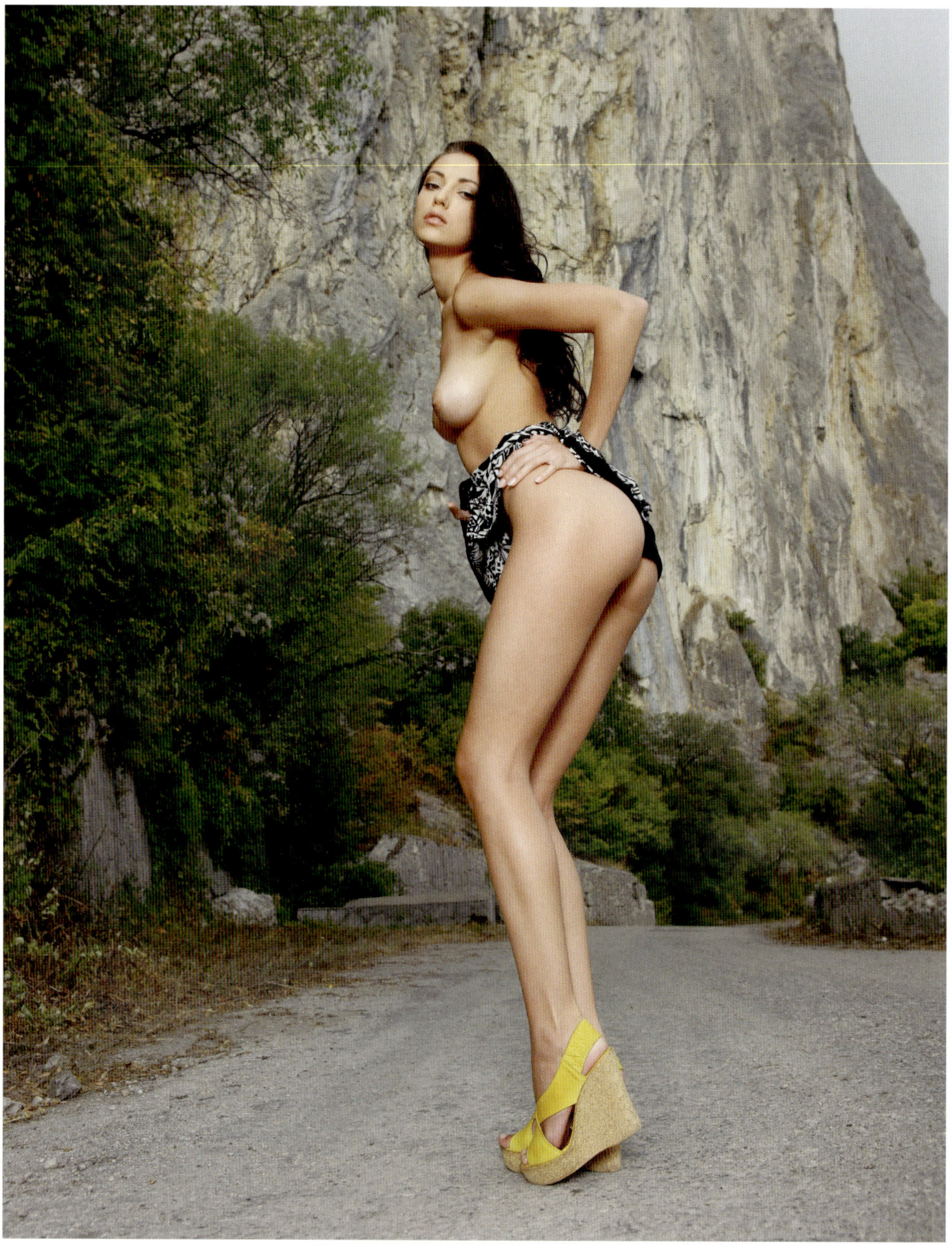

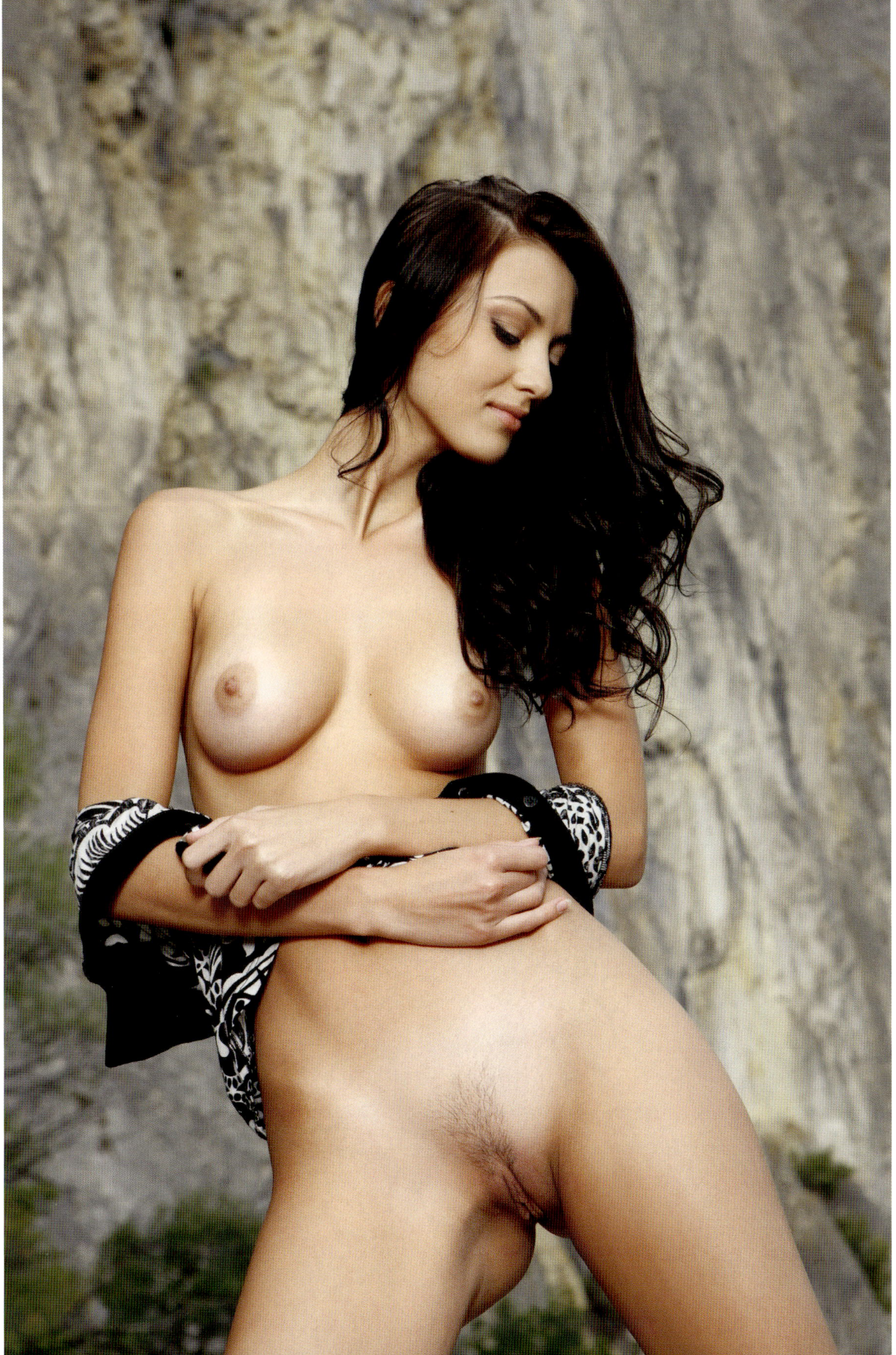

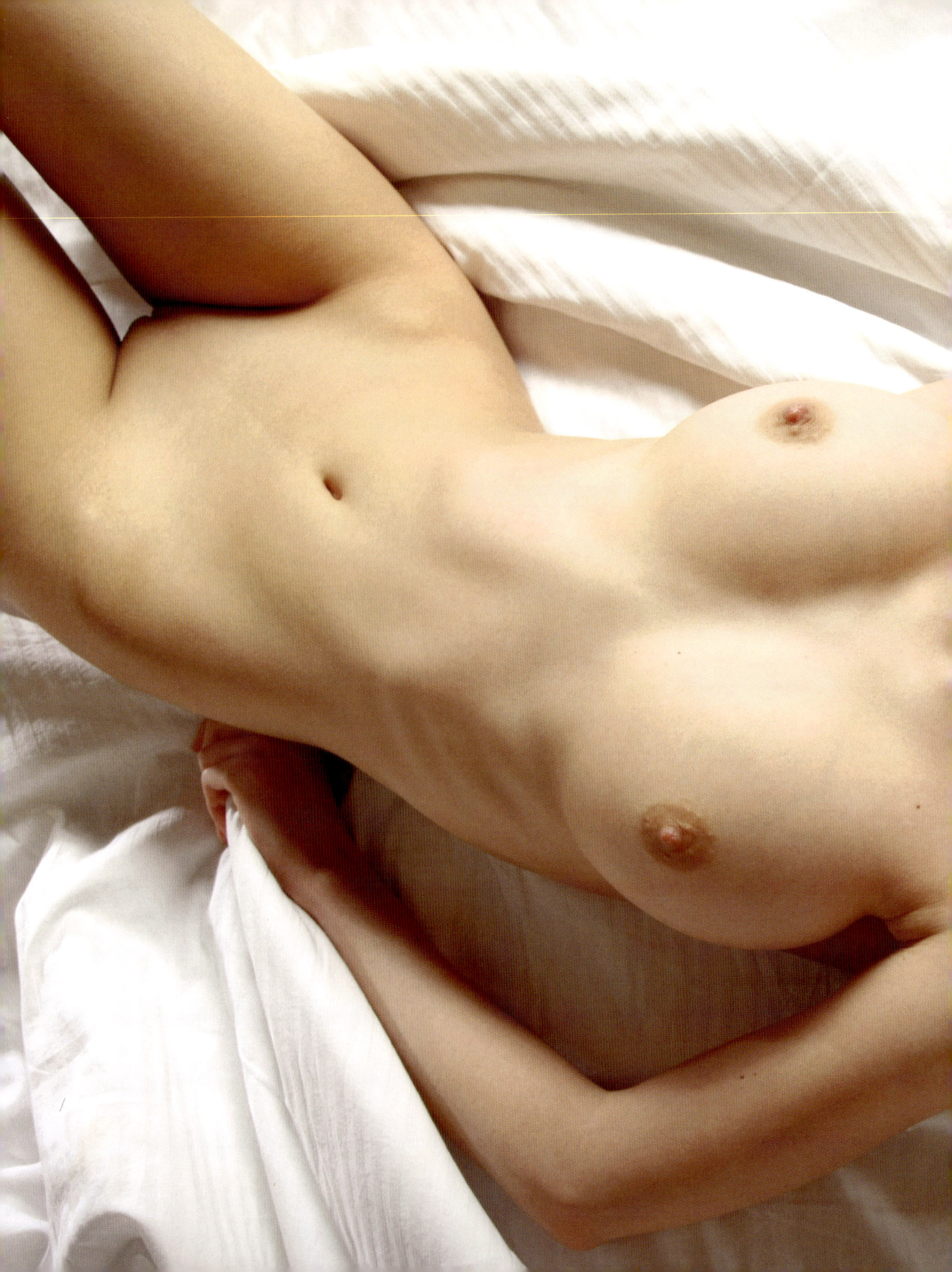

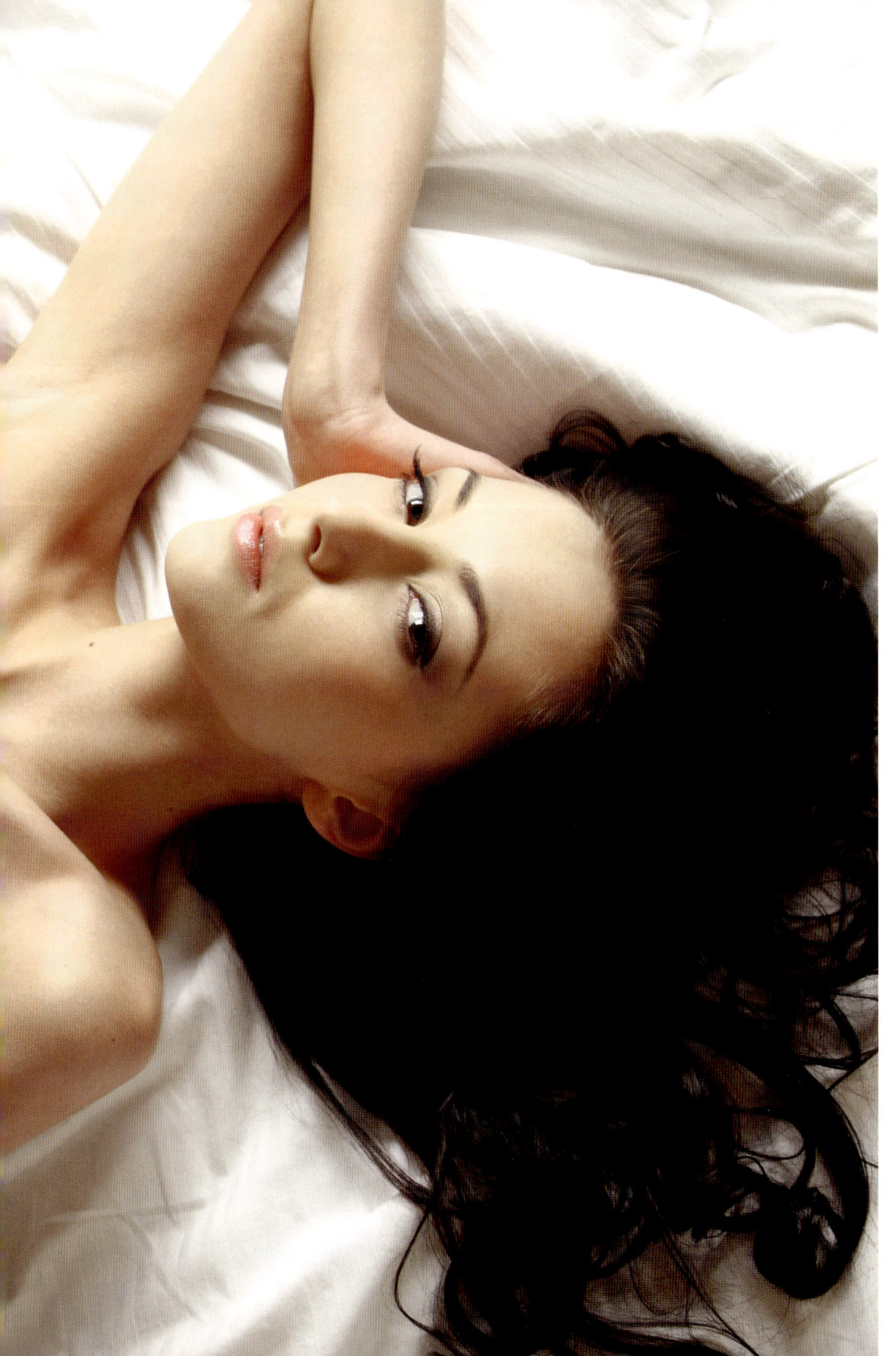

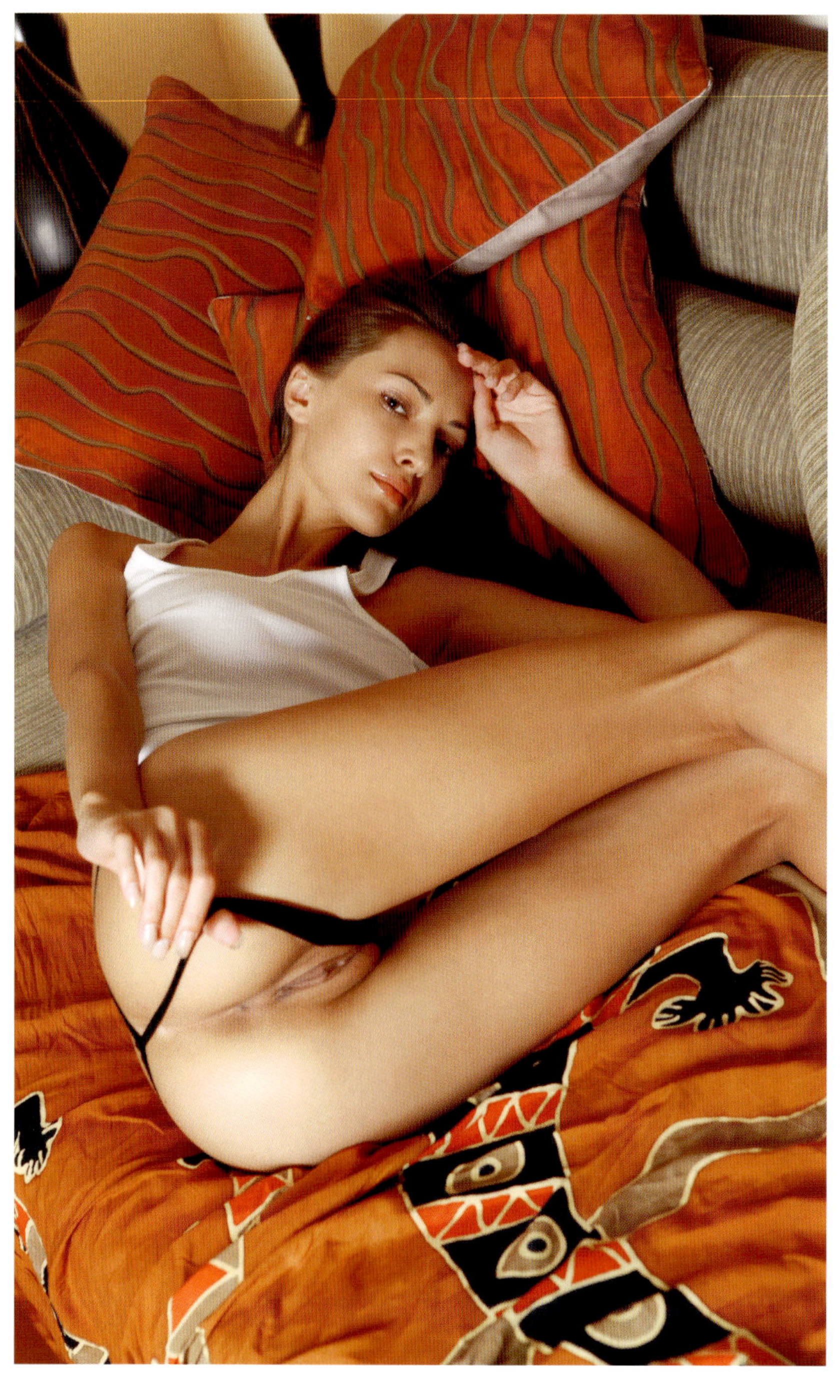

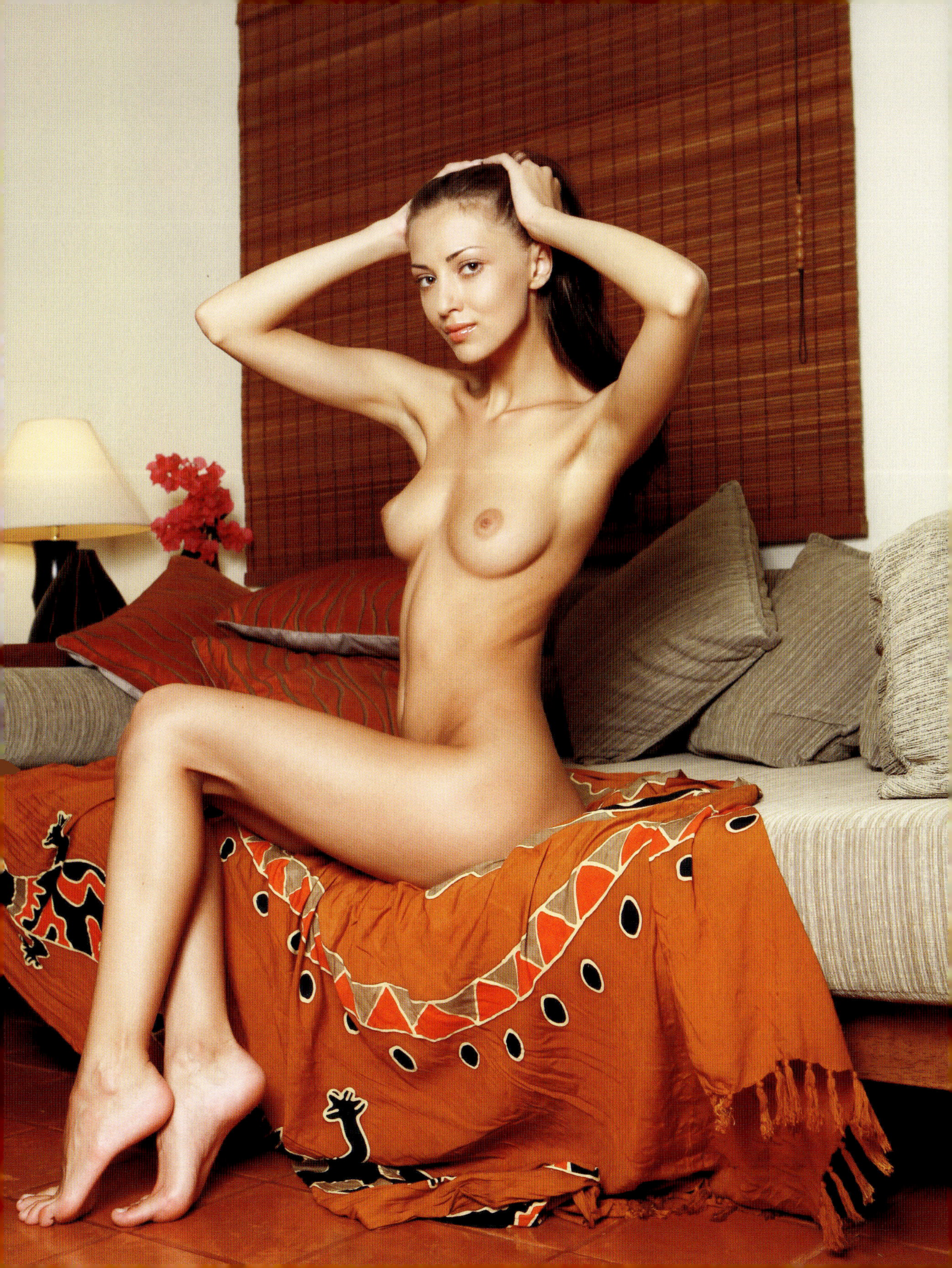

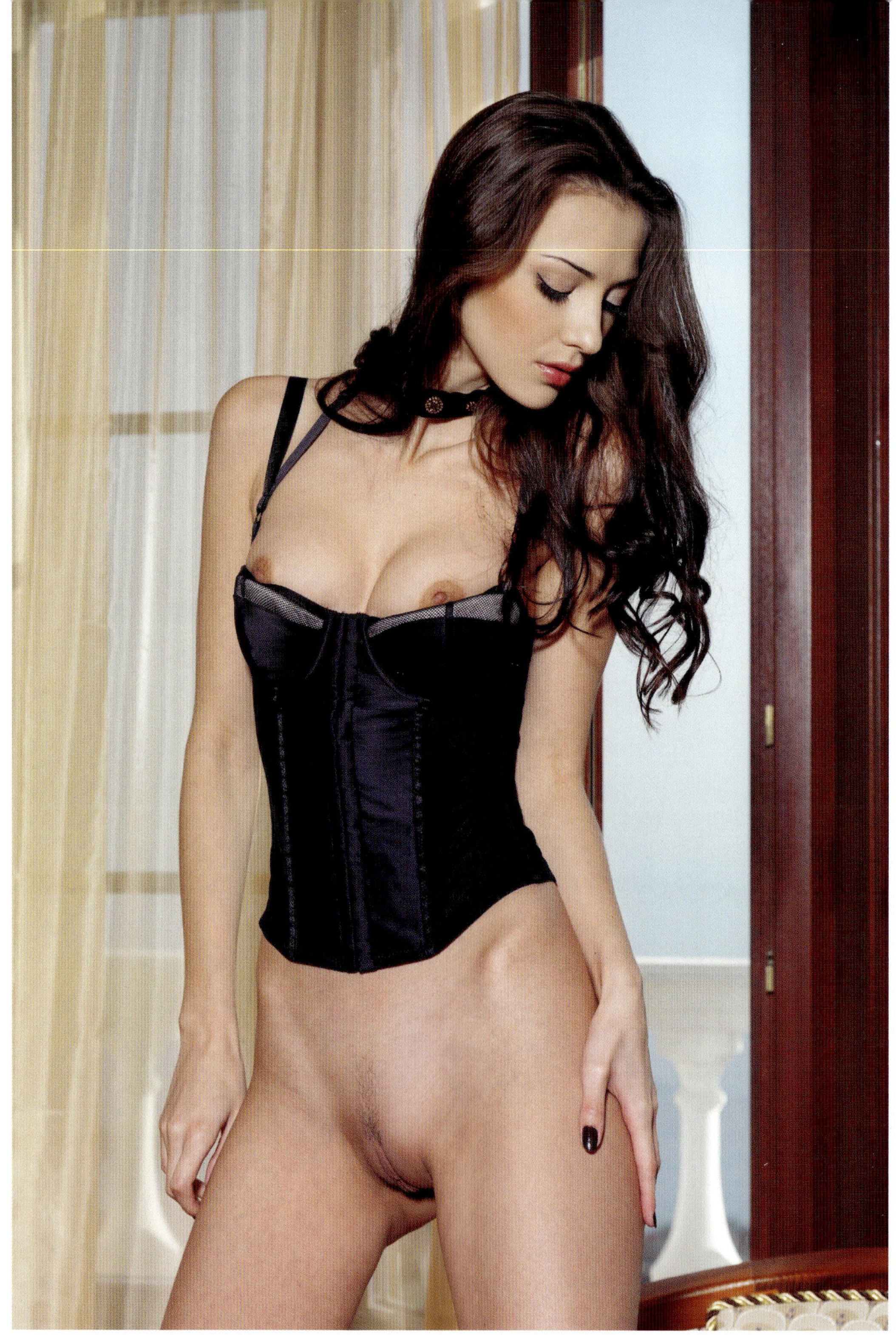

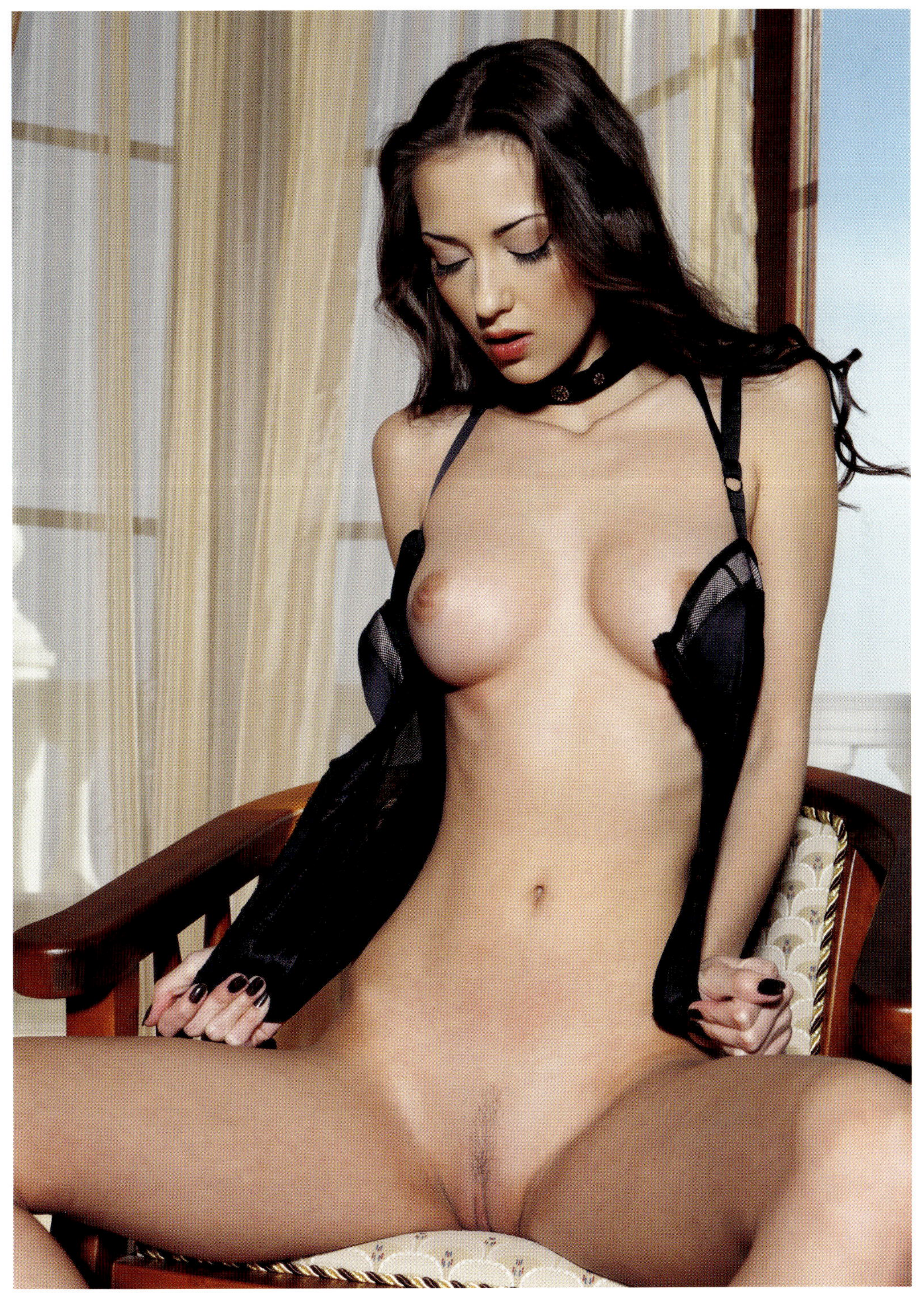

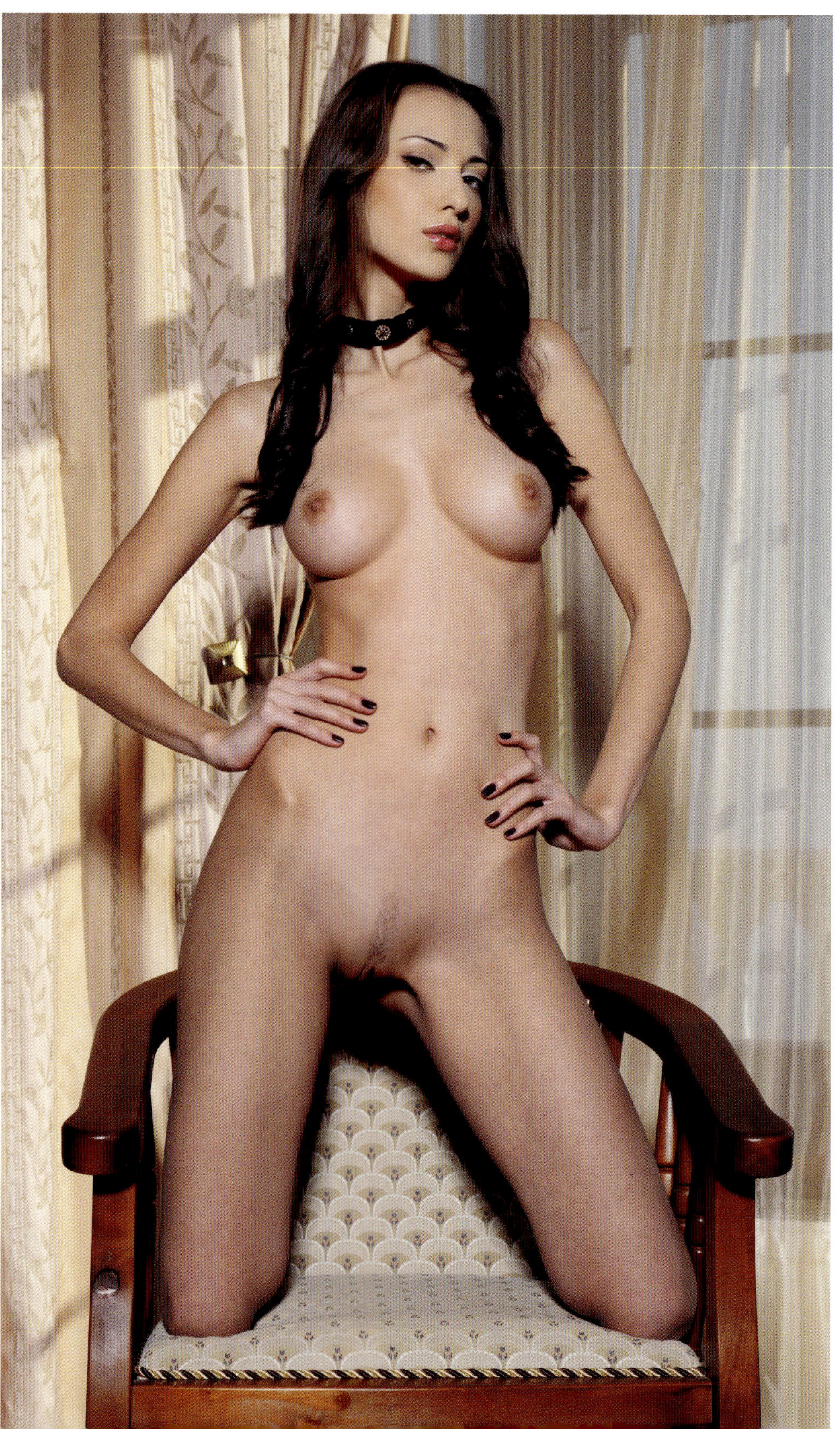

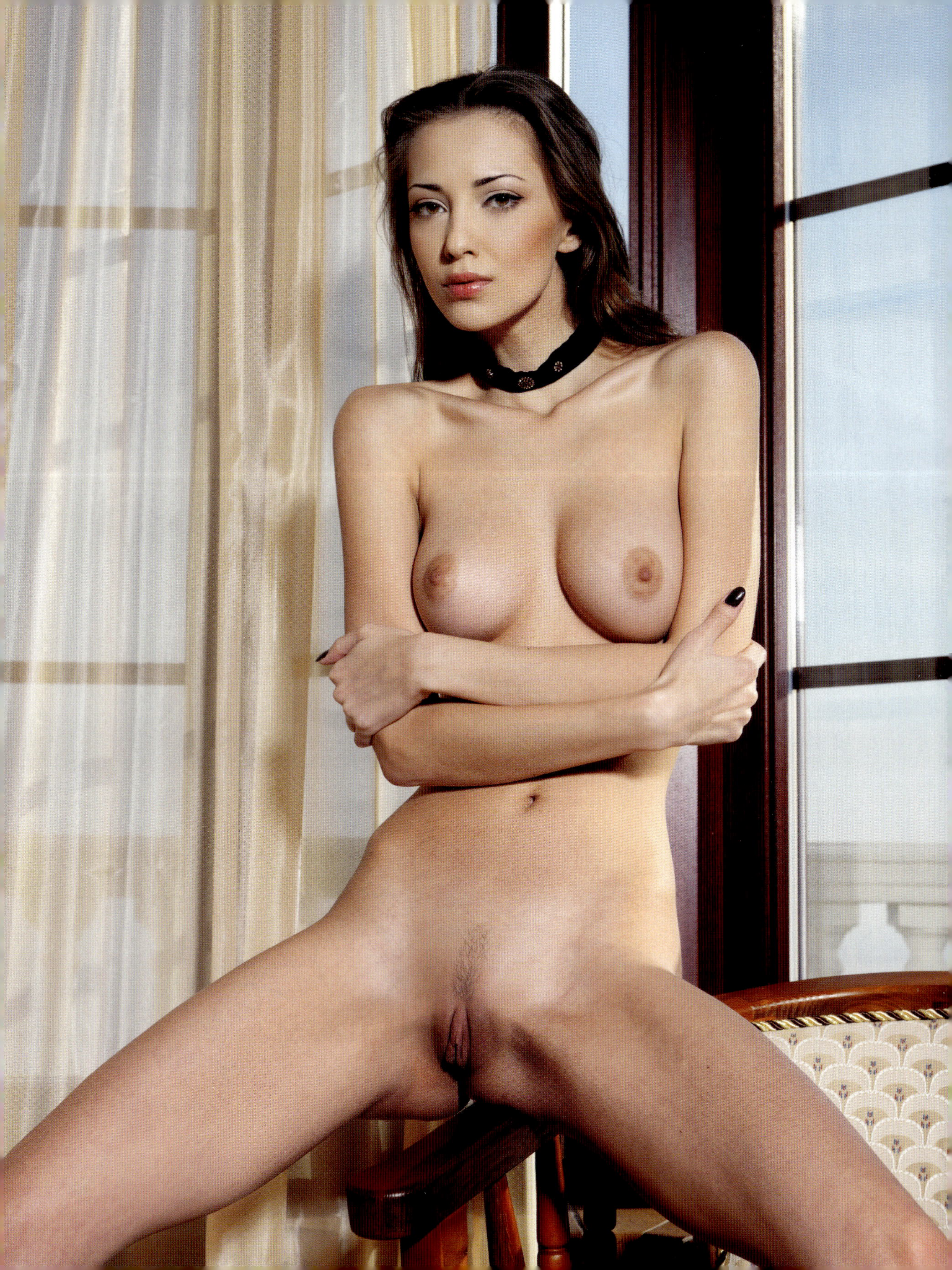

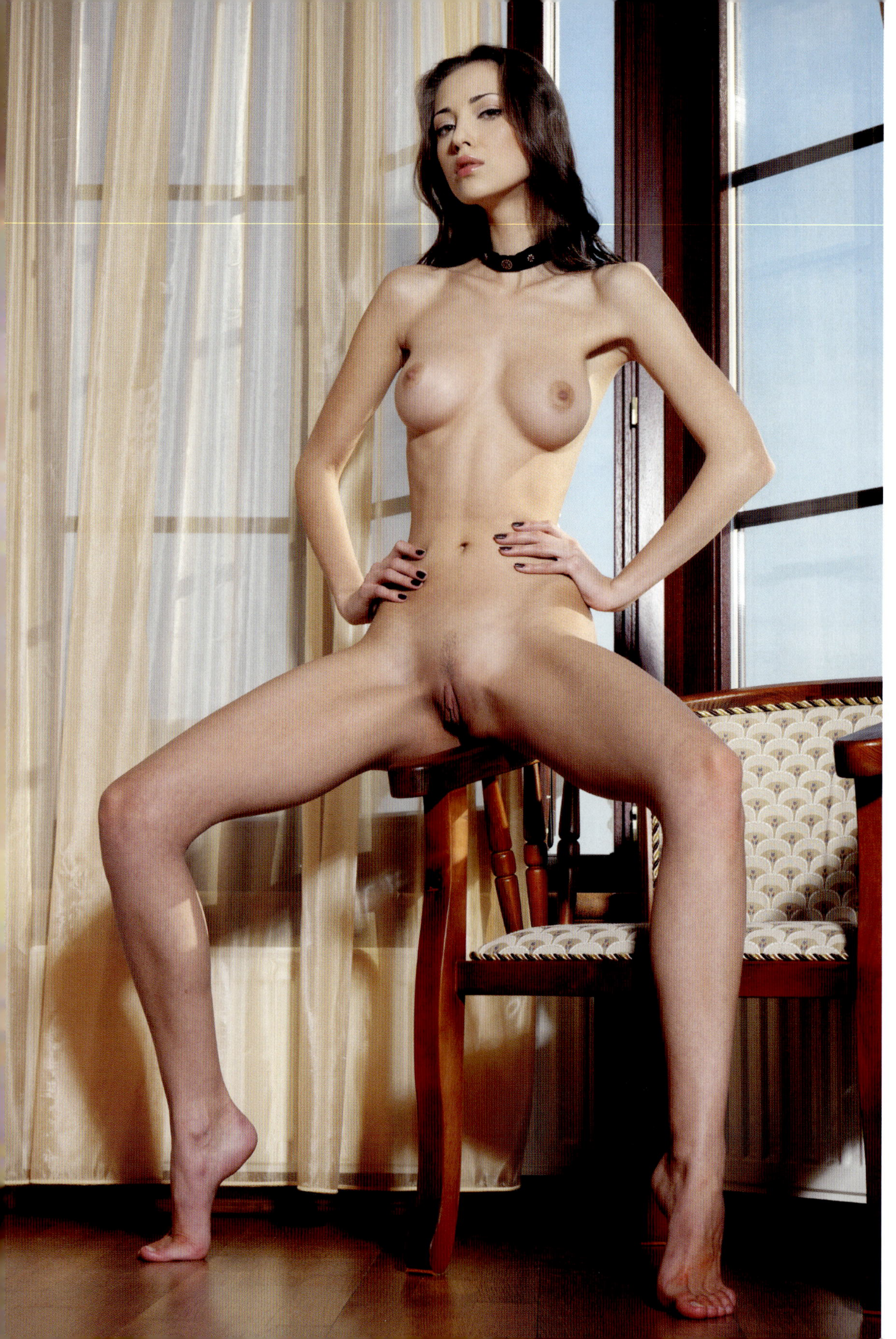

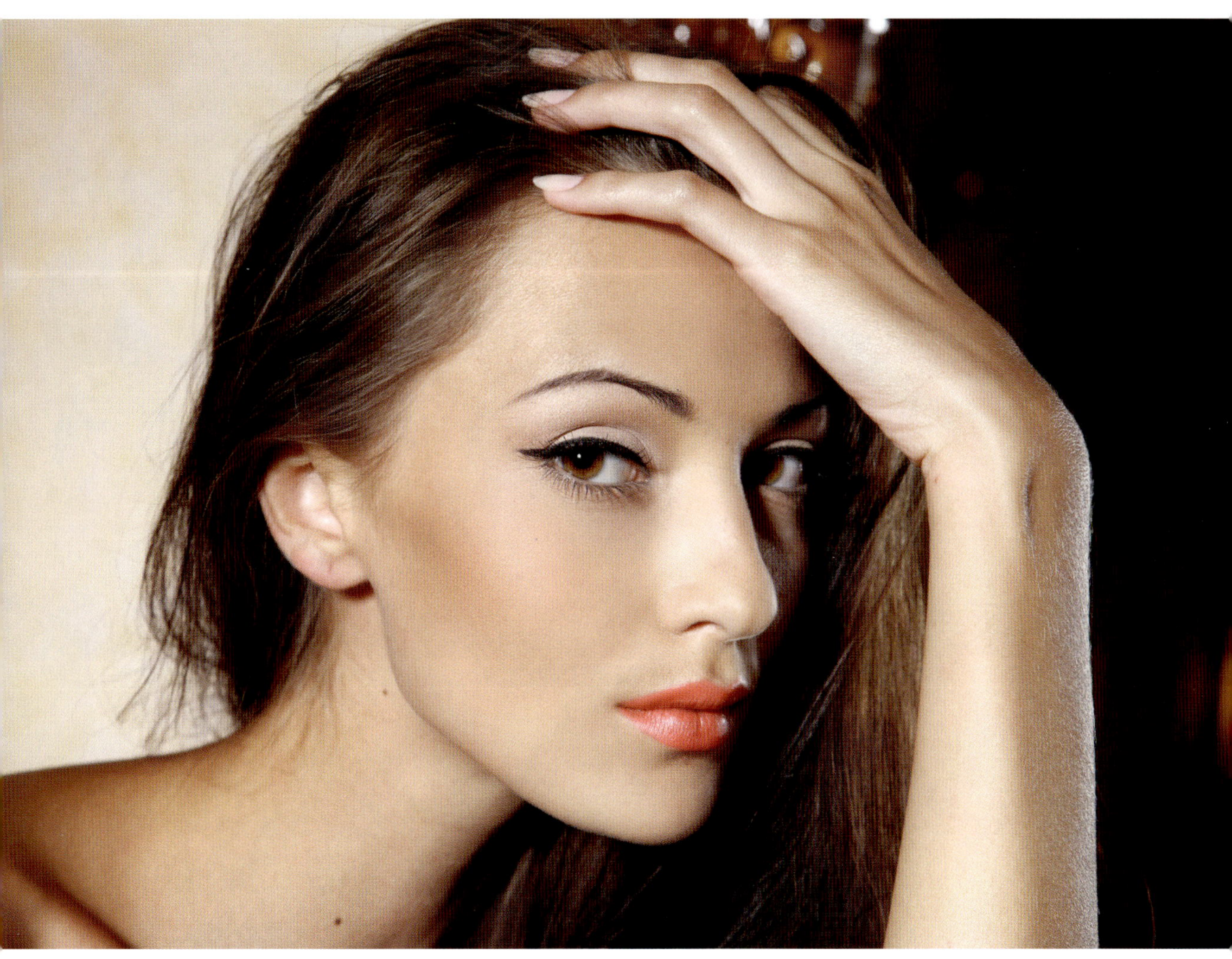

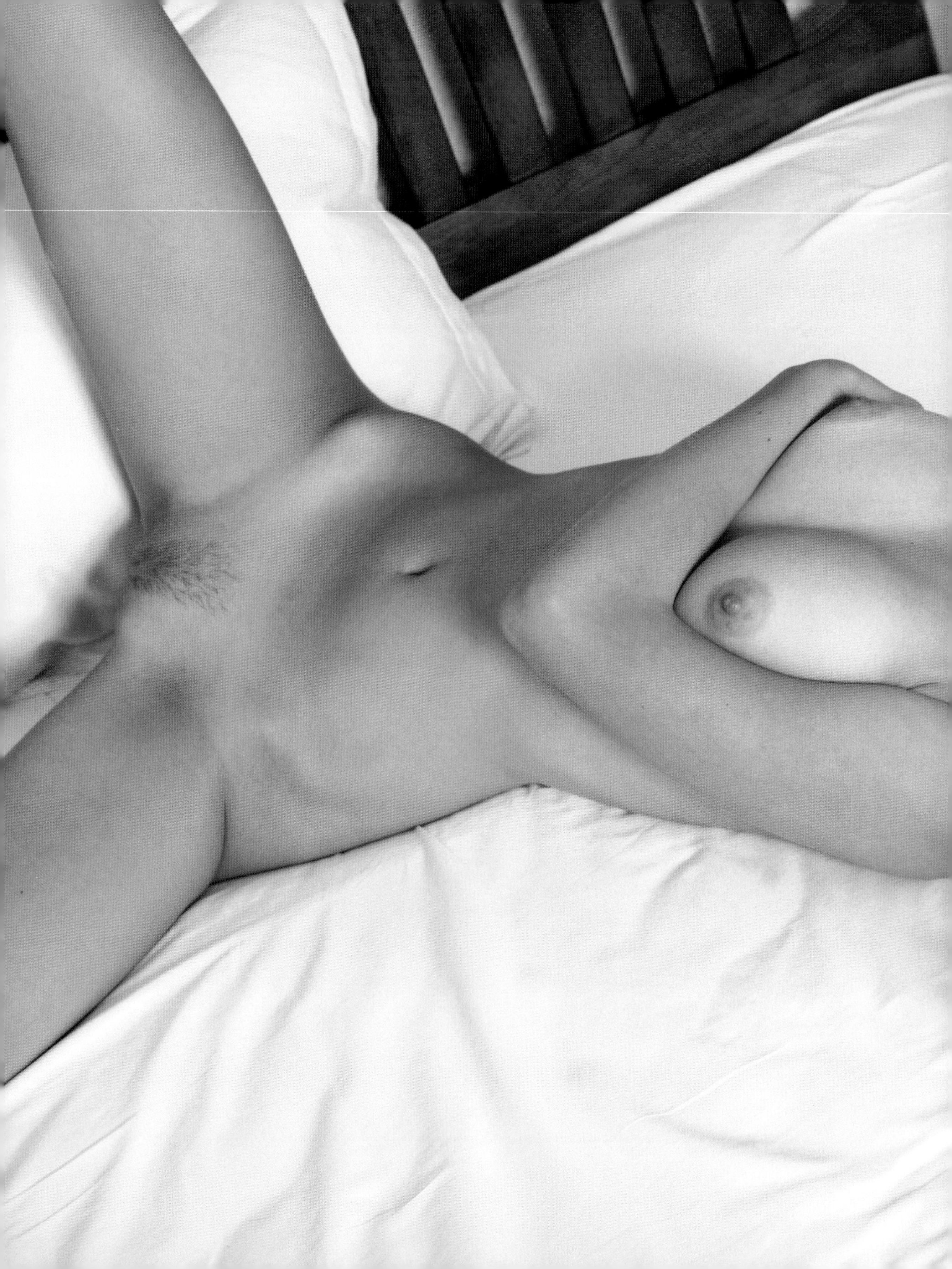

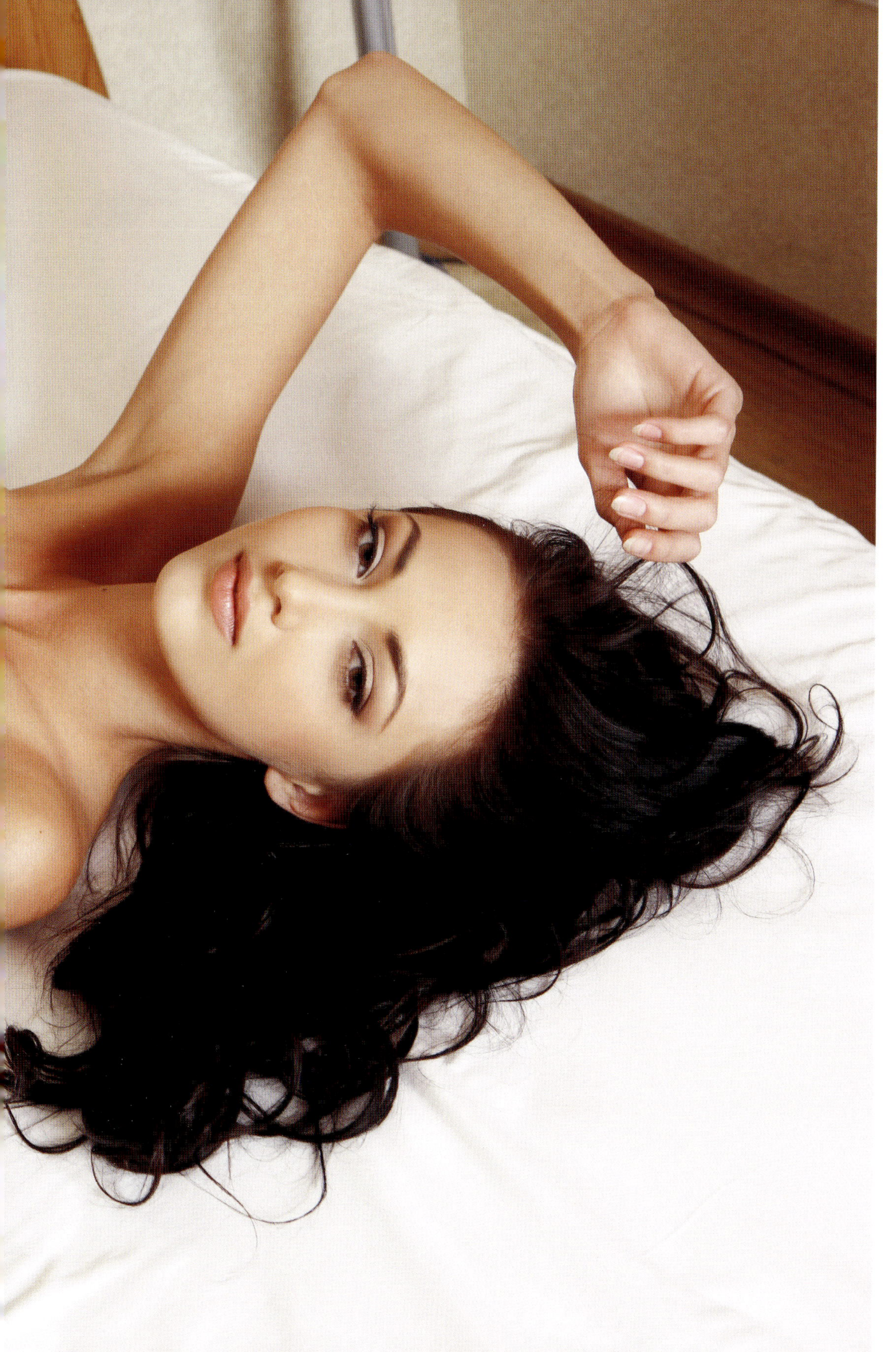

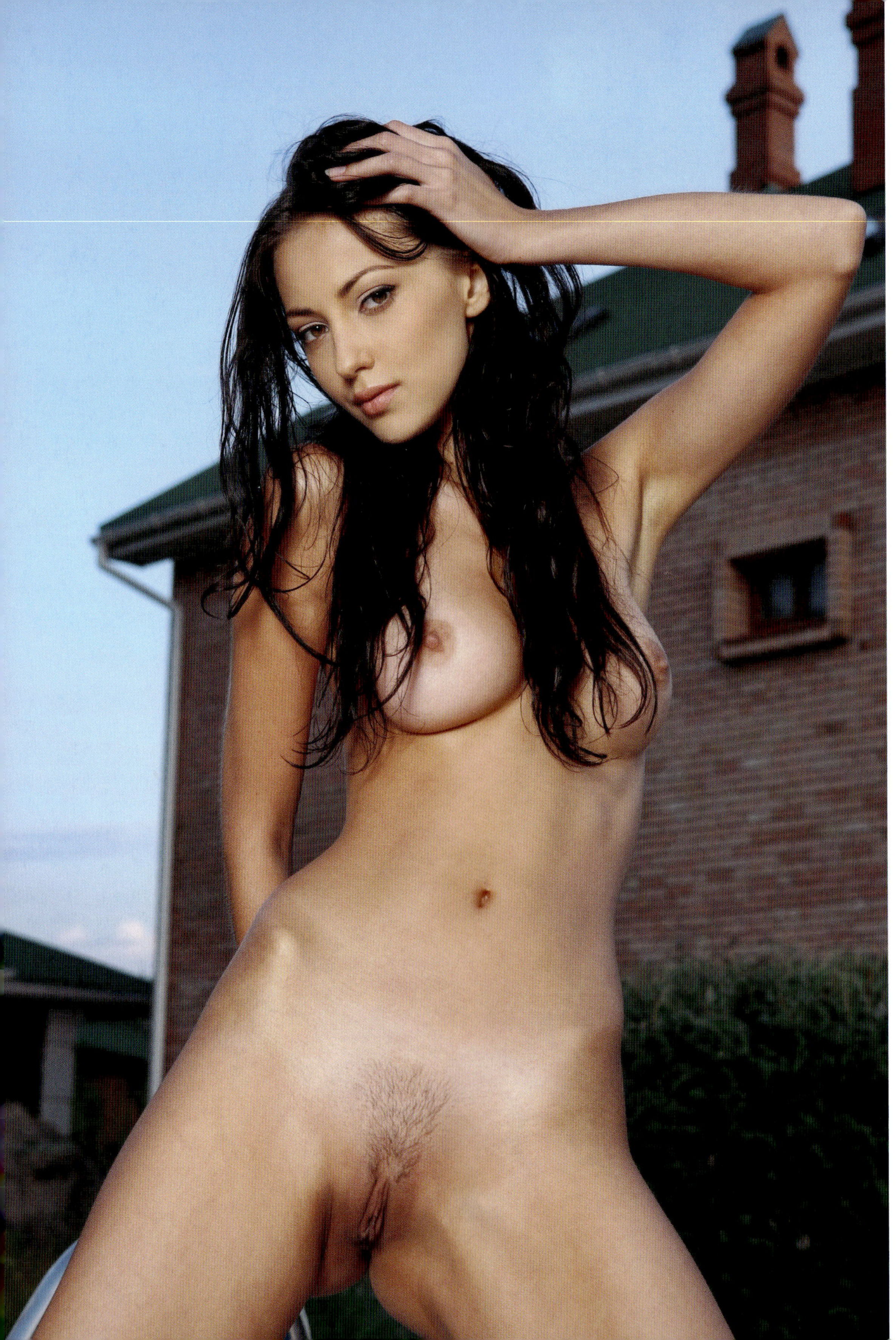

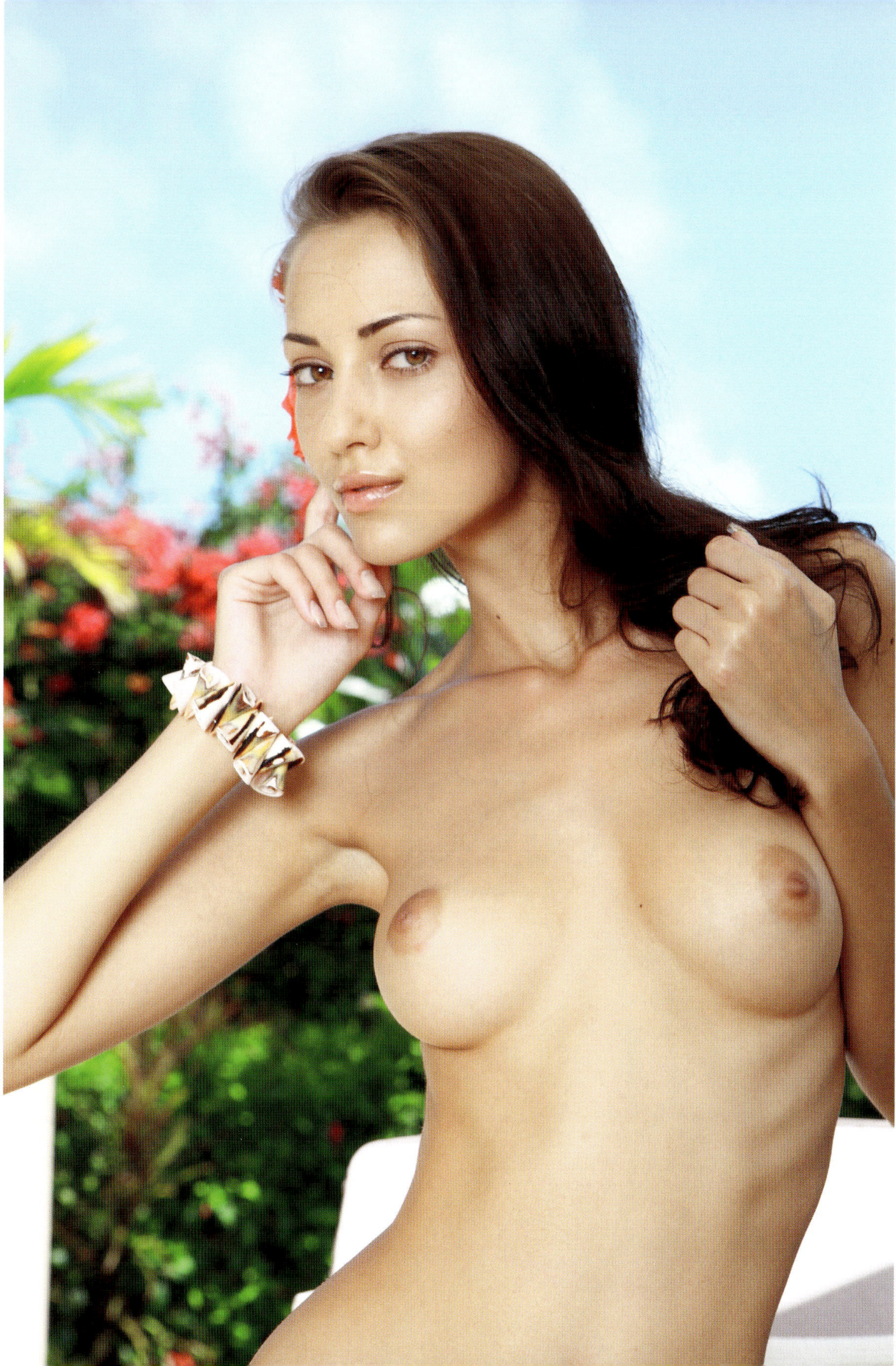

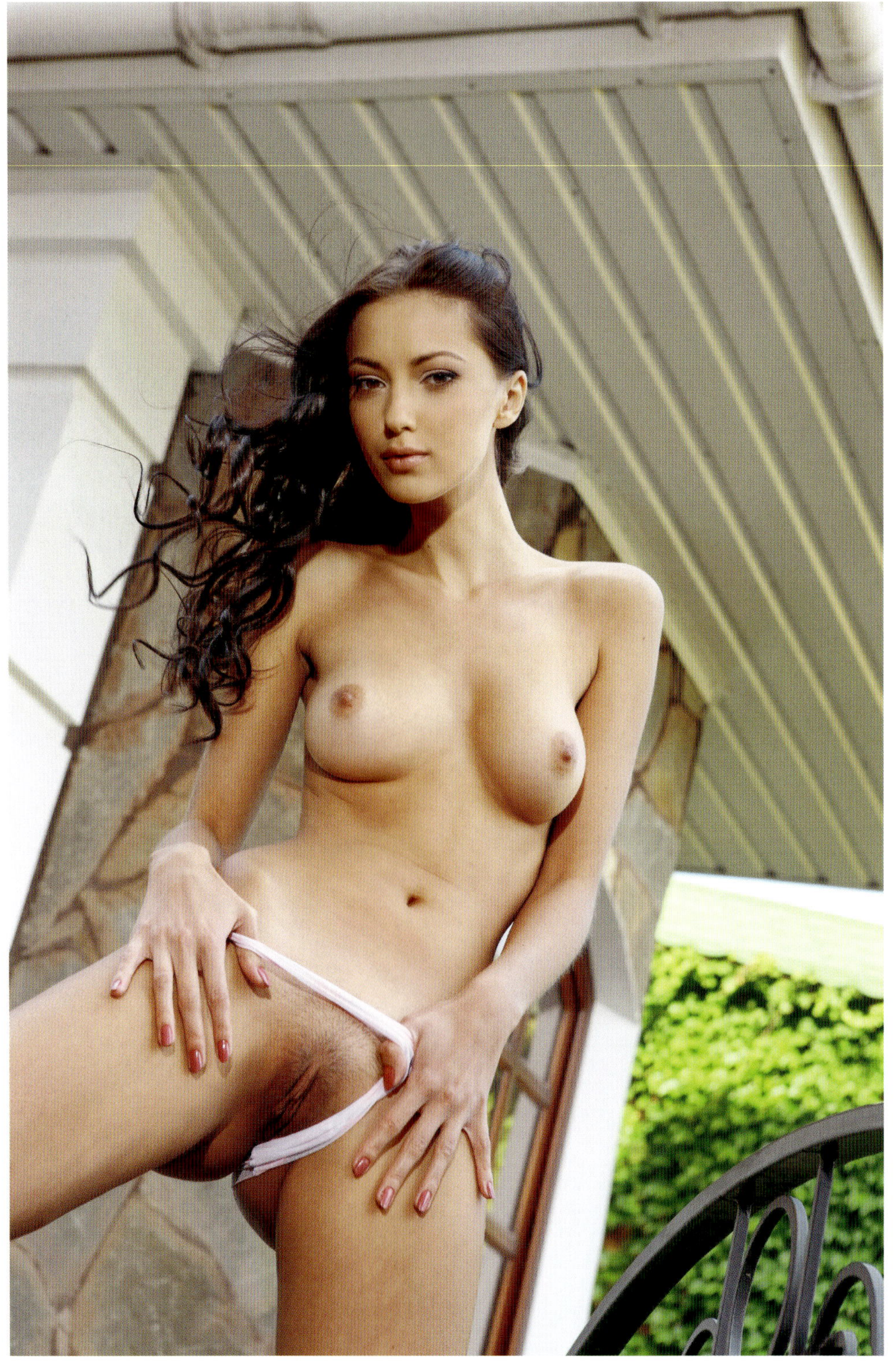

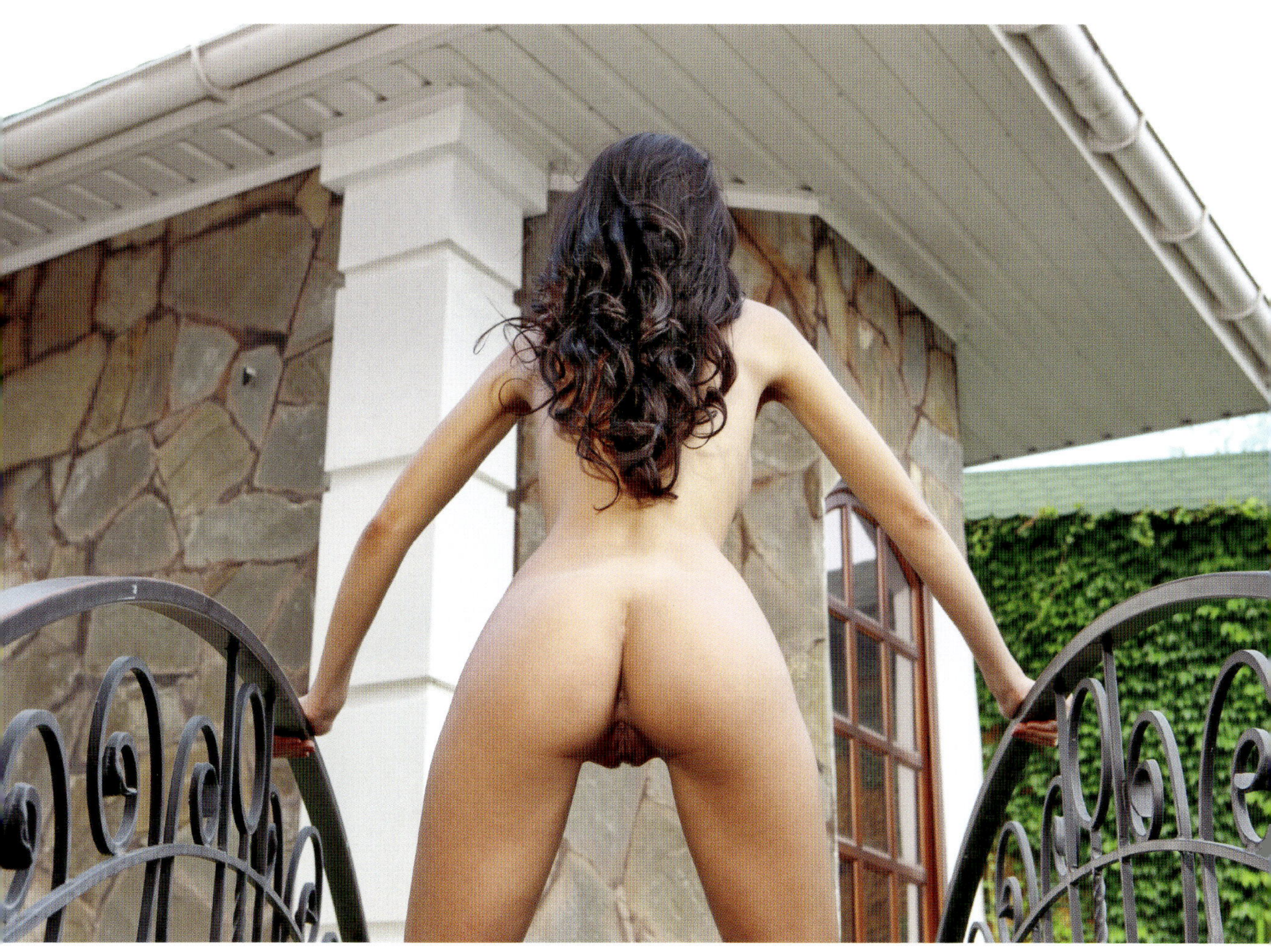

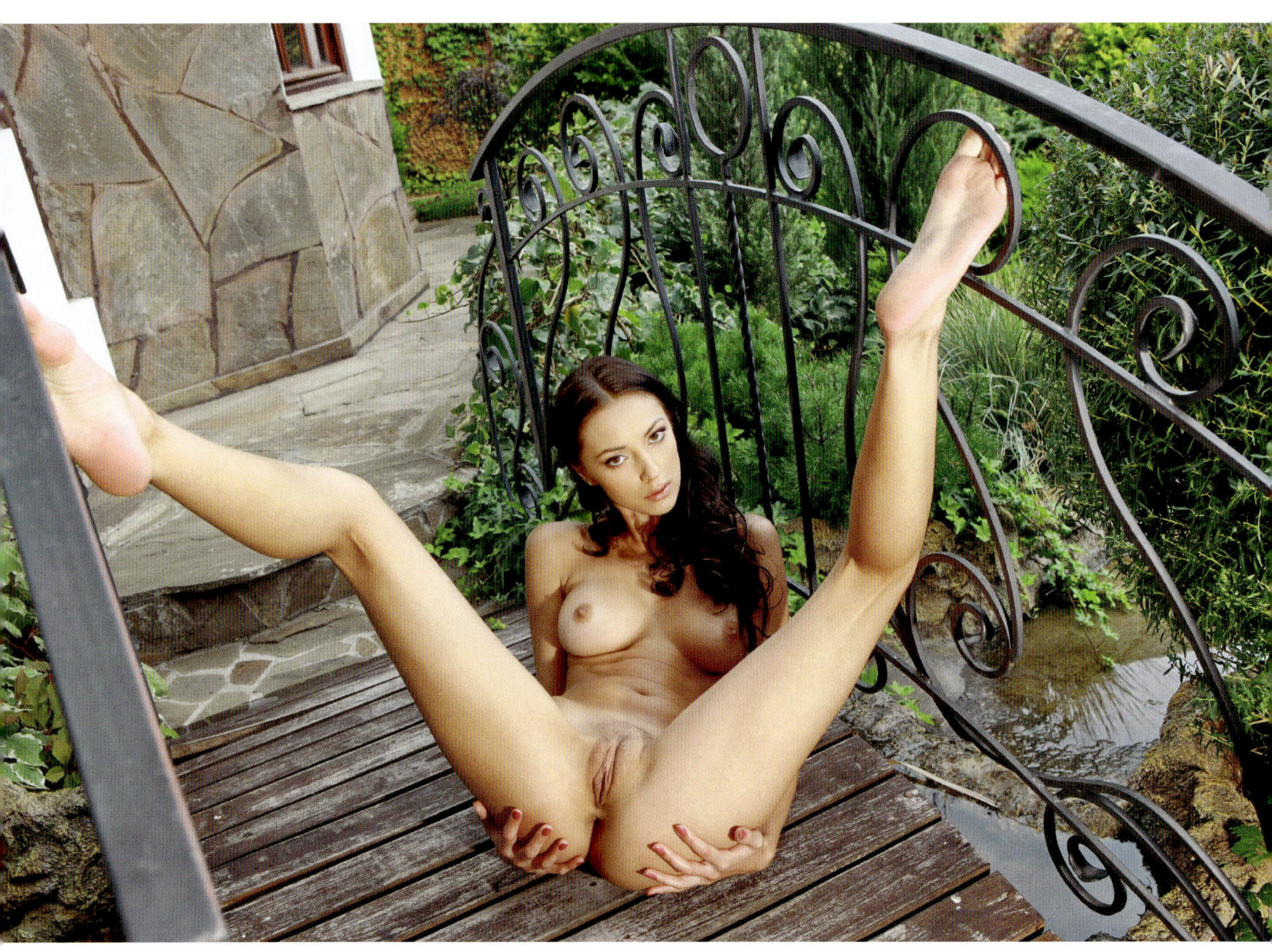

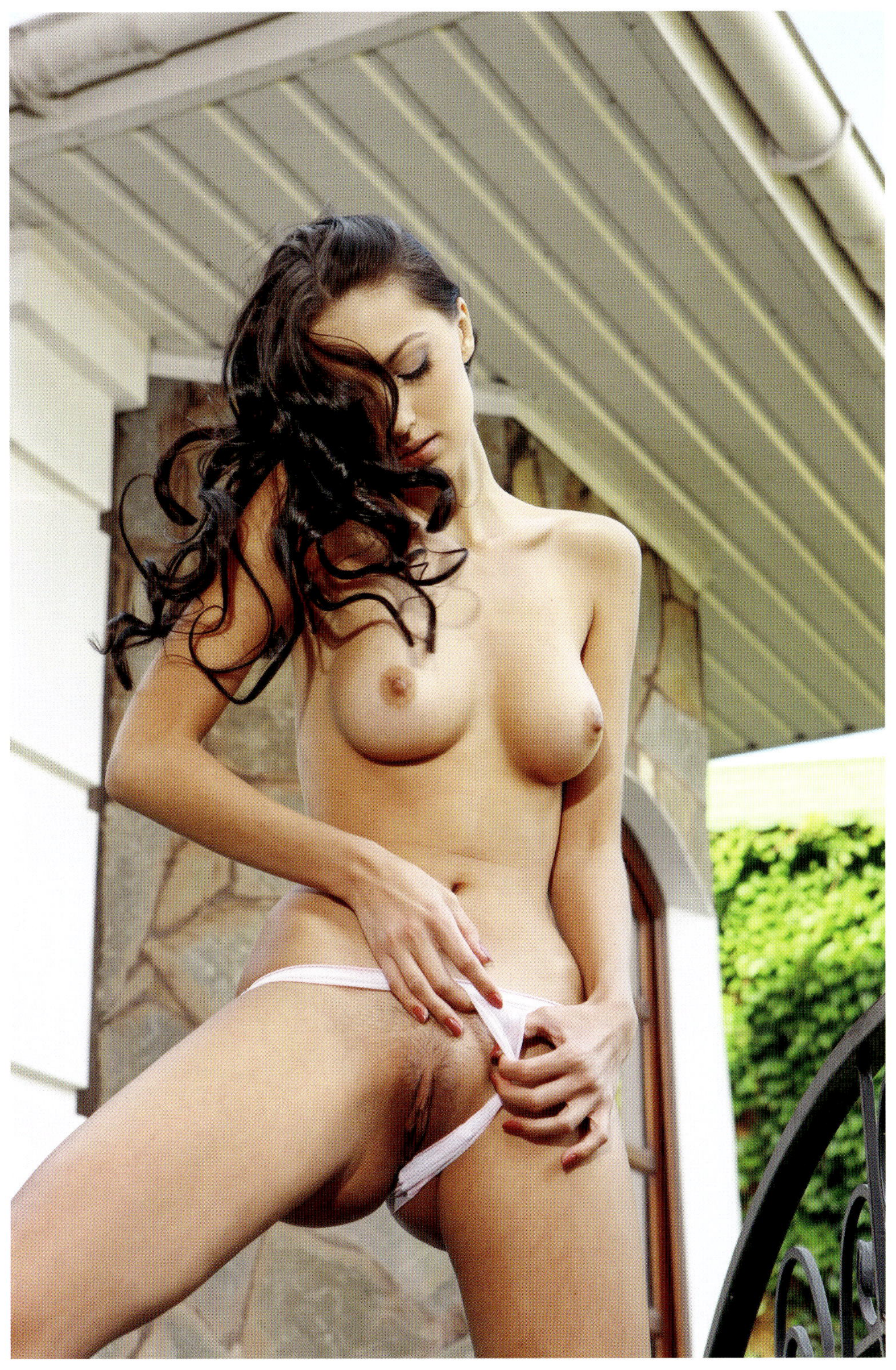

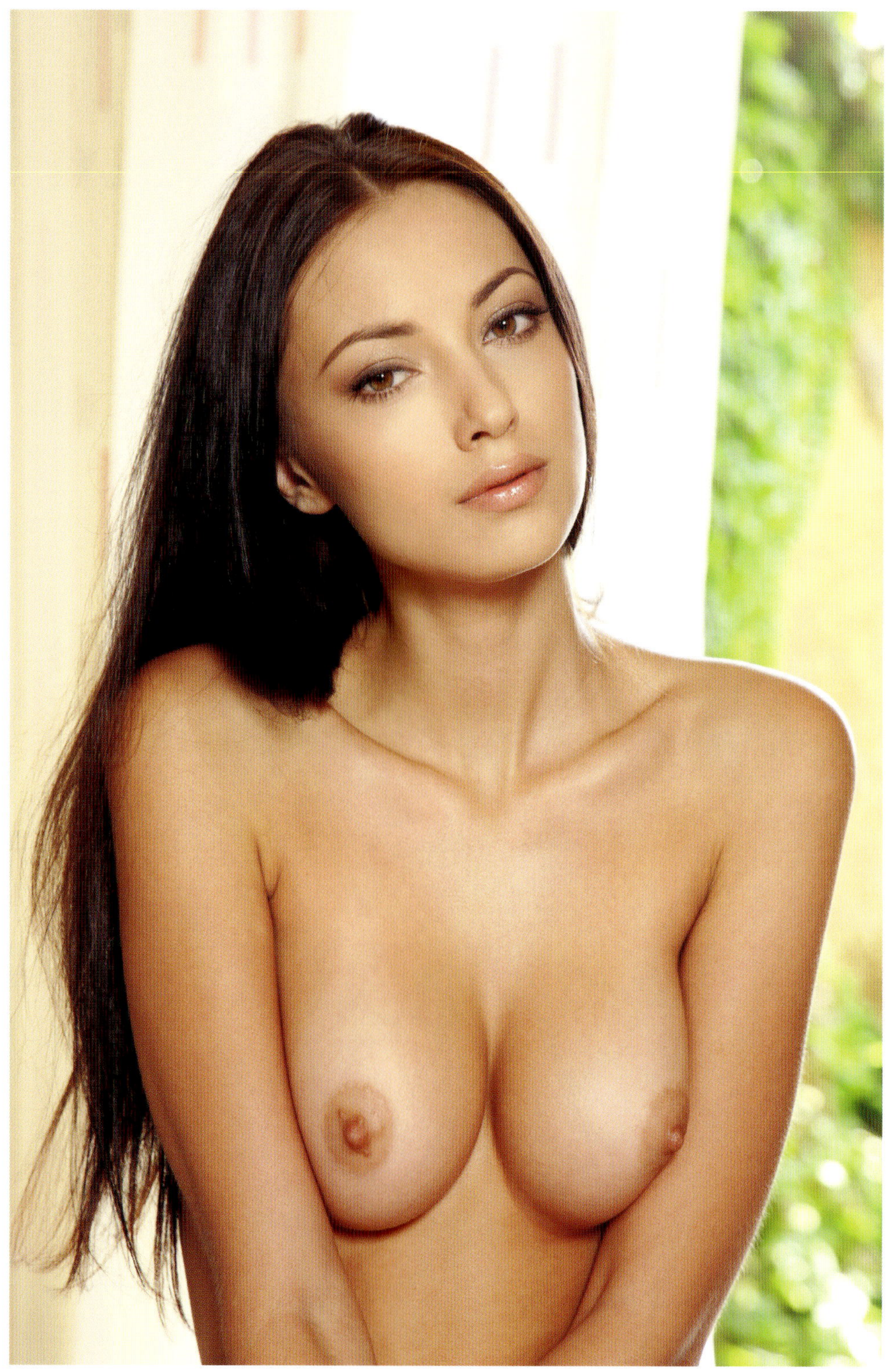

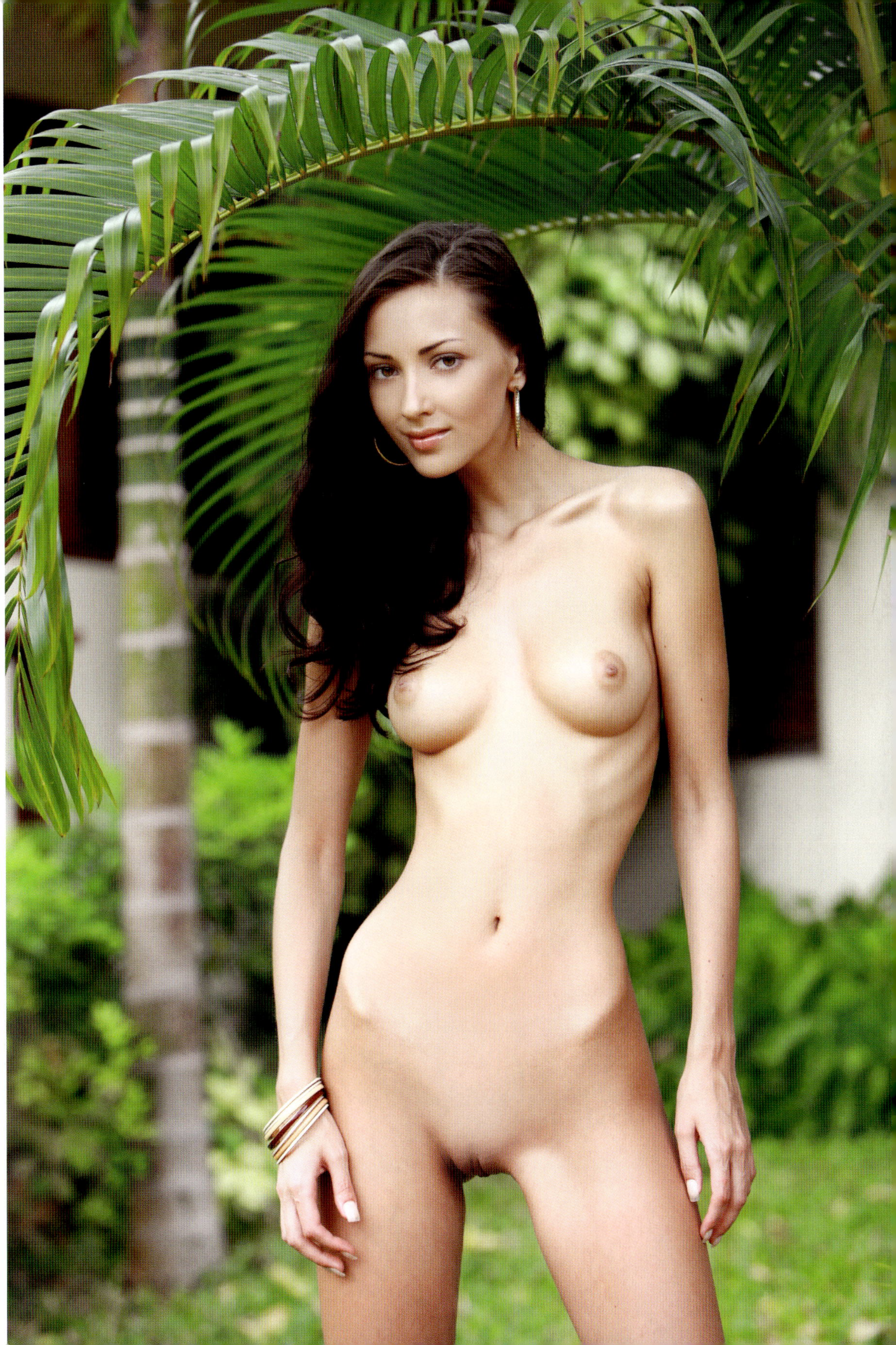

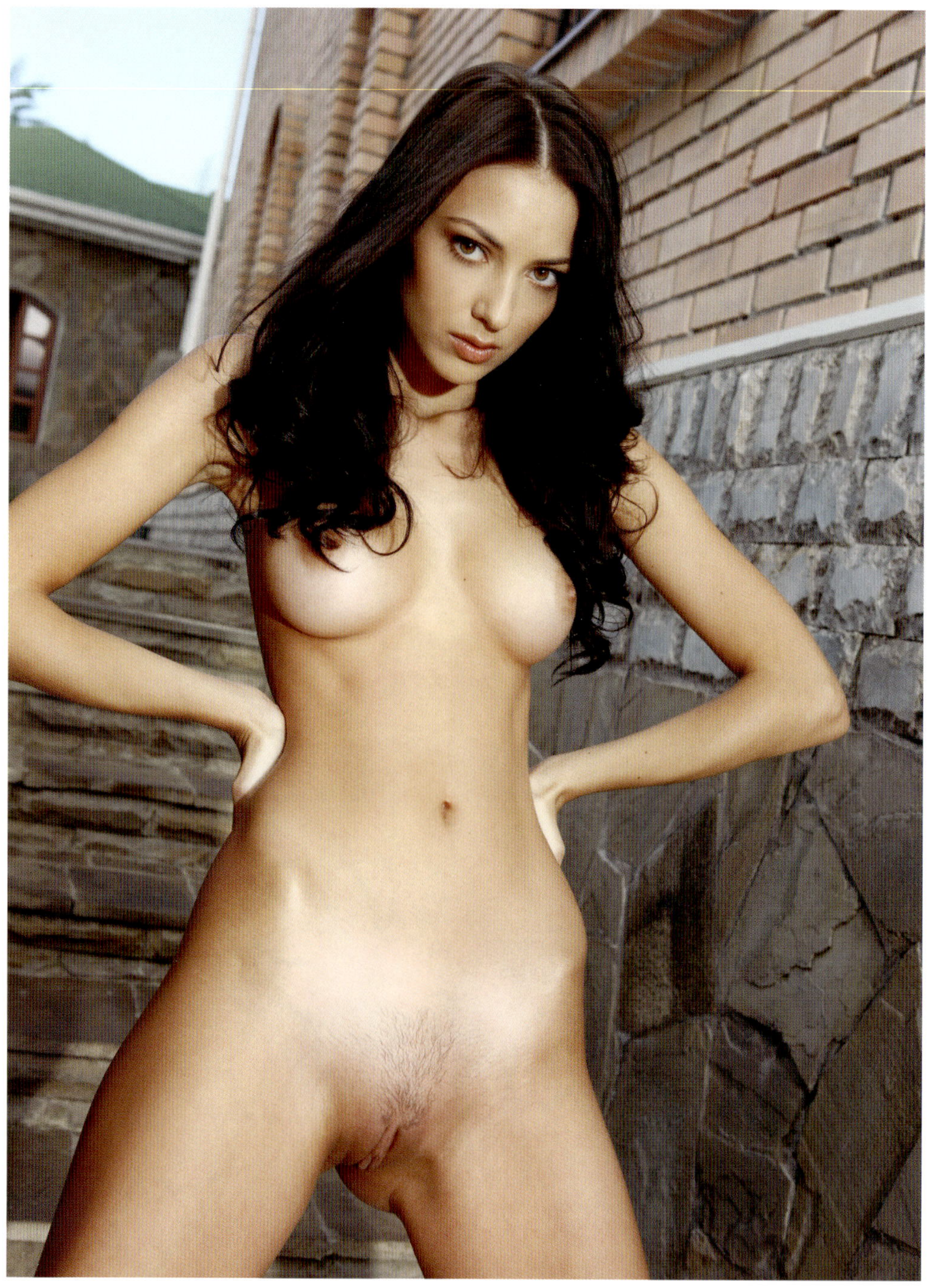

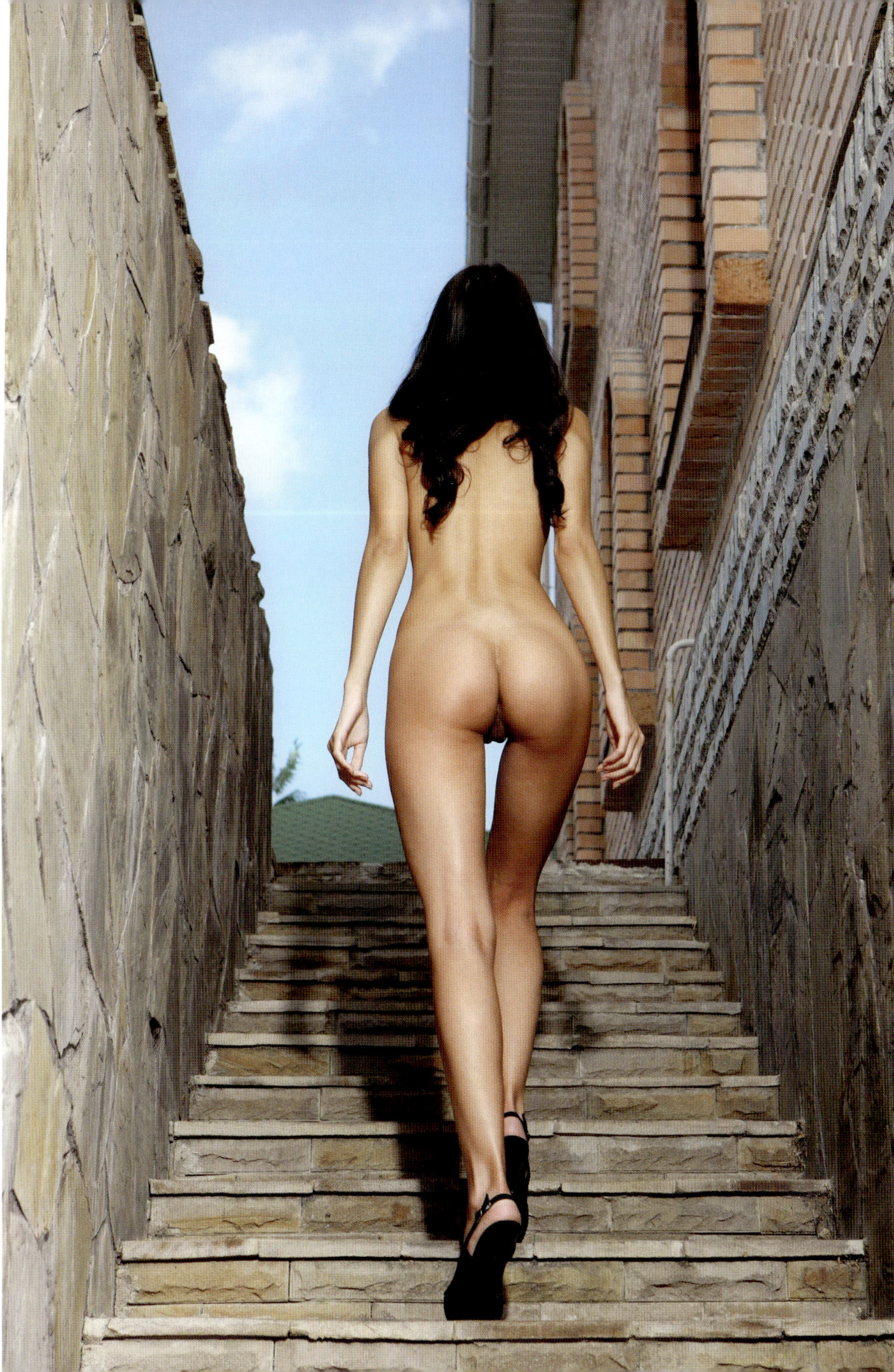

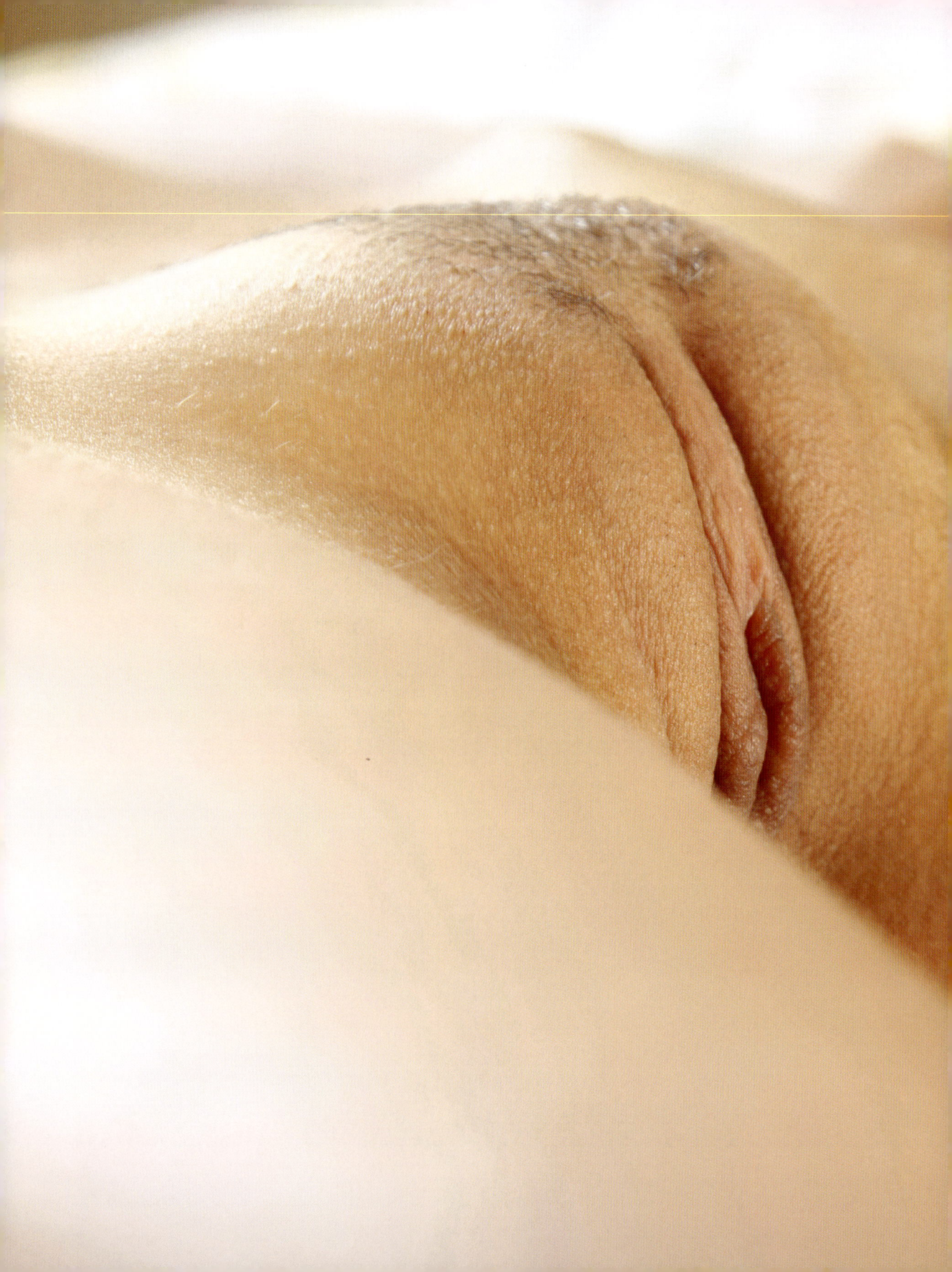

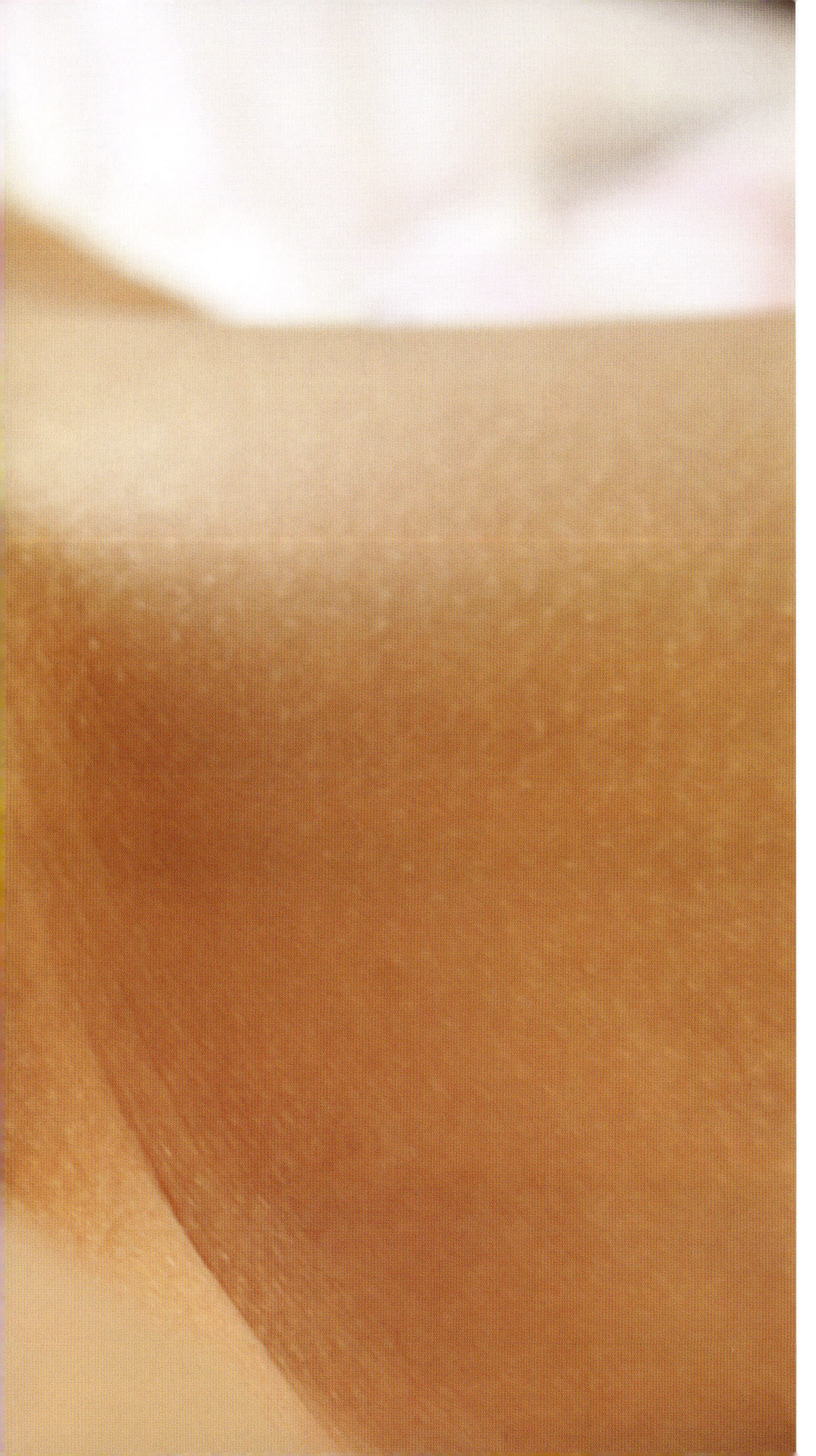

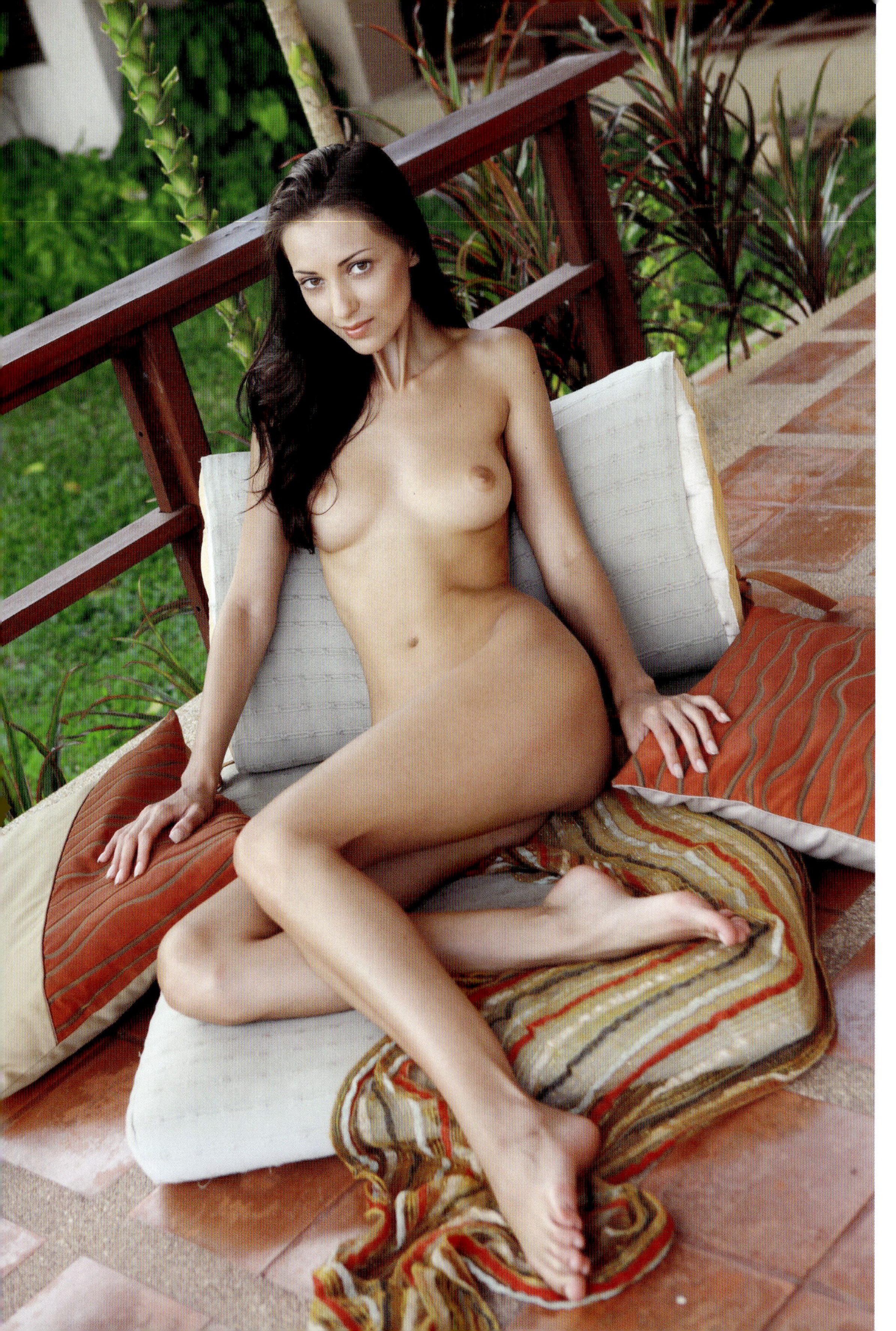

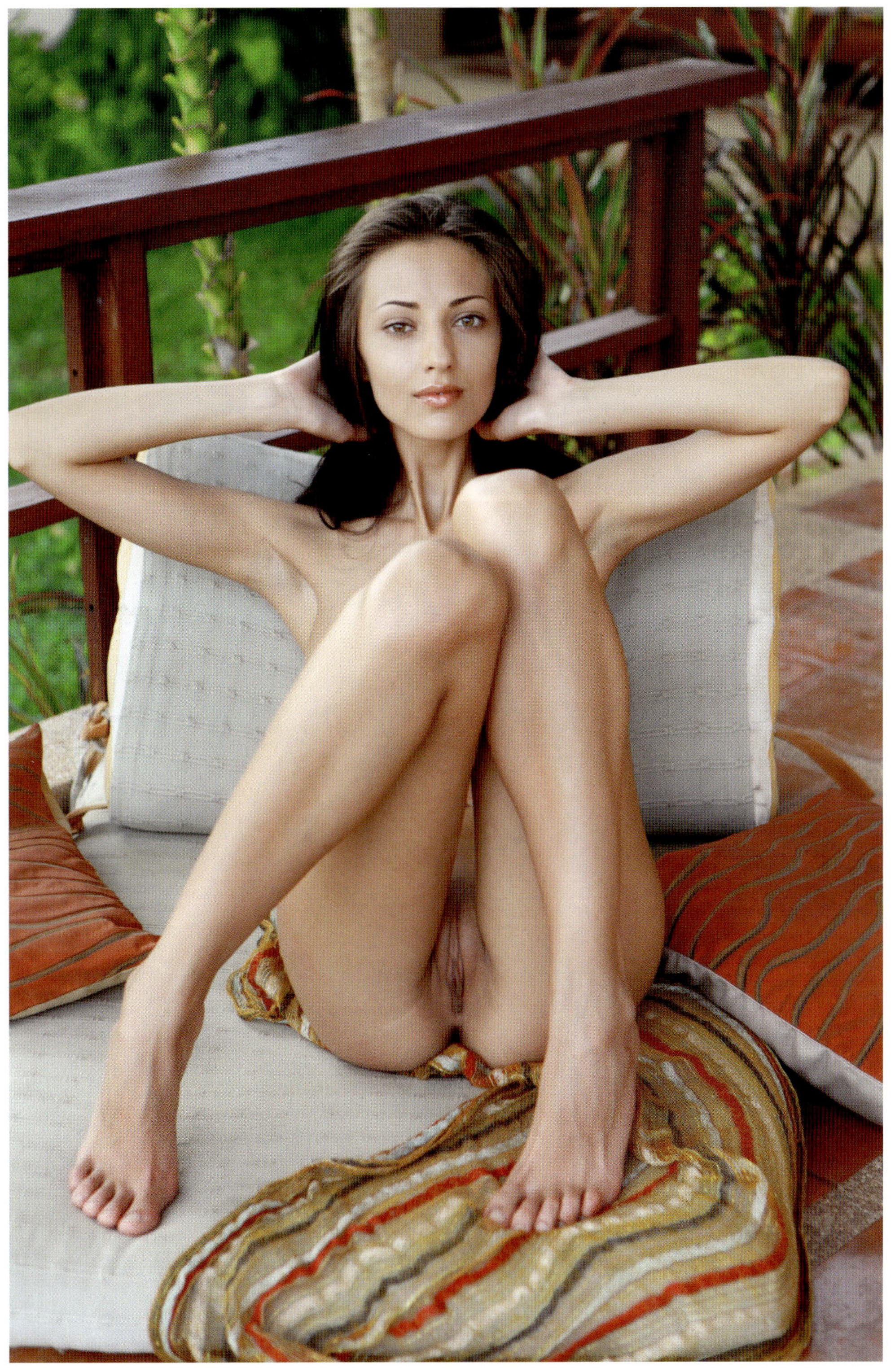

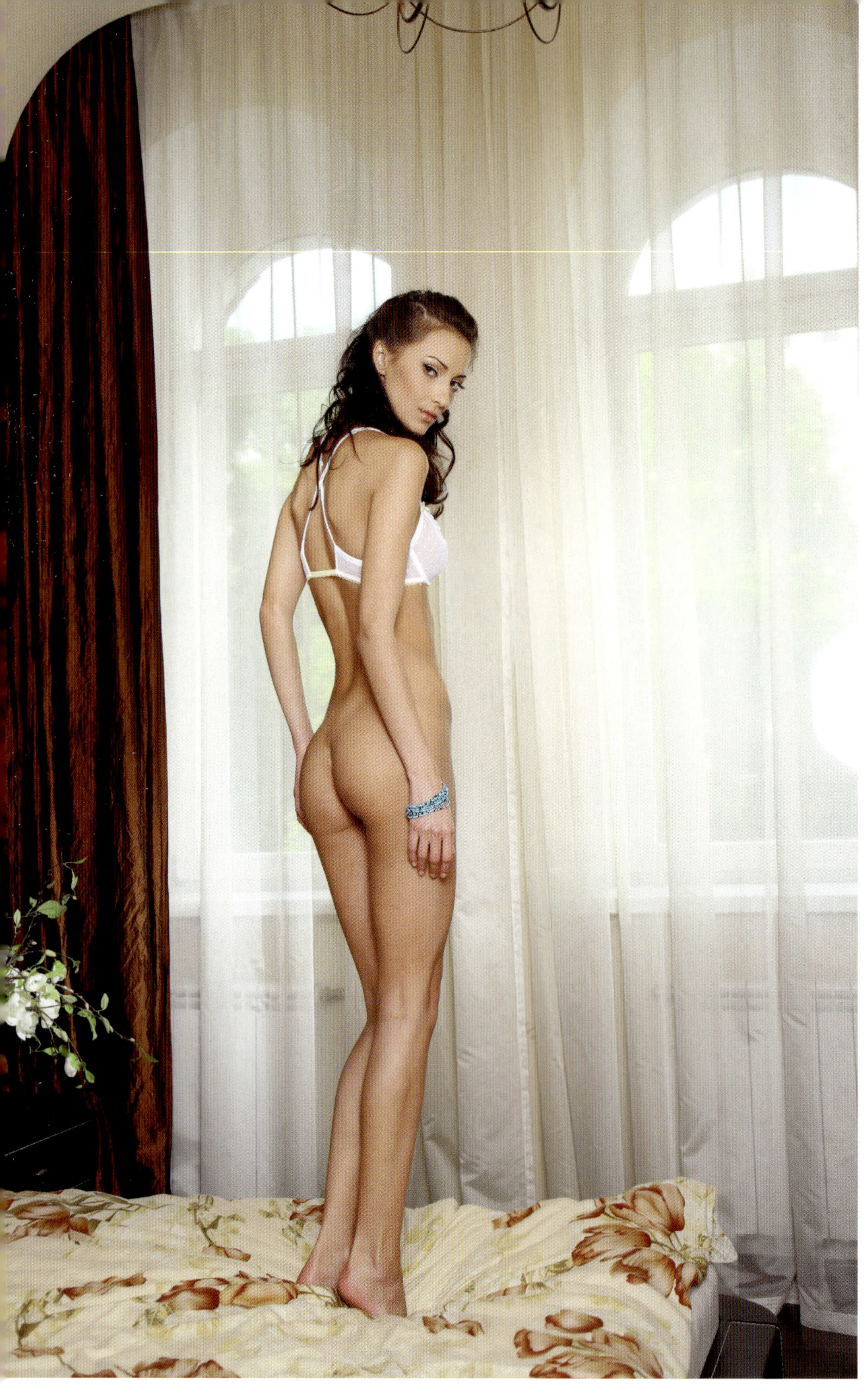

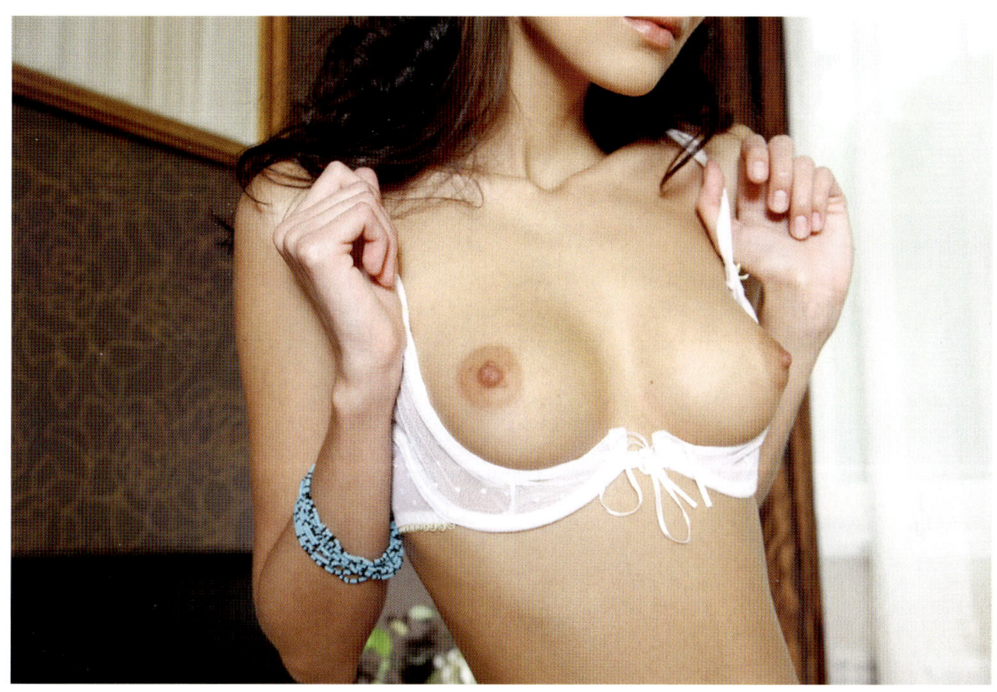

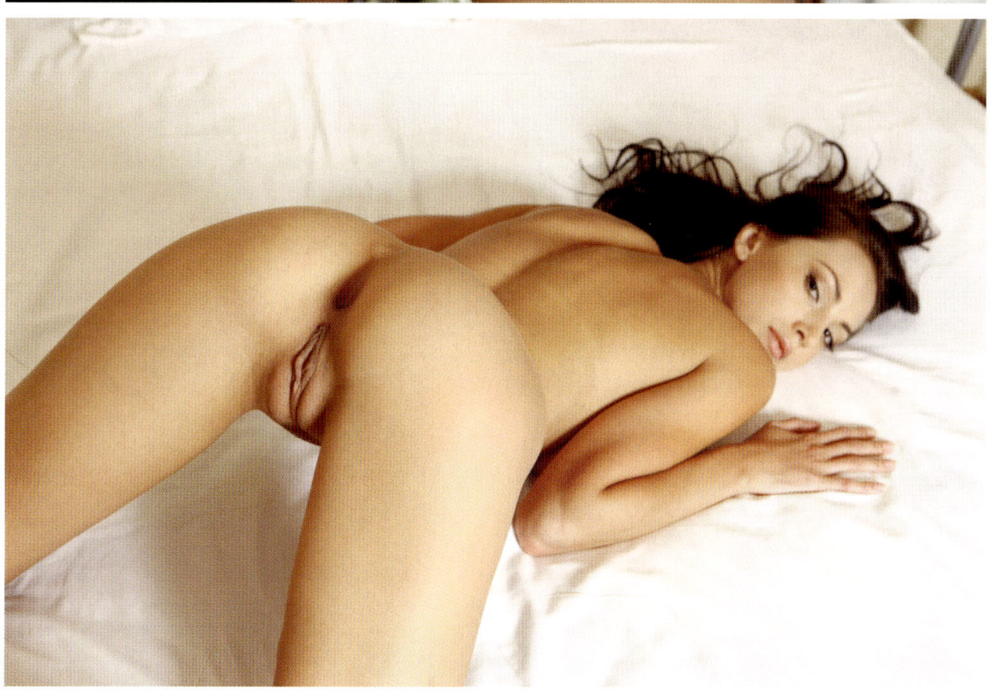

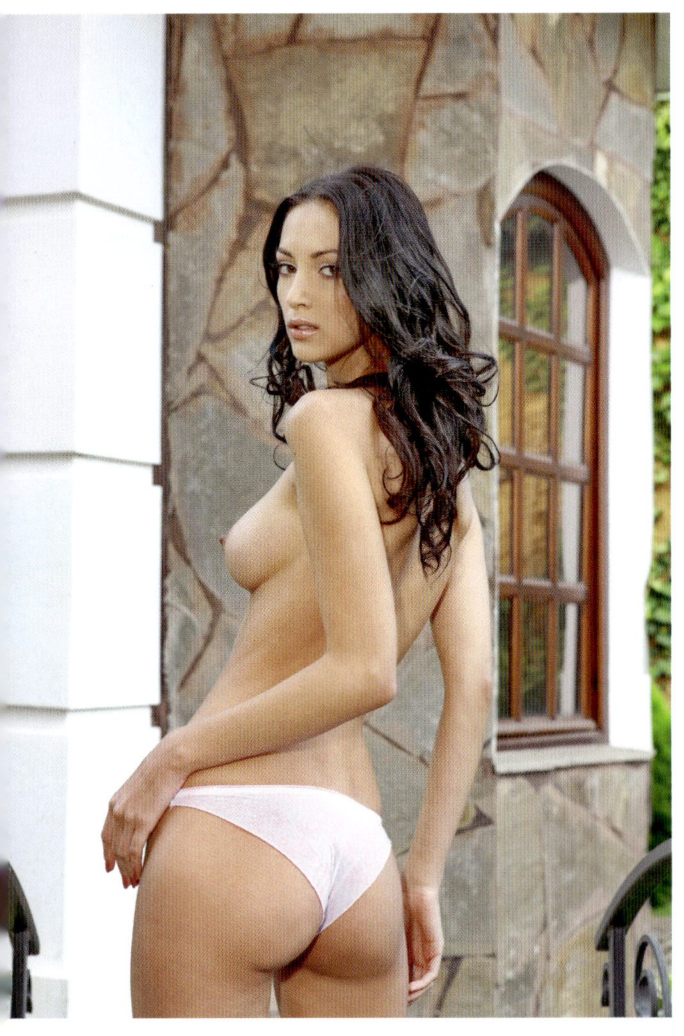

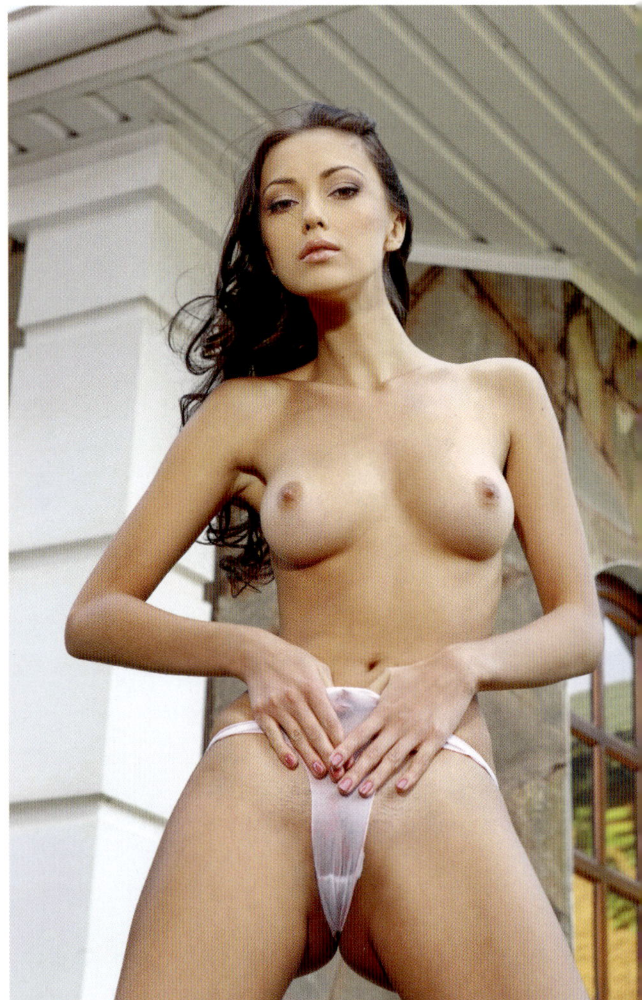

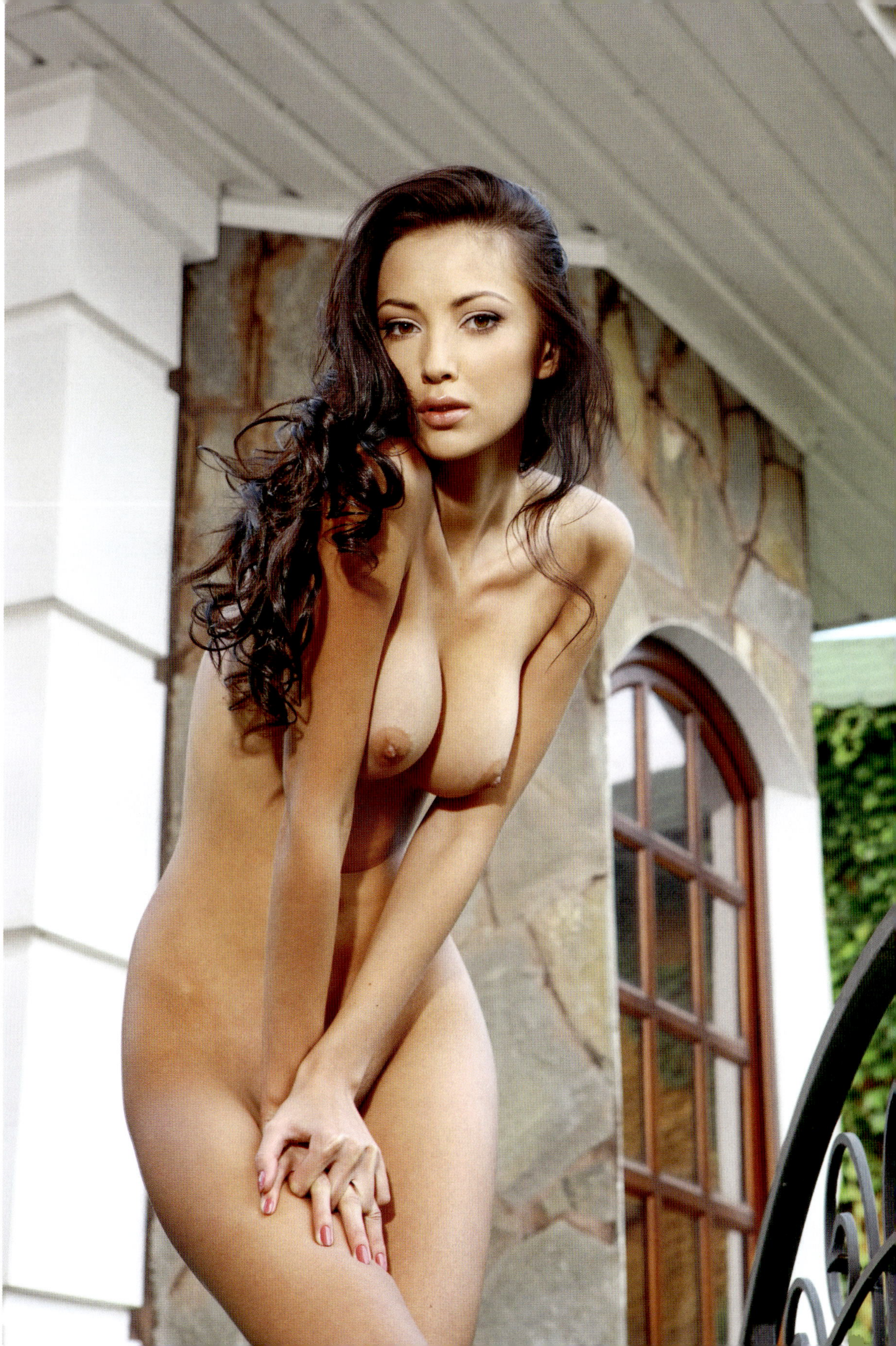

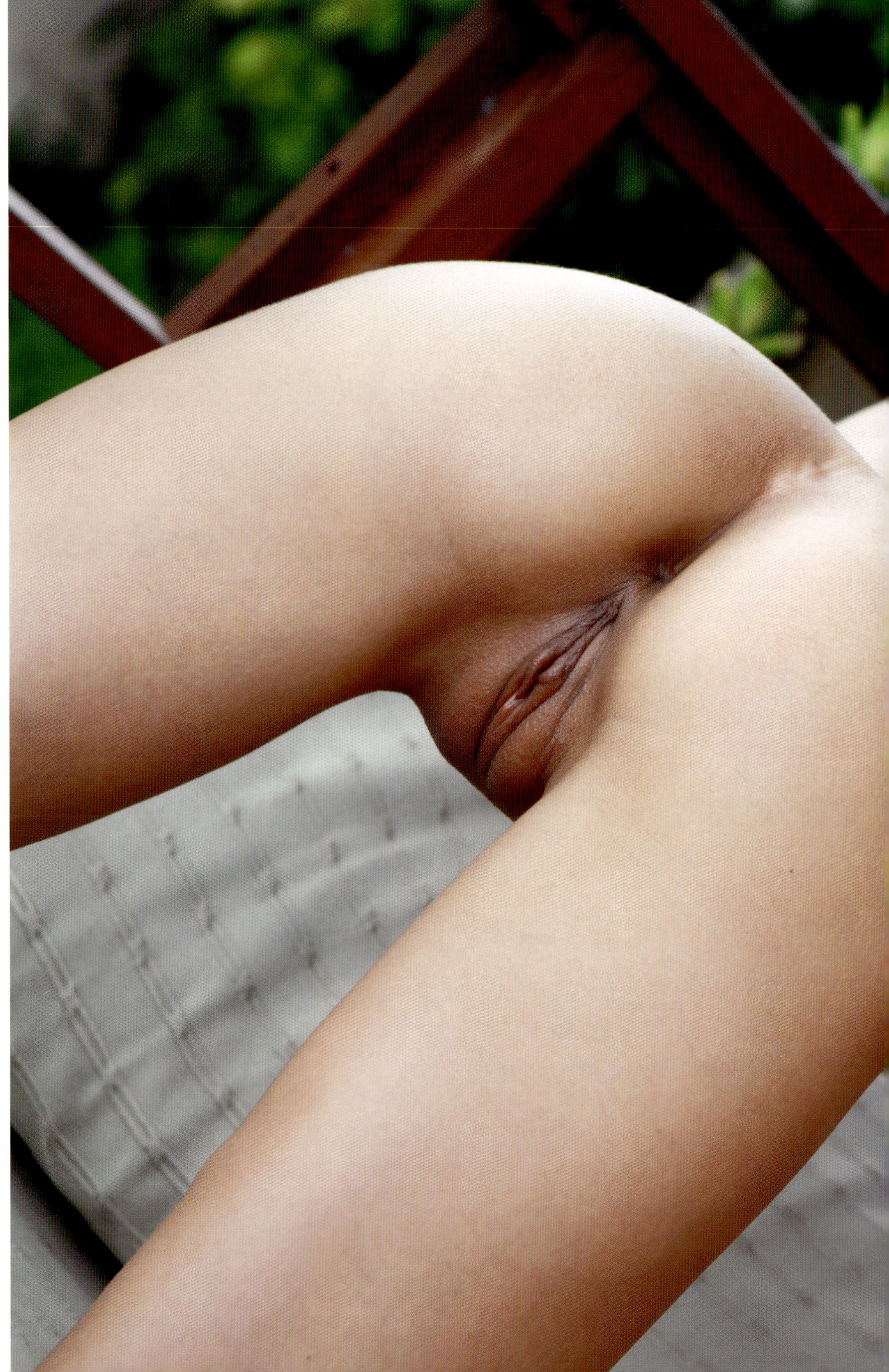

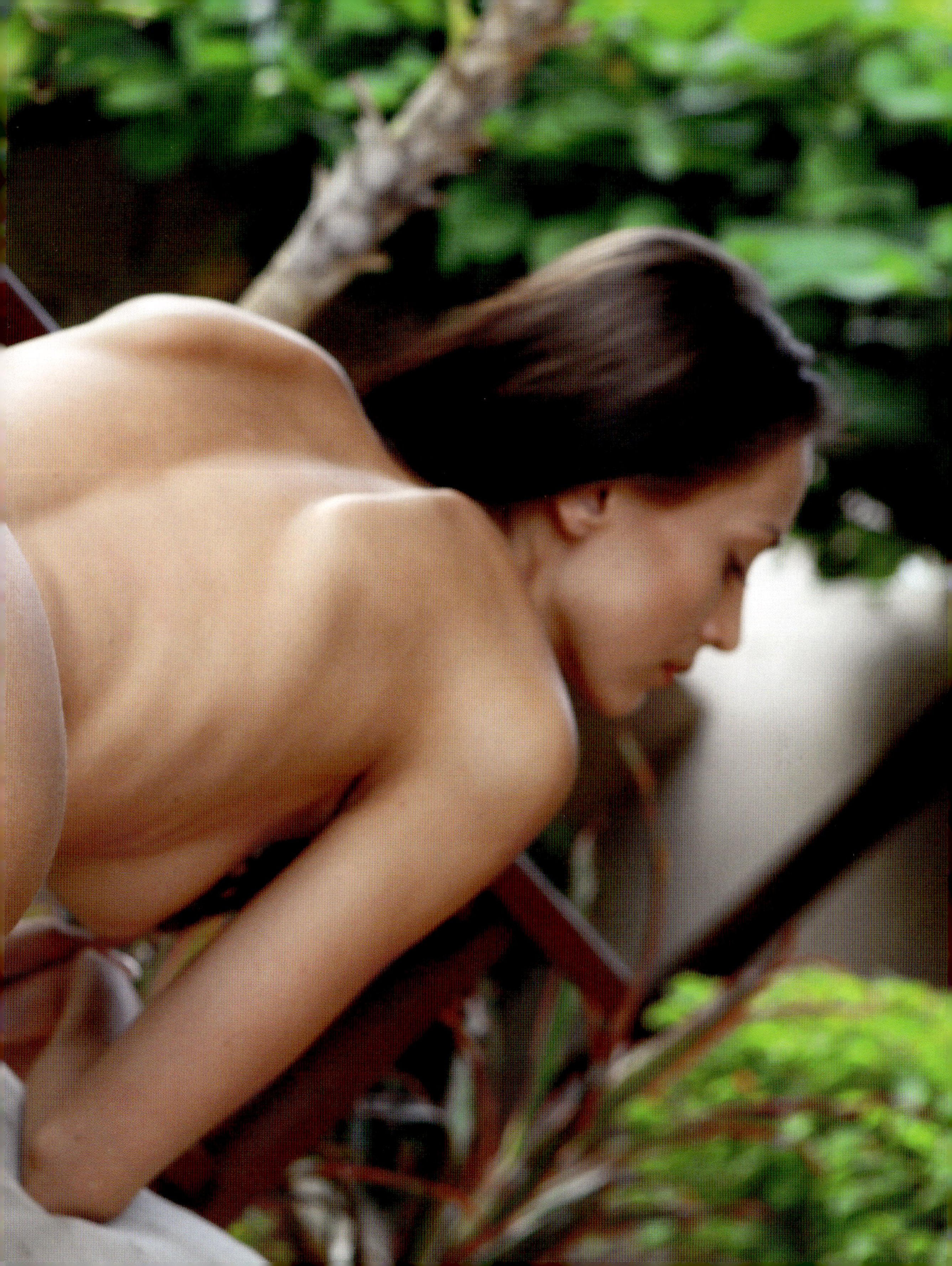

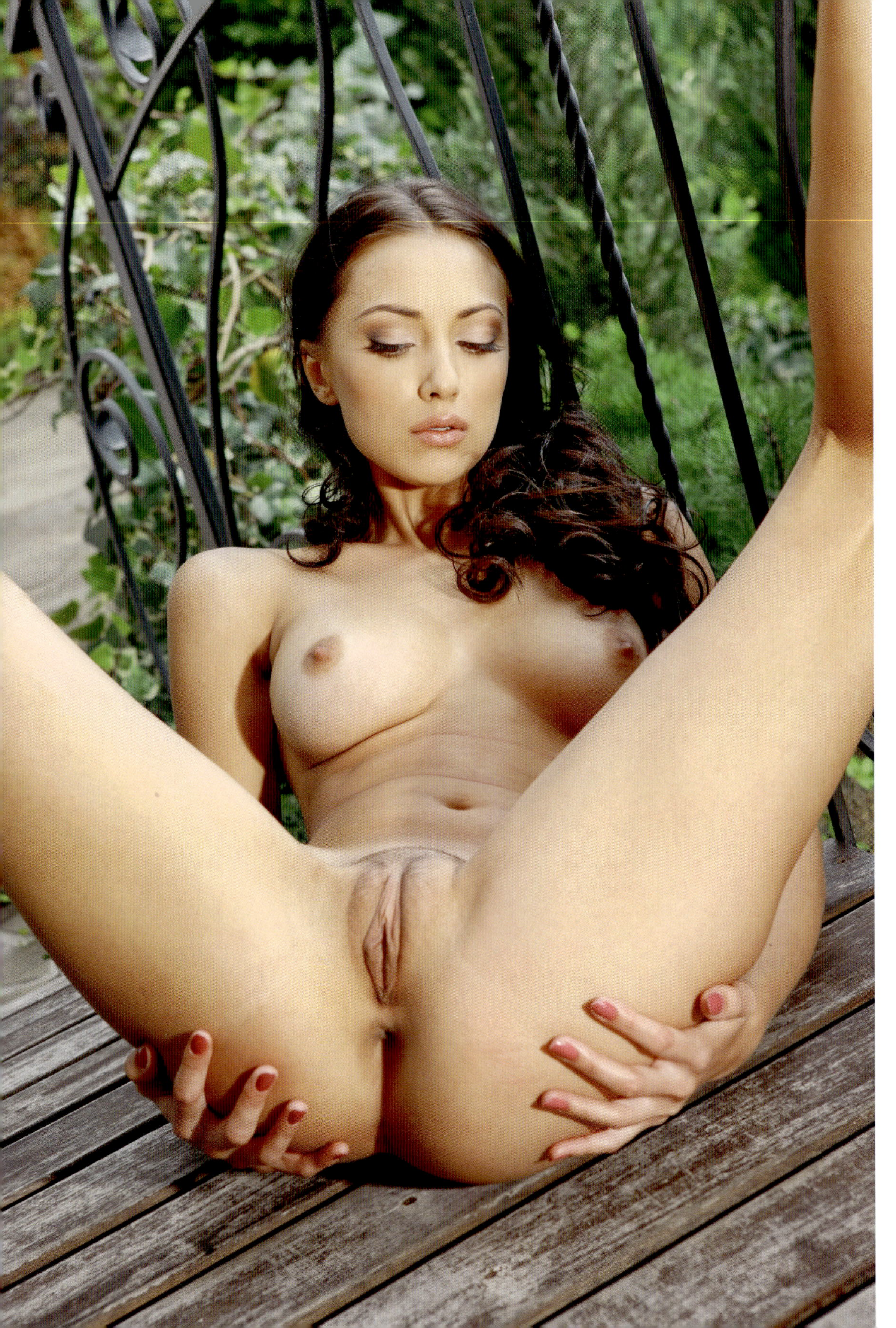

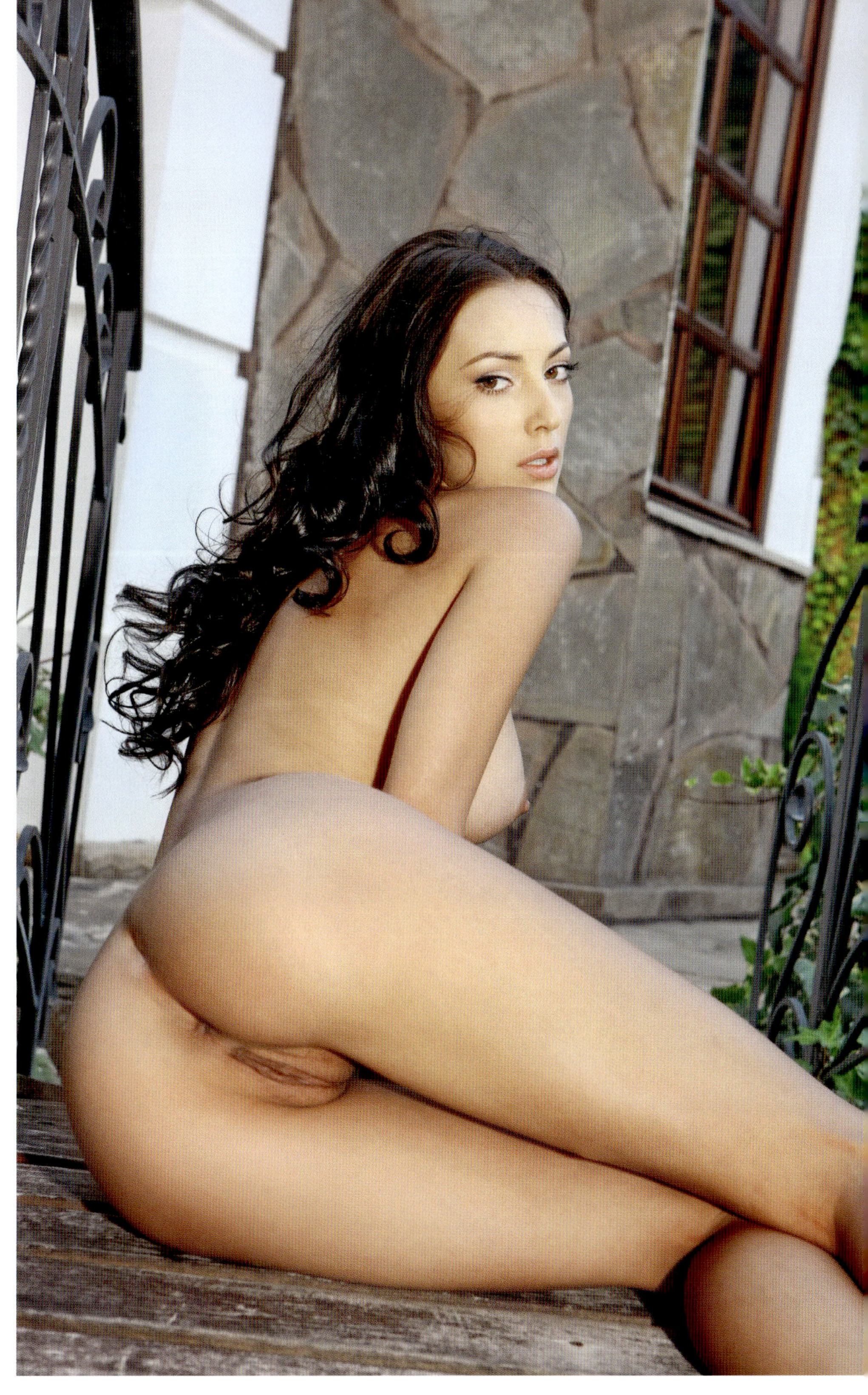

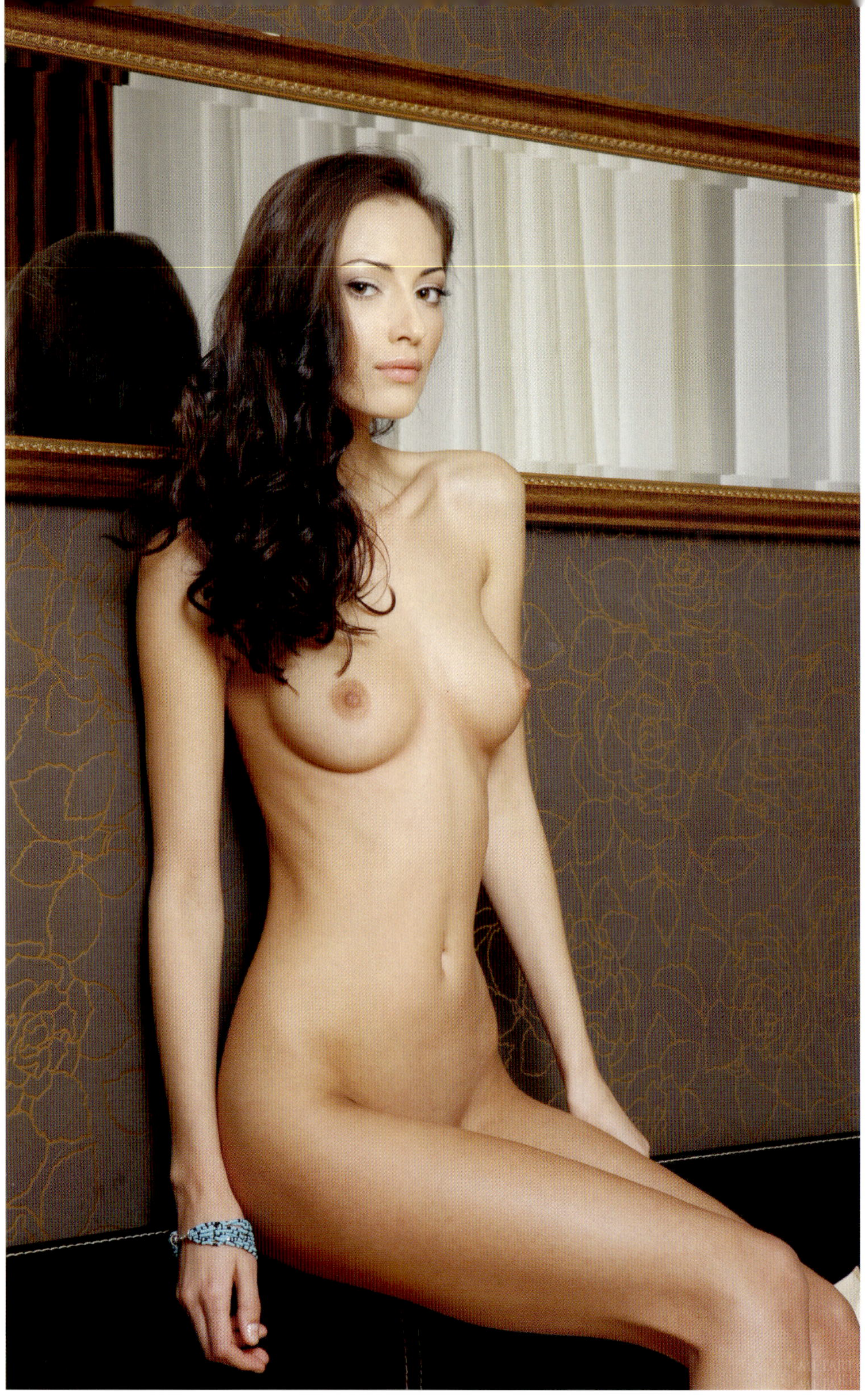

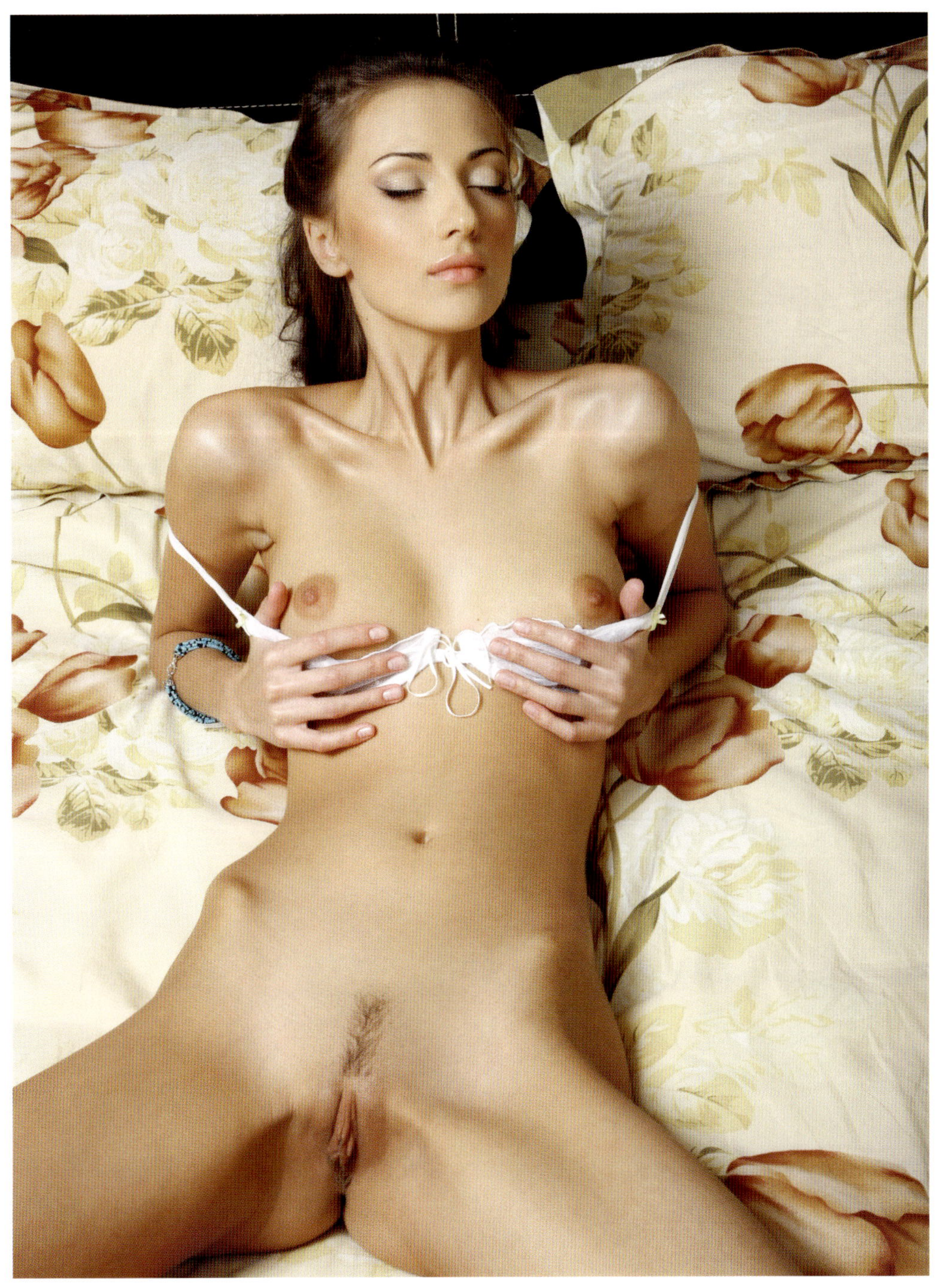

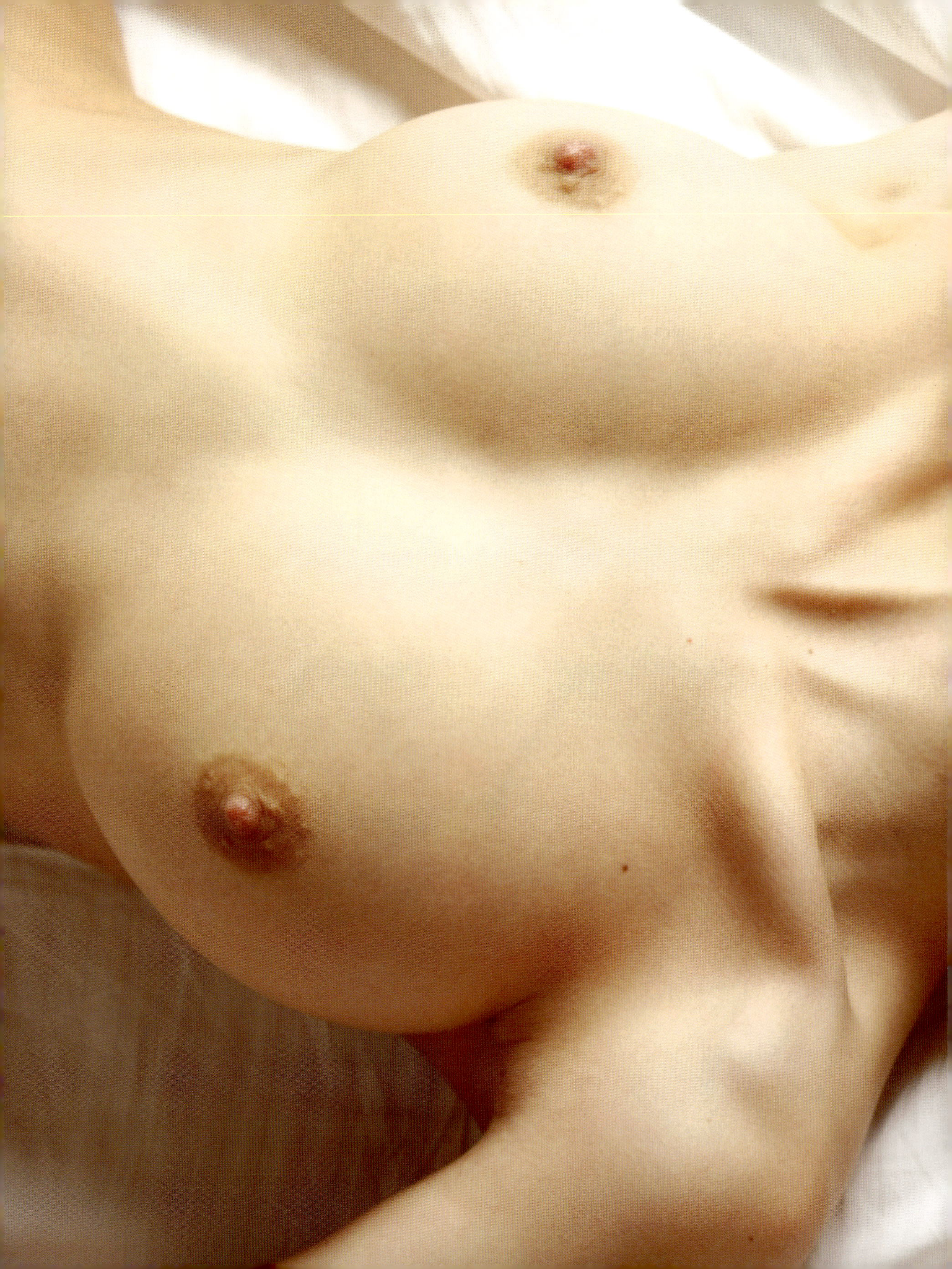

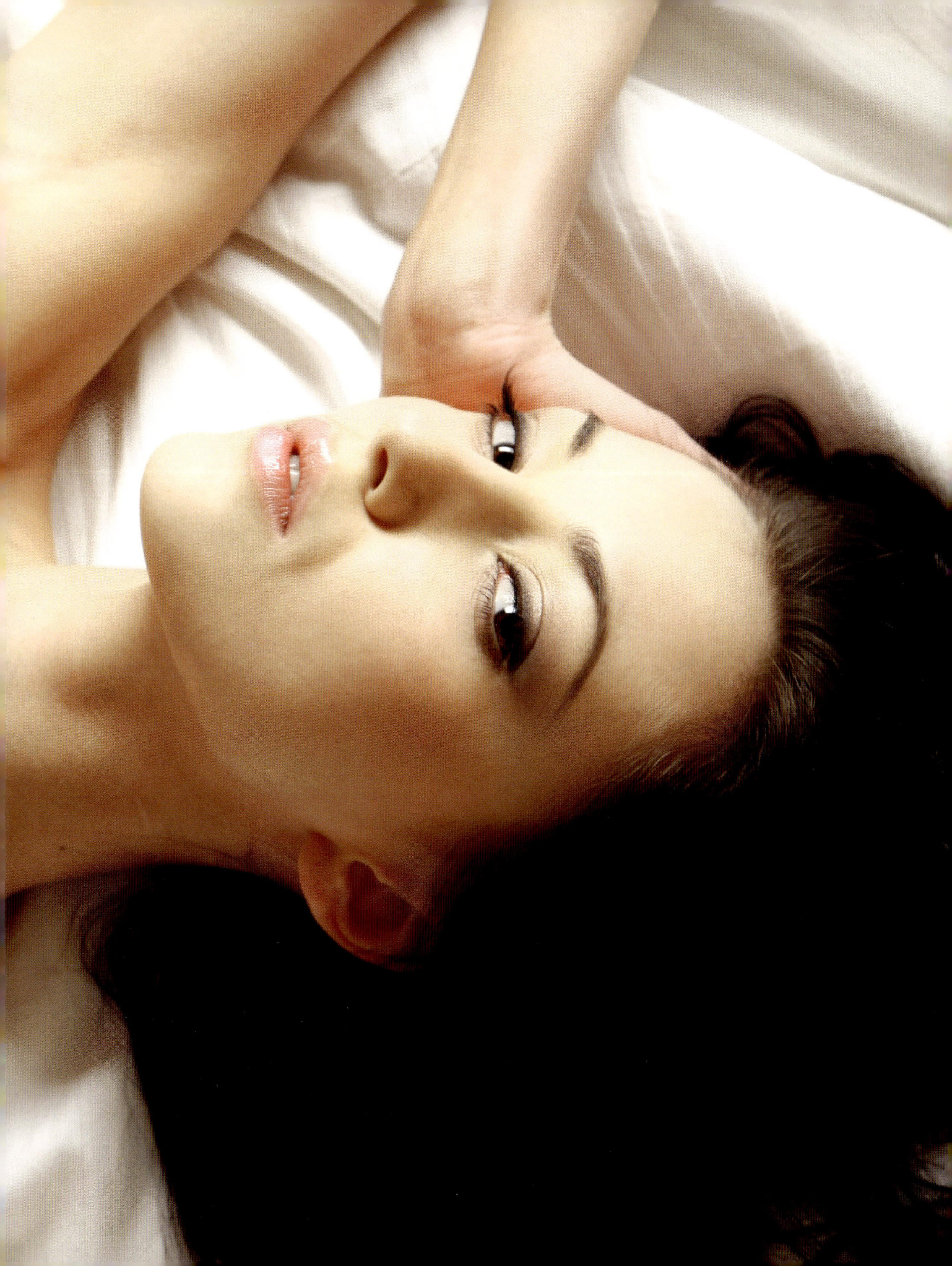

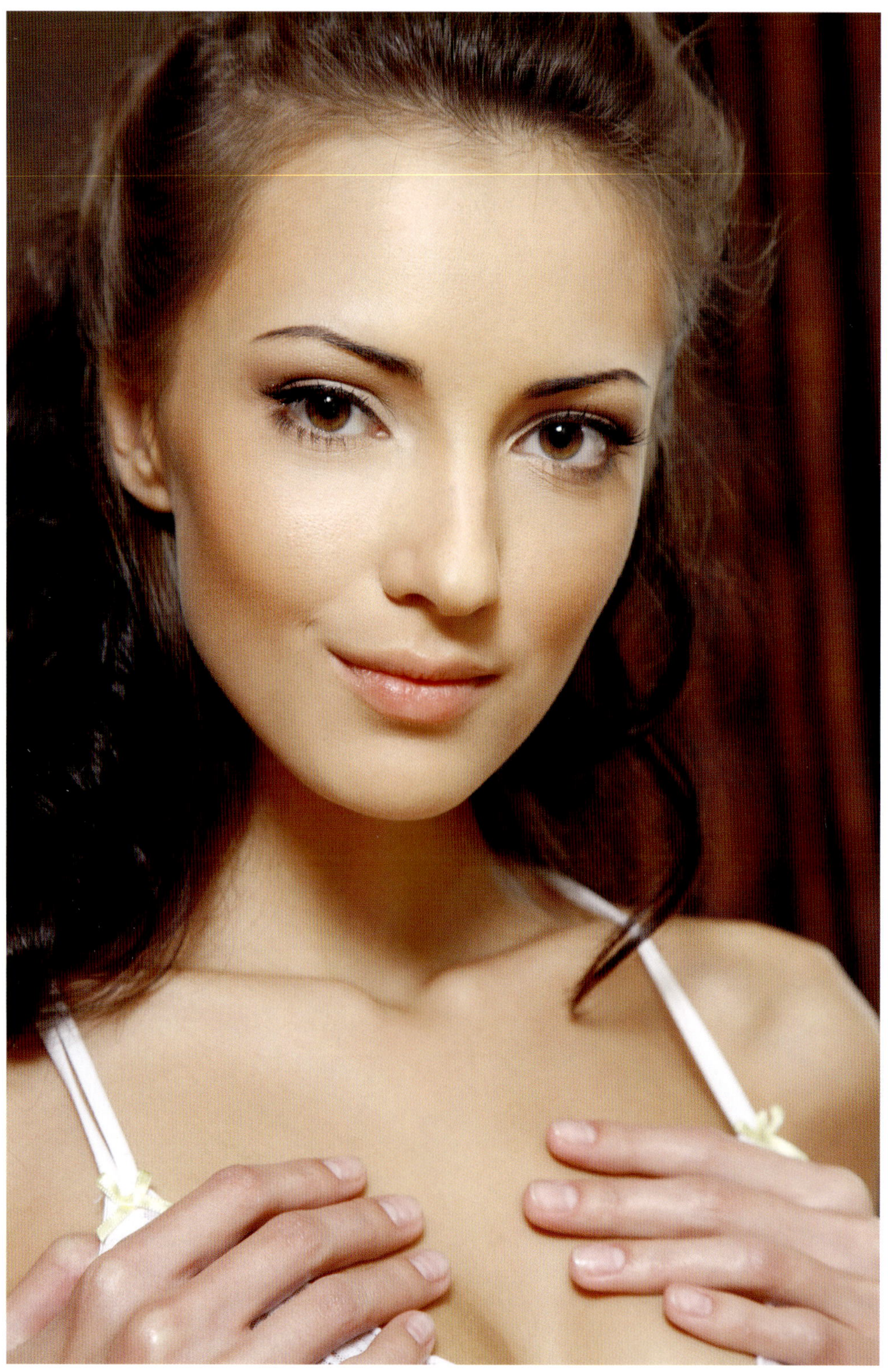

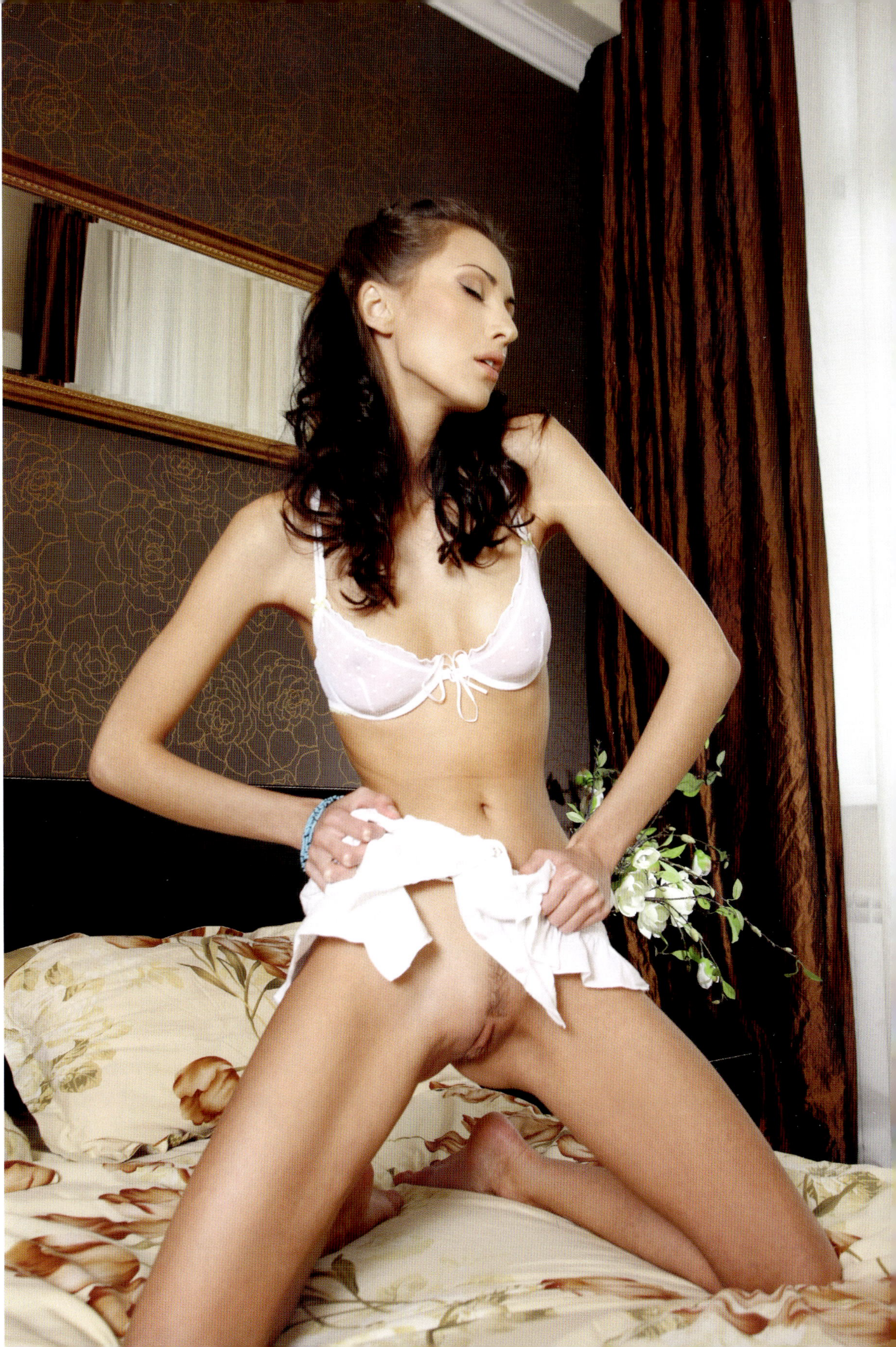

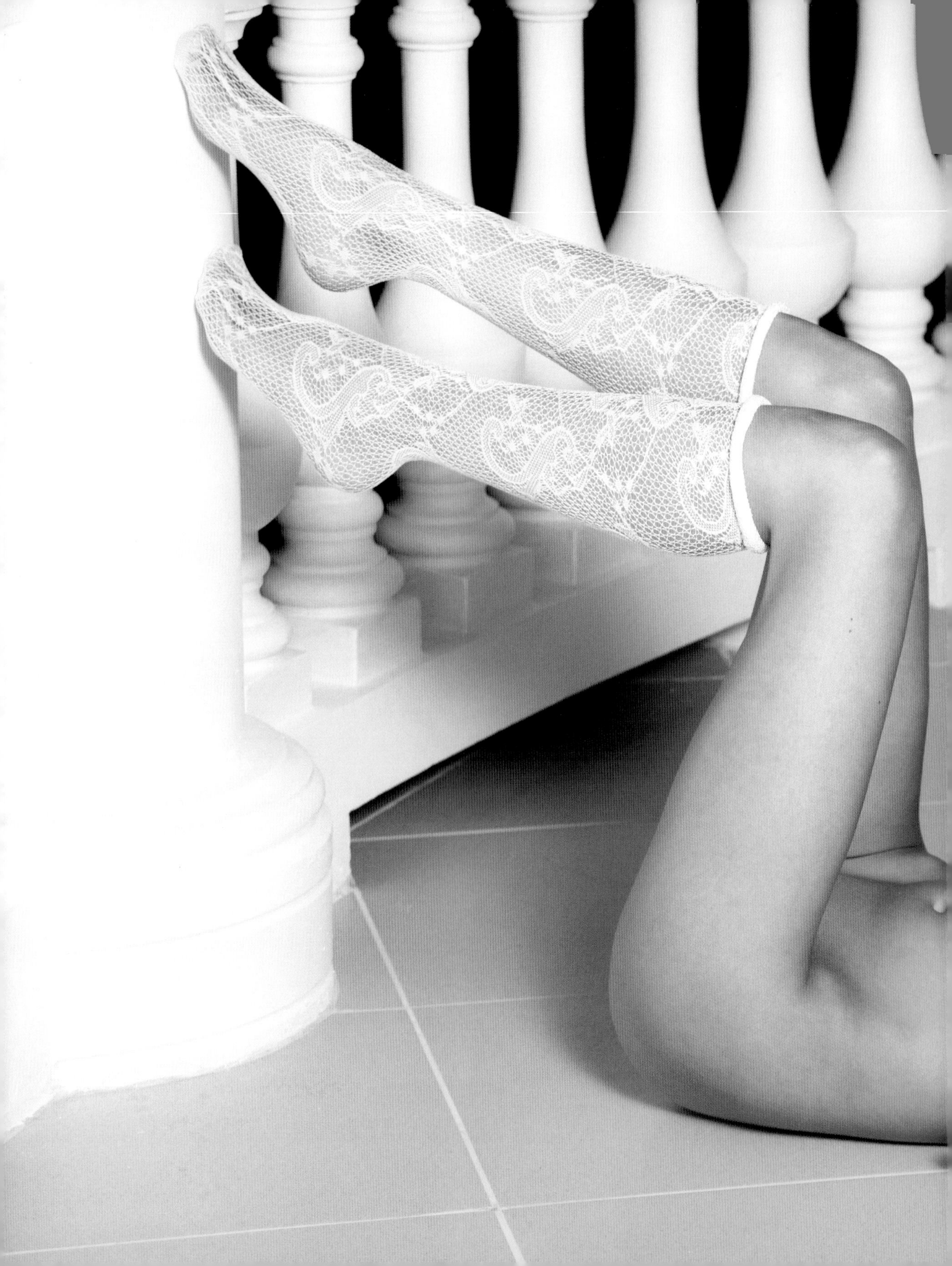

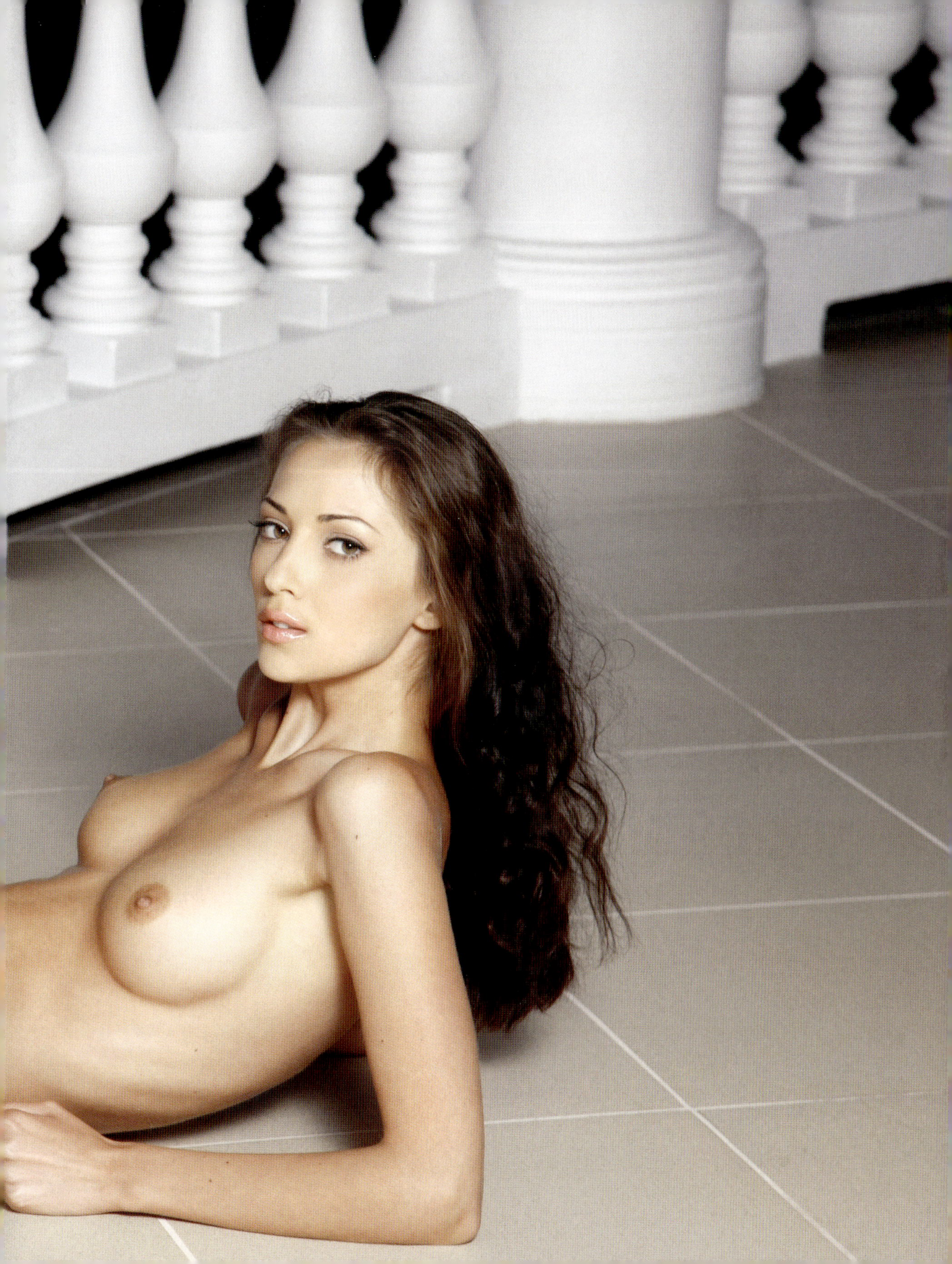

COLLECT THEM ALL: OUR MOST BEAUTIFUL

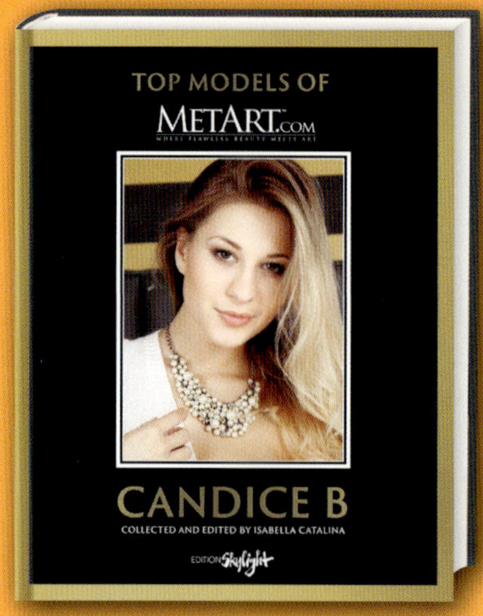

ISBN 978-3-03766-660-9

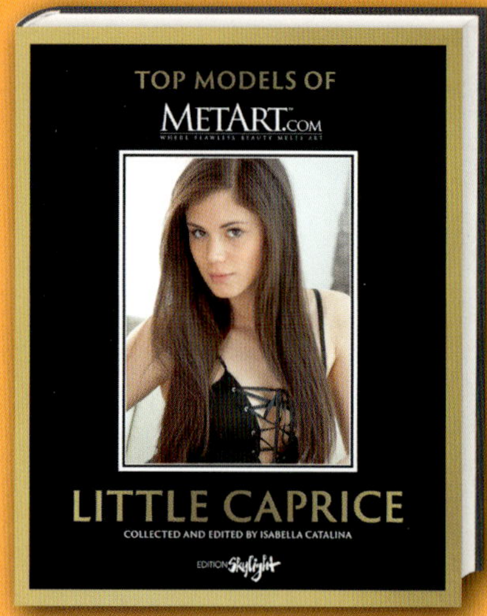

ISBN 978-3-03766-659-3

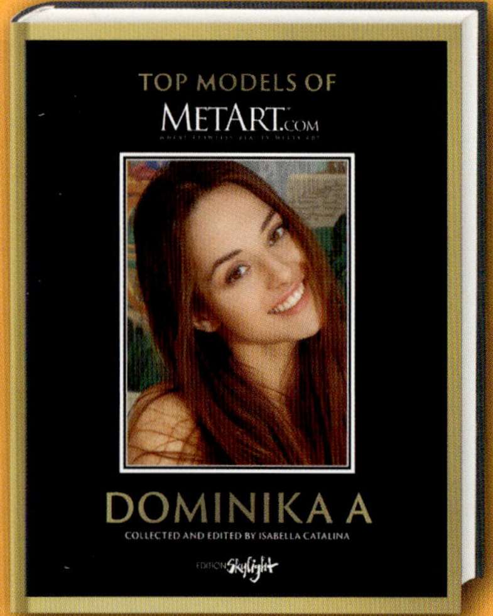

ISBN 978-3-03766-679-1

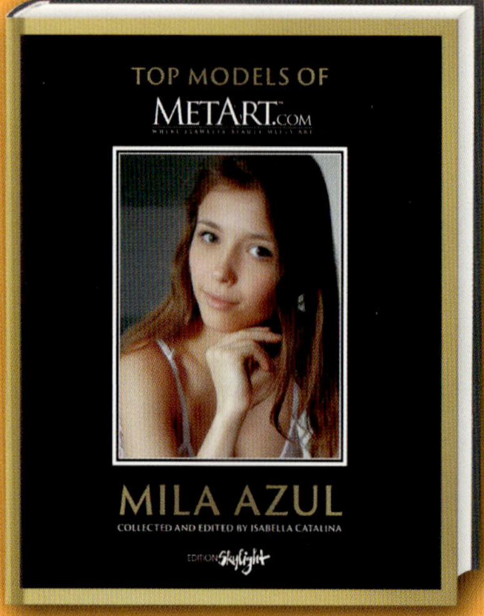

ISBN 978-3-03766-680-7

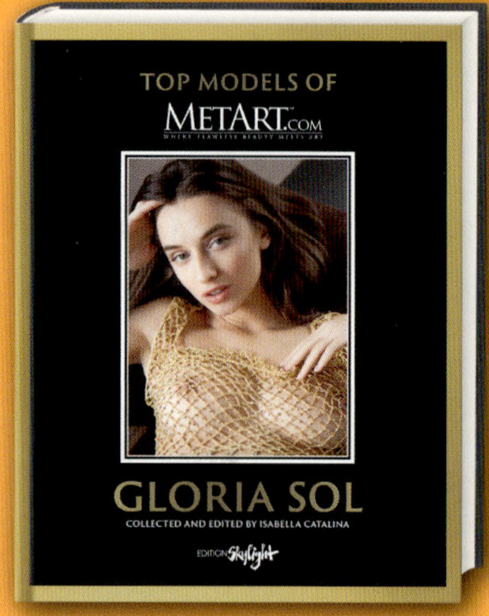

ISBN 978-3-03766-688-3